The Promise of Dawn

The Eschatology of Lewis Sperry Chafer

Jeffrey J. Richards

Wipf and Stock Publishers
EUGENE, OREGON

Wipf and Stock Publishers
150 West Broadway
Eugene, Oregon 97401

The Promise of Dawn
The Eschatology of Lewis Sperry Chafer
By Richards, Jeffrey J.
©1991 Richards, Jeffrey J.
ISBN: 1-57910-910-1
Publication date: March, 2002
Previously published by University Press of America, 1991.

To Debbie

Table of Contents

Preface vii
Introduction 1
Chapter
   I.   Chafer's Life and Career 11
          Early Years
          Education
          Conversion
          Evangelistic Ministry
          Northfield
          Post Northfield Days
          The Latter Years
          The *Systematic Theology*
          Conclusion

   II.   The Sources of Chafer's Eschatological Thought 55
          Chafer's Involvement with the Northfield Conferences
          C. I. Scofield
          Chafer's Eschatological Conclusions as Derived
              from His Personal Study
          Conclusion

Photo Section
          Photographs provided by John A. Witmer, Th.D., archivist
          for the Archives of Dallas Theological Seminary

   III.   Chafer's Dispensationalism 109
          The Dispensational Organization of
              the *Systematic Theology*
          The Dispensations
          Select Dispensational, Premillennial Writers
          Various Views of the Rapture
          The Amillennial Position
          The Postmillenial Position

        Four Distinct Groups
        The Covenants
        The Controversy Concerning Dispensationalism
        Conclusion

IV.   **Chafer's Millennialism** 163
        Historical Context
        The Role of Prophecy
        The Second Advent
        The Resurrections
        The Tribulation Period
        The Judgments
        The Millennium
        Dispensational Premillennialism as Central
           to Chafer's Thought
        Conclusion

Conclusion 205
Bibliography 211
Indexes 245
        Names
        Subjects
        Scripture

Biographical Sketch 259

Preface

Lewis Sperry Chafer earned the title "The Apostle of Grace." God used Chafer to bequeath to the world a spiritual legacy of grace and hope. Throughout his life, he relentlessly pursued his goal of proclaiming the promise of hope and renewed spiritual life in Jesus Christ.

During the eleven years I researched Chafer, the burning question before me was: "What motivated Chafer to achieve such extraordinary accomplishments?" For example, how was it possible for this one-time itinerant evangelist eventually to become the founder and first president of one of the world's largest seminaries? Or, how was it possible for this individual who had no formal theological education to write a highly regarded eight-volume systematic theology? Besides being obviously gifted, my conclusion rests with Chafer's view of the *eschaton*, the New Testament Greek word for the end, or his view of how the Christian message of the any-moment coming of Christ for the saints was a fact rooted in the warp and woof of the New Testament Scriptures. Chafer had a very practical approach and answer for the current questions of time management, motivation, strategic planning and goal setting: the end is near!

The burden of the book concerns his views of the end, rather than emphasizing the person of Chafer. His theology continues to have a massive, world-wide impact upon the thinking, teaching and preaching of many well-known contemporary evangelical pastors, teachers, evangelists, Bible and Christian liberal arts colleges, seminaries, para-church ministries, mission boards, Christian professional organizations, and innumerable lay persons.

If Chafer were alive today, he would view the rise of Israel to a position of a world player with extreme interest, and perhaps with Bible in hand, he would point to passages in both the Old and New Testaments which he believed predict such a rise. But having died in 1952, Chafer was not able to comment on this phenomenon although his writings are filled with the subject of Israel and her relationship to biblical prophecy. Without doubt, Chafer would be fascinated with the current democratic movement in Europe. Today we are reminded that the European Common Market will be a reality. Such an occurrence would not have surprised Chafer since throughout his life he claimed that the Bible predicts the formation of such an alliance. Convinced that Revelation 17 speaks of an unholy alliance against Christ and His armies, Chafer was certain such a confederacy is an event near the end time. Chafer believed the world's last great war, Armageddon, will involve Iran, Iraq, Israel and several other Middle Eastern countries.

Lewis Sperry Chafer's greatness lies in his ability to take what he considered the timeless truths of the Bible and align these truths with contemporary events with unusual insight, scholarship, practicality, and spirituality. Lewis Sperry Chafer, this apostle of grace, believed and proclaimed the coming promise of dawn, the return of Jesus Christ, with clarity, certainty, and conviction.

Salisbury, North Carolina

Introduction

On June 12, 1990 a program entitled "World Without Walls" with Ted Koppel as the host was televised. The program had been recorded on May 19, 1990 at the University of Pennsylvania. Ted Koppel and five distinguished guests discussed global issues. Mr. Koppel closed the discussion with the summary statement that the entire debate centered on the issue of "Futurology." The group attempted to discern what awaits our world in the twenty-first century. Obviously, the topic of the future has a globally interested constituency.

Lewis Sperry Chafer has become a significant religious figure not only in the twentieth century but continuing especially into the twenty-first century. The impact of his life seemingly has set into motion a domino-like influence upon individuals, denominations, Christian organizations, and institutions worldwide. While there are several scholarly works and authors which mention Chafer, the allusions are brief. Stewart G. Cole in *The History of Fundamentalism* merely refers to Chafer's association with the League of Evangelical Students.[1] Ernest Sandeen alludes to Chafer twice but relegates him either to a footnote or includes him in a list with other individuals who hold similar theological positions.[2] Likewise, Timothy Weber only includes Chafer in a list of names.[3] George Marsden, mentioning Chafer once, gives additional insight by citing Benjamin B. Warfield's scathing criticism of Chafer's *He That Is Spiritual*. Warfield believes Chafer to be an Arminian even though Chafer claims his system is Calvinistic.[4] Clearly then, Chafer has been all but ignored by current scholarship. Perhaps one reason for this is that he has not been widely read outside of evangelical religious environs. Upon closer inspection, one becomes aware of the theological profundity Chafer possessed. As an evangelical theologian, he was involved with those of similar persuasion such as A. C. Gaebelein, W. H. Griffith Thomas, A. B. Winchester, W. B. Riley, R. A. Torrey, D. L. Moody, C. I. Scofield, and H. A. Ironside.

For a period of years Chafer served on the faculty of the Northfield Schools founded by D. L. Moody and ministered in music at the Northfield conferences. Here he came in contact with and was influenced by the leading evangelical theologians and ministers of the United States, Canada, the British Isles, and Europe. At Northfield, Chafer met and formed a close relationship with C. I. Scofield, who became Chafer's theological and biblical mentor. Chafer was an associate of C. I. Scofield in a Bible institute in New York City and then at Philadelphia School of the Bible (now Philadelphia College of the Bible). Scofield also introduced Chafer to the Southland Bible Conference in Florida. He was largely responsible for Chafer's transition from itinerant evangelism to itinerent Bible teaching and Bible conference ministry.

During this period of his life, 1915 - 1925, Chafer published most of his books on doctrinal subjects. His works reflect a fairly well-defined theological position since they cover aspects of angelology, anthropology, soteriology, ecclesiology, Christology, pneumatology, and eschatology.

Chafer taught theology in the seminary he led in establishing in Dallas, Texas. This teaching responsibility had been initially assigned to W. H. Griffith Thomas, the British Anglican scholar, whose death in 1924 thrust it upon Chafer. In preparation for his classes in systematic theology, Chafer immersed himself in the standard works in systematics and dogmatics as broadly and deeply as time and energy permitted. His rigorous study continued for many years and led to the production of his own *Systematic Theology* in 1947 - 1948, only four years before his death.

Why should a book be written concerning Chafer's eschatology, or his view of the end? He made his greatest theological contribution in this area since he gathered massive themes, materials, and actually the collective dispensational, premillennial thought of the latter nineteenth century and first half of the twentieth century. Many fine sermons had been preached and articles written concerning dispensational premillennialism, but there was no systematic theology written from this viewpoint. Chafer did not merely collect, but he interpreted creatively and forcefully evangelical eschatology. Missing from Chafer's writings and life is the negative, militant, narrow approach to theology in general and eschatology in particular. He is not representative of the common caricature of a

Introduction

conservative theologian during this period. Rather, one finds in Chafer a theologian collecting and interpreting in a scholarly, practical, and positive style the entire field of theology and particularly eschatology.

What theological characteristics identify Chafer? He had much in common with the entire Reformed tradition. Excluding eschatology, Chafer is similar theologically to such Princeton divines as Warfield, Hodge, and Machen. He claims such doctrines as the sovereignty of God, the inspiration of the Scriptures, the virgin birth, total depravity of humanity, election, irresistable grace, and the perseverance of the saints. But strict Calvinists have accused him of Arminianism because Chafer adheres to a position of unlimited atonement, or the view that the death of Christ is for the world and not for a select few.

In reference to eschatology, Chafer is premillennial, and this is another position in which he differs from his otherwise Reformed articulation of theology. His works depict Christ's return before the establishing of the millennium. Neither technological progress nor the preaching of the gospel will usher in this period. Christ will actually reign over the earth as king, and during the millennium the Jewish people will experience the fulfullment of the promises made to Abraham and David. Postmillennialism, as represented by James H. Snowden and Loraine Boettner,[5] states that the millennium will be realized by means of a universal proclamation of the gospel and the conversion of the majority of humankind during the present age. By a method of spiritualizing, those who hold to amillennialism either find the millennium fulfilled in the present age on earth in the Church or fulfilled in heaven by the saints. Chafer, of course, rejects both postmillennialism and amillennialism, claiming that a literal historical-grammatical means of analysis results in a premillennial interpretation.

Chafer is a dispensationalist in his understanding of the Bible. Where does the idea of dispensationalism originate? Arnold D. Ehlert has compiled a thorough bibliography of dispensationalism. Ehlert believes the entire concept of the dispensations can be traced back to the creative days and seventh day of rest as found in the book of Genesis. Six creative days followed by a day of rest, prophetically symbolizes six periods of time followed by a time of utopia. He cites David Gregory of Oxford who believes the Hebrew letter *aleph* since it is found six times in the first verse of the first chapter of the book of Genesis, and since in Jewish arithmetic the *aleph* symbolizes one thousand, Gregory concludes the world would last six thousand years. The seventh thousand, then, would be a period of rest. Ehlert cites several references from the Church Fathers which in his opinion depict the importance of the six thousand-year periods followed by a seventh thousand time of rest. From the time of the Reformation, Ehlert examines the writings of William Gouge and Pierre Poiret and claims there is a dispensational scheme in their writings. Ehlert believes John Edwards wrote the first extensive work on dispensationalism. He also believes Jonathan Edwards in his *History of the Work of Redemption* gives a semblance of dispensationalism. John Nelson Darby gives a seven-part dispensational scheme; however, in terminology of each dispensation, there is a lack of similarity with Scofield and Chafer.[6] This subject will be discussed more in depth in subsequent chapters.

Instead of interpreting the Old and New Testaments according to a two or three covenantal scheme, Chafer divides the Old and New Testaments into seven distinct periods. Chafer, however, primarily emphasizes only three of the dispensations: law, grace, and kingdom. The reason for emphasizing only three of the dispensations is because he feels only these three are found in the majority of the Old and New Testaments. The three dispensations, or time periods, are found from the book of Exodus to the end of the book of Revelation. Chafer believes the saints will be taken out before the time of tribulation begins. The tribulation will be a seven-year period which could begin at any moment, and immediately before the commencement of this period, the Church-age saints along with the then living saints will be taken. Understanding the last week of the seventy weeks of Daniel chapter nine as a yet future event, Chafer claims I Thessalonians 4:16-17 speaks of the initiation of this period. Dispensational premillennialists have disagreed concerning how this seven-year period should be interpreted. Chafer recognizes the period will be very similar to the dispensation of law, the period from the giving of the law to Moses to the crucifixion of Christ. Chafer claims since the sixty-nine weeks are part of the dispensation of law, the seventieth must be also. The age of grace is not part of these seventy weeks, but is a parenthesis which could end at any time.

Central to understanding Chafer's eschatology is the division between Israel and the Church. The latter is merely an intercalation in his

Introduction

thought, and of this period the Old Testament prophets were unaware.

Only the blindest form of covenant theology would ignore the overwhelming evidence in the Scriptures that the Church is not in Daniel's 483 years, or in any period of the Old Testament history. Those who would thrust the Church into the last 7 years of Gentile times are guilty of introducing an element into that period which has no place in that period since it is not to be on earth during the eventful years which that period consummates.[8]

I have critically examined the writings of Lewis Sperry Chafer in order to determine Chafer's understanding of the events surrounding the end time. Chafer wrote hundreds of articles for *Bibliotheca Sacra*, *The Sunday School Times*, *Our Hope*, and the *Revelation* magazine. He also wrote several books which cover a variety of subjects such as evangelism, Satan, and the spiritual life of the Christian. The culmination of his thought is the *Systematic Theology*.

Chapter one, "Chafer's Life and Career," is biographical. Although his works are becoming better known, Chafer remains an enigma to many, simply to be shrugged off as another obscure southern Bible teacher and preacher. This chapter endeavors to ascertain just who Lewis Sperry Chafer was. An inquiry into the formative influences of his life is essential. There are many sources which discuss him, some on a personal level. Regarding the writing of the *Systematic Theology*, C. F. Lincoln offers some helpful insights:

> The discipline and training which Dr. Chafer received as a background for the writing of this extensive work on Systematic Theology was that of many years of faithful study. In his early years he was known among Bible teachers as especially given to doctrine and was invited on several occasions to become a teacher of Bible doctrine in leading institutes of this country ...
> Dr. Chafer himself said that "the very fact that I did not study a prescribed course in theology made it possible for me to approach the subject with an unprejudiced mind and to be concerned only with what the Bible actually teaches." This

independent research has resulted in this work which is unabridged, Calvinistic, premillennial, and dispensational.[9]

How Chafer saw himself is an important question. His father was a Congregational minister, and Lewis Chafer, though ordained in the Congregational Church, remained the majority of his career in the Presbyterian Church, U. S. This chapter gives insight into the influences which molded Chafer's character.

Chapter two, "Chafer's Sources," discusses the theological influences upon Chafer. What initiated his intense desire to write a systematic theology from a dispensational, premillennial perspective? The question of how he came to this conclusion concerning eschatology is pertinent to this chapter. It is necessary to discuss the contribution various individuals made upon his theological thinking. His father, the Reverend Thomas Franklin Chafer, graduated from Auburn Theological Seminary and his mother's father, Asa Sperry, was a licensed Welsh Wesleyan preacher. Chafer did not simply imbibe his father's theology; rather, he came to radically different conclusions than those of his father. Was Chafer an iconoclast with somewhat of a rebel spirit, or were his conclusions based upon genuine conviction?

Chafer founded a seminary in the midst of the theological controversy between modernism and fundamentalism, but he did not wish to have the institution identified with fundamentalism since he believed the movement had become somewhat radical. But there is a need to understand why he took a moderately fundamental position.

Chafer was unusually well-rounded in his professional acquaintances. Two very close associates during these years were A. B. Winchester and W. H. Griffith Thomas. The latter was a noted Anglican scholar. This chapter explores the question of whether or not C. I. Scofield exerted a considerable contribution to Chafer's understanding of eschatology.

Chapter three, "Chafer's Dispensationalism," concentrates on this subject, as found throughout his writings. Chafer wrote several works which specifically address the issue, but the primary statement of his position is contained in the *Systematic Theology*.

Chafer's system of eschatology is primarily found in volume four of the *Systematic Theology* though his analysis of dispensationalism is

Introduction

dispersed throughout the volumes. Daniel Fuller states: "In the writings of Lewis Sperry Chafer, and especially his eight-volume *Systematic Theology*, is to be found the most complete systematization of dispensationalism."[10] Likewise, Norman Kraus claims Chafer's *Systematic Theology* is the first work in which dispensational distinctions have been employed as the "unique structural and interpretive principle."[11] For those whose courage shrinks when they ponder the task of wading through eight volumes of systematic theology, they will welcome the news that in 1988 Chafer's *Systematic Theology* was abridged and is now available in two volumes consisting of about nine hundred pages.

Since this book focuses upon Chafer's eschatology, only those facets of dispensationalism which are concerned with the subject will be discussed. Chafer found prophetic Scripture within each dispensation, but perhaps the prophetic element is more appropriate to his millenialism. This chapter, then, concentrates on the division of biblical history into specific periods rather than upon eschatological content within each dispensation which Chafer saw as prophetic.

Chapter four, "Chafer's Millennialism," focuses upon his understanding of premillennialism. The chapter briefly covers the historical development of premillenialism. The essential tenets of postmillennialism are also viewed. Other subjects related to Chafer's understanding of premillennialism are also discussed. Chafer's view of the ordering of events which precede the millennium, or the thousand-year reign of peace, is pertinent to this chapter as well as the events within this period and those which close it.

Many of the disciples of Chafer's teachings are currently better known than Chafer, including Charles R. Swindoll, Charles C. Ryrie, Hal Lindsey, Lawrence (Larry) O. Richards, Tony Evans, David Jeremiah, J. Vernon McGee, Howard Hendricks, Charles Stanley, and Joseph Stowell. Chafer's influence is readily apparent in the ministries of these individuals, but there are literally hundreds of thousands of others Chafer has directly or indirectly influenced.

Notes: Introduction

1. Stewart G. Cole. *The History of Fundamentalism* (New York: Richard R. Smith, 1931), p. 257.

2. Ernest R. Sandeen, *The Roots of Fundamentalism* (Grand Rapids: Baker Book House, 1978), pp. 221, 243.

3. Timothy P. Weber, *Living in the Shadow of the Second Coming* (New York: Oxford University Press, 1979), pp. 88, 161.

4. George M. Marsden, *Fundamentalism and American Culture* (New York: Oxford University Press, 1980), p. 98.

5. James H. Snowden, *The Coming of the Lord* (New York: Macmillan Co., 1919): Loraine Boettner, *The Millennium* (Philadelphia: Presbyterian & Reformed Publishing Co., 1957)

6. Arnold D. Ehlert, "A Bibliography of Dispensatinalism," *Bibliotheca Sacra* 101 (January 1944): 95-101 and serially through January 1946.

7. Lewis Sperry Chafer, *Systematic Theology*, vol. 1: *Prolegomena-Bibliology-Theology Proper* (Dallas: Dallas Seminary Press, 1947), pp. 40-41.

8. Lewis Sperry Chafer, *Systematic Theology*, vol. 4: *Ecclesiology-Eschatology* (Dallas: Dallas Seminary Press, 1948), p. 364.

9. C. F. Lincoln, "Biographical Sketch of the Author," in *Systematic Theology*, by Lewis Sperry Chafer, vol. 8: *Biographical Sketch and Indexes* (Dallas: Dallas Seminary Press, 1948), pp. 5-6.

10. Daniel Fuller, "The Hermenuetics of Dispensationalism" (Th.D. dissertation, Northern Baptist Seminary, 1957), p. 378.

11. Norman Krause, *Dispensationalism in America: Its Rise and Development* (Richmond: John Knox Press, 1958), p. 57.

Chapter One
Chafer's Life and Career

Lewis Sperry Chafer's life spanned eight decades, and during his career, he contributed enormously to the area of eschatology by virtue of writing and publishing a dispensational, premillennial eschatology. He experienced and witnessed a vast upheaval in American religion from the 1870s until 1952. But Chafer was no mere spectator to what was occurring religiously; he was deeply involved throughout his life as an evangelist, pastor, author, systematic theology professor, and seminary president.

As is true with many gifted individuals, he possessed paradoxical qualities. His father was a graduate of Auburn Theological Seminary, but Chafer, though he was awarded three honorary doctorates, was not a seminary graduate. Nevertheless, his lack of formal theological education did not hinder him, but served as a catalyst to encourage him to study theology intensely. Short in stature and light of frame, he was fearless of spirit in controversy and debate. He was an ardent evangelist during an era when evangelism was replete with gimmickry and had acquired a reputation of charlatanism. However, Chafer continually spoke against the use of methods in evangelism and in his book, *True Evangelism*, voices his concern over the indiscriminate use of coercion in evangelism.

Chafer retained his membership in the Presbyterian Church, U. S. though he himself was a devoted evangelical who perhaps would have been more comfortable in a more theologically conservative denomination. Born and raised in the Midwest and New England, he was instrumental in establishing a seminary in the heart of the southwest, Dallas, Texas. Although he was a southern Presbyterian, one of his closest colleagues was an Anglican, W. H. Griffith Thomas. Even though Chafer had no children, it is impossible to calculate how many recognize him as their spiritual father, perhaps even millions revere his teachings.

Early Years

Born at Rock Creek, Ashtabula County, Ohio, on February 27, 1871, he was the son of the Reverend Thomas Franklin Chafer and Lois Lomira Sperry. Thomas Franklin graduated from Auburn Theological Seminary with the class of 1864 and was the local Congregational minister. Thomas Chafer was born in 1828 and lived until 1882. Thomas Franklin's father, William Chafer, was born in York, England and came to the United States in 1837. Lewis's mother was born at Rock Creek, Ohio in 1836 and lived until the fall of 1915. Her father, Asa Sperry, was a licensed Welsh Wesleyan preacher. His maternal grandmother of Irish descent was Ann Sperry.[1]

When Lewis was eleven years old, his father died, leaving a family of three children: one daughter, Maryette, and two sons, Rollin and Lewis. Lewis, the youngest, inherited many of the finer traits of his father. He wrote his sermons with great care; discipline marked his thinking and writing style. C. F. Lincoln claims: "This trait of painstaking study on the part of the father reflected and magnified in the untiring devotion of Doctor Chafer to ceaseless searching of the Scriptures in the severest of inductive study."[2]

Education

The details of Chafer's formative years, however, have not been documented. He attended public school until age twelve, just one year after the death of his father. He assumed his share of the household responsibility by working on a nearby farm. His early years apparently were filled with heavy responsibilities, which he took seriously. Dr. Edwin C. Deibler, a former student of Chafer and one who traveled four years with Chafer in evangelistic and Bible conference ministries, describes Chafer as "small of stature but tough . . . had spent years on the farm."[3]

From 1885 - 1888 he attended New Lyme Institute of New Lyme, Ohio. Here he discovered a talent which characterized his entire ministry — music. "An old photo shows him in the New Lyme Band, playing the violin, and his sister Maryette playing the triangle."[4] His natural ability in music proved to be of importance in his eighty-one years as an evangelist, pastor, and even seminary professor and president. Chafer was a gifted musician, and he believed the gospel could be presented also through the medium of music, since people are less defensive while listening to music than while listening to an evangelist or minister speak. Also, he believed music is edifying to the saints.

His widowed mother moved the family to Oberlin, Ohio with the intention of providing Lewis an opportunity for education at Oberlin College and Conservatory of Music. Lewis attended this school from 1889 - 1892, and here his ability in music matured. The years at Oberlin meant more to Chafer than just the acquiring of proficiency in music since he met his future wife, to whom he was married in 1896. They eventually co-authored and published seventeen hymns between 1909 - 1917, which are contained in their work entitled *Selected Hymns*.[5]

Edwin C. Deibler states concerning this musical team: "Prior to his [Chafer] days as an evangelist, he was a gospel musician, with his wife Loraine. They served as a musical team; he the choir director, song leader and soloist, she as the accompanist and arranger."[6]

Oberlin College was founded by the revivalist Charles G. Finney. One might suppose that the Arminian theological atmosphere greatly influenced Chafer's theological thought. But Chafer did not enroll in one theology course. Also, his professors of music were not necessarily evangelically or even theologically minded "because the teachers were hired for their musical ability rather than their piety."[7] But Sydney Ahlstrom spoke of Oberlin as a "center of influence for revival theology,"[8] and it cannot be doubted that the influence of the atmosphere of Oberlin had an impact upon the evangelistic thinking and career of Chafer. He spent one year in the preparatory school and two years in the conservatory. In 1892 he graduated from Oberlin Conservatory of Music and ended his formal academic career.

Conversion

Central to the entire career of Lewis Sperry Chafer was his

conversion experience. Dr. John A. Witmer, who personally knew Chafer, believes Chafer was only seven at the occurrence of his conversion and that his conversion experience was the result of responding to an evangelistic message preached by an evangelist named Scott.[9] Howard also suggests this age when he speaks of a religious crisis in Chafer's life at the age of seven. Howard writes:

> At seven he had a definite religious crisis but no one showed any interest in him at the time. "If there had been child evangelism then," he notes, "they would have landed me high and dry, but people weren't interested in children then and I don't know just what happened."[10]

One cannot be definite concerning this "religious crisis" although it does appear Chafer indeed had a religious experience as a child of seven. Throughout his life Chafer believed God had directed His grace toward him at the time of his conversion, and the theme of grace became a dominant emphasis in his ministry; thus, he welcomed the title "Apostle of Grace." Toward the end of his life, Chafer wrote in his culminating work, the *Systematic Theology* :

> Sovereign grace originates and is at once a complete reality in the mind of God when He, before the foundation of the world, elects a company who are by His limitless power to be presented in glory conformed to the image of His Son. By so much they are to be to all intelligences the means by which He will manifest the exceeding riches of His grace (Eph. 2:7). This manifestation will correspond to His infinity and will satisfy Him perfectly as the final, all-comprehensive measurement of His attribute of grace.[11]

However, grace for Chafer was intimately related to eschatology, since he believed the individual's ultimate salvation is derived solely from the grace of God.[12] At the conclusion of his volume on eschatology in the *Systematic Theology*, Chafer writes:

The location of the third heaven has never been revealed, but it is the home of the Father, the Son, and the Holy Spirit, and has never been inhabited by any created being until the present age. When a believer dies, he goes at once to be with Christ (2 Cor. 5:8; Phil. 1:23) and therefore takes up his abode in that sphere. Thus all believers will be brought into that place of glory at the coming of the Lord, and the third heaven is being populated at the present time. Salvation consists in fitting individuals for that heavenly sphere.[13]

Evangelistic Ministry

After his studies at Oberlin were completed, Chafer pursued the career of evangelist for the next seven years. He had been prepared for this profession early in life because of the years he had spent in the parsonage as the son of a minister, his personal conversion experience, and the talents which he developed further at Oberlin College, a school which was very much part of the revivalistic tradition. He became an evangelistic singer until approximately the turn of the century.

Chafer was associated with many well-known evangelists, but he was particularly involved with Arthur T. Reed.[14] In 1896 he married Ella Loraine Case. She had been a vital part of his ministry since his studies at Oberlin.

Music was central to his ministry throughout his life but especially during his first seven years as an evangelist when he was forming specific opinions of the use of music in evangelism. Years later in 1918, writing from East Orange, New Jersey, he explains:

> Science has not gone far, and perhaps cannot, in discovering and analyzing the underlying cause of the vital force in music; but the effectiveness of music may easily be traced through its three fundamental elements — rhythm, melody, and harmony....
>
> ... The varying effects produced in the mind by these elements of music constitute the evidence that music is a

language of the soul....

... There must be strong agreement between the words of a hymn and the effect of the music. Thus truth is often more effective when it is sung that when it is spoken. Certainly the blessing of God has accompanied the singing of the Gospel.[15]

Chafer's ministry as an evangelist spanned twenty-two years, 1892 - 1914. Until the late 1890s, however, he was not preaching but was convinced his gift in evangelism was music. A crisis occurred in 1897, and this event was a significant factor in his desire to begin a preaching ministry; he contracted tuberculosis.

The theme of eschatology was interwoven in this experience because for the first time in his life, Chafer became aware of his own mortality. Finally, he fully resigned himself to what he perceived as the will of God for the rest of his life. Chafer's entire preaching and teaching ministry was essentially eschatological in nature. Yes, he spoke of the grace of God, power for living, forgiveness, the Spirit-filled life, and essential doctrines, but all these topics and subjects were controlled by the overarching theme of humanity's mortality, the need for salvation, and the ultimate encounter with the living God.

His episode with tuberculosis marked a turning point in his ministry because he realized his personal limitations and that he must commit himself fully to the ministry of evangelism. Seeking ecclesiastical endorsement, he was ordained into the Congregational ministry at the age of twenty-nine in the First Congregational Church of Buffalo, New York. After his ordination in 1900, he briefly pastored a church in Lewistown, New York, but since he believed his true gifts were in evangelism, he once again returned to this ministry.[16] There was a great difference now in his ministry — he returned as a preacher of the Word. He was convinced of his call, and from this time until his death in 1952, fervency and conviction characterized his life and efforts. Although at this point in his life, he did not have the awareness he would have in later years concerning expository preaching and teaching, he was committed to proclaiming the Word of God; he had heard the call of God and he submitted to that beckoning.

Soon after his commitment to a career of preaching and teaching,

Chafer's Life and Career

Chafer began examining and changing his opinion of evangelism. Chafer continually questioned the popular evangelism of his day. He became skeptical of evangelistic techniques and in his work *True Evangelism* speaks of "false forces in evangelism."[17] Of particular interest is his view of the true message of the evangelist:

> The New Testament evangelist is given a particular message to proclaim. That message is the "good news" of the Gospel of Grace; it is therefore a distinct body of truth for this age. His evangel is one of "glad tidings," because it offers freedom from the bondage of the law, with attempts at self-fitting for the presence of God, and because it proclaims a perfect salvation by the power of God through faith in Jesus Christ and His redemption on the cross.... [18]

Chafer, then, in contrast to many of his contemporary evangelists, believed in a positive and affirmative message. Howard gives added insight into Chafer's thinking concerning evangelism:

> Chafer had ample opportunity to watch the "methods" of the high-powered evangelists of those days. J. Wilbur Chapman was applying his "machinery" to gospel preaching, organizing his meetings to the point of spotted trained personal workers in every fifth row to converge on the audience during the invitation. He stormed the big cities with 25 evangelists holding simultaneous meetings. For a while Chafer was one of 25. But soon, he claims, he began to see dangers in the ordinary methods of "getting decisions," counting raised hands and promptly leaving town. There seemed to be no place for the grace of God or the work of the Holy Spirit, and he began to question the use of methods which do not recognize the Spirit's ministry of revealing the Gospel.[19]

Chafer's book, *True Evangelism*, although not published until 1911, was written in 1901. He came to be known as the evangelist "without methods" and stressed "an entire dependence upon the Spirit to do every phase of the work that has been assigned to Him in the purpose of God."[20] He comments further on the use of methods:

> Likewise, an undue emphasis upon methods in modern evangelism is almost universal. The erroneous impression exists that the evangelistic efforts should be confined to stated times and seasons, and that impression has led to a far more serious one, namely, that God is only occasionally "on the giving hand"; whereas the Scriptural forces in true evangelism depend upon the unchanging promises of God, the constant abiding presence of the Holy Spirit in the Church, and His continual working through members of the body of Christ.[21]

Many years later, in 1947, Chafer wrote an article defending the writing of *True Evangelism*. He stated the reason for writing the book as follows: "The purpose in the main being to record the experiences through which the author had passed in evangelism in relation to the methods of the day and to provide a constructive message on the unchanging truth that souls must be enlightened by the Holy Spirit."[22] The book virtually contains no eschatological or dispensational themes. The work was written before his introduction to C. I. Scofield and his personal study of the Scriptures through a dispensational, premillennial method.

It is apparent that Chafer, though very much within the then current evangelistic tradition, had definite and firm convictions concerning evangelism, convictions which placed him at odds with many if not most of his contemporaries. Because of his reservations with methods in evangelism, many accused him of refusing to give an invitation, as was a common practice among the evangelists of that era. Edwin Deibler states: "Relative to the canard that Chafer was not interested in evangelism and refused to give an invitation, I heard Chafer preach a message in the summer of '38 at the First Baptist Church in San Diego and give an invitation afterward to which there was a considerable response."[23]

Chafer appeared as a fervent evangelist, polished but unpretentious. One easily obtains the impression that although Chafer was comfortable with evangelism, this was not the area in which his gifts could be used to the fullest. He was too methodical, organized, creative, and perhaps not fully spontaneous to limit himself solely to evangelism. One sees a progression in his personal realization that his best gifts lay in Bible teaching and writing. He wrote his work, *True Evangelism*, in order to correct the flagrant abuses in evangelism. The work was indeed a precursor of his intense desire to fashion a biblical philosophy of his personal faith.

Northfield

The last quarter of the nineteenth century was a period when Bible and prophetic conferences were very popular. Kellogg writing in 1888 speaks of

> An impressive visible illustration in the premillennial conference held in The Church of the Holy Trinity, New York, in 1878, when the great assembly at its closing meeting, rising to their feet, passed with great enthusiasm the following resolution: "That the doctrine of our Lord's premillennial advent instead of paralyzing evangelistic and missionary effort, is one of the mightiest incentives to earnestness in preaching the gospel to every creature till he comes." Nor is this a matter with them of mere words....[24]

D. L. Moody, who was virtually a household name in the United States and Great Britain during the last quarter of the nineteenth century, exerted a powerful influence upon the theological climate at Northfield, both by his personal teachings and the speakers he brought to Northfield. Through the influence of D. L. Moody, premillennialism became the dominant eschatological position at the Northfield conferences. Sandeen writes: "By 1886 the leaders of the millenarian movement had practically taken over the Northfield conferences and transformed it into another of their familiar premillennial gatherings."[25] Theologians and clergymen who took part were not only from the United States but also from Canada and Great Britain. Moody selected leading British clergy to lead evangelistic meetings at Northfield.[26] Northfield indeed became an important chapter in Chafer's life.

In 1903, the Chafers moved to East Northfield, Massachusetts. Chafer transferred his ministerial membership to the Presbytery of Troy, New York. Lincoln relates the important relationship which commenced at Northfield:

> At that time Dr. C. I. Scofield was pastor of the Congregational Church of Northfield, which had been organized by D. L. Moody, and there was cemented between the two men [Scofield and Chafer] a closeness of fellowship... which lasted until Dr. Scofield's death in 1921. When Dr. Chafer moved to East Northfield he began at once his service as music leader, along with Ira Sankey, D. B. Towner, George Stibbins, and others, in the great Moody Summer Bible Conferences. Mrs. Chafer was the official organist for the conferences.[27]

Chafer was affiliated with Northfield from 1903 - 1909. During those years, the Northfield Bible Conference featured such biblical expositors and theologians as H. W. Webb-Peploe, G. Campbell Morgan, W. Graham Scroggie, and F. B. Meyer of Great Britain; W. H. Griffith Thomas and A. B. Winchester of Canada; and A. T. Pierson, William B. Eerdman, C. I. Scofield, H. A. Ironside, and George E. Guille of the United States. In later years, Chafer acknowledged the influence of these dispensational, premillennial theologians when he wrote: "The association and close acquaintance with some of the world's greatest expositors ... placed before me the ideals of expository preaching based on extended knowledge and familiarity with the Scriptures."[28]

D. L. Moody organized Northfield in 1880 with a view to giving the average church member an opportunity for spiritual renewal. Chafer had this to say about the impact of Northfield:

> Not only does the summer Bible conference minister to the hunger of many, but it has been one of the greatest agencies in transforming Christian lives. In these gatherings, more than

has ever been estimated, lives have been dedicated to God, and true spirituality entered into which has resulted in ministries for God which have gone out to the ends of the earth. A book of personal testimonies from Keswick, Northfield of the earlier days, and from the conferences of later days, would disclose how wonderfully God has provided for the present needs of his people through the summer Bible conferences. What an unnumbered company of Christians are thanking God for the vision and spiritual change which they have received at these great Bible study, missionary and Victorious Life gatherings![29]

During these years at Northfield, Howard relates that Chafer owned a farm in the Northfield area, and he spent the winters in evangelistic campaigns, farmed in the spring, and in the summer led the singing at Northfield with such well-known musicians as Ira Sankey.[30] Mrs. W. R. Moody, daughter-in-law of D. L. Moody, states of Chafer: "I always consider the peak of our singing here was reached under Mr. Chafer. I shall never forget 'Master, the Tempest is Raging,' and so many other hymns which they [the audience] never sang so well for anyone else."[31]

From 1906 - 1909 and for three weeks in the fall of 1910, he was a teacher of music and Bible at the Mount Hermon School for Boys. Mount Hermon was a secondary school affiliated with Northfield which had a basic curriculum along with Bible. Chafer apparently was very approachable as a teacher and his students readily confided in him. His students found him capable, helpful, and likable. He was repeatedly asked if he would consider taking a pastorate in the area and allow interested individuals to be taught pastoral subjects under his supervision.[32] He did not grant their request, but the suggestion that he teach pastoral subjects became a powerful though somewhat latent force in his life. Years later he was the primary personality in the founding of a theological seminary in Dallas, Texas.

As a man in his mid-thirties, what changes had taken place in his thinking and life? First, he had not limited himself solely to music but was developing as a preacher and Bible teacher; second, he was meeting and influencing an ever-widening circle of friends and acquaintances; third,

The Promise of Dawn

he was beginning to see himself as a professional teacher; and fourth, he was developing a critical awareness to speak against and correct abuses in religion such as with the writing of *True Evangelism*.

Chafer did not disclose just how early he accepted dispensational premillennialism. It is known that he heard many who held to such a position at Northfield, and at this location he met C. I. Scofield and formed a close relationship with him, which was nurtured through the years. Perhaps all that can be said with certainty is that Chafer was essentially in agreement with dispensationalism by this period in his life, but he lacked the solid scholarship behind that belief. He was personally convinced but had not studied the full range of dispensationalism. Time would eventually eliminate that lack.

By this period in his career, there were no outstanding achievements. There were no accomplishments which would serve as an anticipation of his future greatness. After all, he had no formal theological training and was trained in music. Perhaps at this time in his life, Chafer himself was not aware of the great potential he possessed. One quality which served him well throughout his life was his great ability to organize, and this characteristic was evident even at a very young age. All the ingredients for a career of prominence appeared to be crystallizing, but there was no clear-cut direction in achieving specific goals. He displayed ability in speaking and writing. His first book, *Satan*, was written in 1909 and is a biblical summary of what the Scriptures teach concerning this being. *True Evangelism* was published in 1911. People apparently were drawn to him, as testified to by his closeness with his students at Mount Hermon.

Witmer believes the Northfield years were crucial for the career of Lewis Sperry Chafer; these years marked a certain *rite de passage* in his life. Witmer cites Chafer's intense belief in the great need for expository preaching and the strong desire to start a school for the training of ministers as the two major results of the Northfield years. Witmer writes:

> In the years that followed as Dr. Chafer itinerated the evangelistic and Bible conference ministry he made a point of quizzing countless pastors concerning areas in which they felt their seminary course of study failed to prepare them. Invariably the

response was that they were not taught the English Bible in order to be able to minister its truths. The conviction slowly crystallized that a seminary was needed with a distinctive curriculum that would equip men to be expositors of the Word of God. Through these contacts and experiences God prepared Lewis Sperry Chafer for a quarter-century to be His instrument in founding Dallas Theological Seminary.[33]

A dispensational and premillennial eschatological foundation would eventually characterize this school. These distinctive emphases were formulated by Chafer himself.[34]

Of all the people Chafer met in his itinerating work as an evangelist during the Northfield days, the one who influenced him the most was Dr. C. I. Scofield, the editor of the *Scofield Reference Bible*. Chafer often likened this relationship to that of a father and a son.[35] The exact date cannot be fixed, but an important meeting took place between Scofield and Chafer which changed the entire direction of the latter's life. At the time, Scofield was pastor of the First Congregational Church of Dallas, Texas. Scofield had invited Chafer to hold evangelistic meetings. At the conclusion of the meetings. Scofield convinced Chafer that his gifts in evangelism were not as great as his gifts as a Bible teacher. The two prayed together, and Chafer dedicated his life to a lifetime of biblical study. The commitment to the Lord on the part of Chafer was accomplished on a human level by C. I. Scofield, and in a real sense that commitment on Chafer's part represented a transference of the dispensational and premillennial teachings of Scofield to Chafer. Walvoord places this event during the World War I years.[36] Renfer, however, points out that Scofield was pastor of the First Congregational Church of Dallas between the years 1883 - 1895 and also from 1903 - 1910. The meeting between the two could not have occurred during the first date since Chafer and Scofield did not actually meet until 1901. All that can be stated with certainty is that the meeting took place before 1910.[37]

This unusual meeting with Scofield dramatically altered the course of Chafer's life since the latter apparently took to heart Scofield's advice. Especially from this period until the end of his life, Chafer became a prolific writer and gifted Bible teacher. Chafer must have been somewhat unsure of his gifts to have taken so seriously Scofield's comments. Granted, he had a great admiration for Scofield, but Chafer was no longer a young man.

One sees a gradual awareness on Chafer's part concerning his best gifts and the need to develop them to the fullest. How significant was the impact of Scofield upon Chafer? *The Sunday School Times* editors write that Chafer had "become in a real sense the successor to Dr. Scofield ... and is among the most eagerly sought Bible teachers in the United States."[38] The direction of his life was determined.

Post Northfield Days

Bible Conference Ministry

From 1911 - 1916 Chafer traveled during the winter and spring with Scofield. He was affiliated with Scofield at a school in New York City. Chafer says: "I was constantly with Scofield. We had one time a school in New York and the correspondence part of it was in the hands of Dr. Scofield and Pettingill, and the oral teaching was in the hands of Dr. Scofield and myself."[39]

Gradually Chafer was becoming known as a Bible teacher and not an evangelist. Chafer recalls:

> I had been chosen by Dr. Scofield to be his associate teacher traveling about together.... This took me out of evangelistic work and put me into the Bible teaching field.... The old man was getting feeble and he had a way of making engagements and then having a habit of breaking them at the last moment and sending me as a substitute teacher. And I had that experience of trying to fit into the shoes of Dr. Scofield. It opened the door for me to travel as a Bible teacher.[40]

Chafer left Mount Hermon in 1911, and in the following years he associated with a host of well-known Bible teachers and evangelists in an itinerant Bible conference ministry. Some of the names were: A. T. Pierson, William Eerdman, James Gray, R. A. Torrey, W. H. Griffith

Thomas, A. B. Winchester, W. Graham Scroggie, and G. Campbell Morgan. In addition to Bible conference work, Chafer was also invited to speak at theological seminaries in the United States. In 1912 through the influence of James Sprunt, a board member of the Union Theological Seminary in Richmond, Virginia, Chafer delivered a message at the seminary. Sprunt, in responding to a letter from the study body committee, told of his reason for inviting Chafer to speak:

> When Mr. Chafer came here I was impressed from the beginning of his lectures with his great expository power, as well as his profound knowledge of the Scriptures.... Mr. Chafer presented many messages to me in a clear light which had previously been hidden or confused. I was, therefore, most desirous that others could share this benefit.[41]

The student body of Union Seminary apparently responded very favorably to Chafer since they wrote a letter to James Sprunt concerning Chafer's message:

> It was a continual feast of spiritual blessing the full value of which is inestimable. Judging from the remarks made by members of each class in our student body we have not been favored with a series of lectures more deeply spiritual, more edifying and more inspiring than these which it has been our recent privilege to enjoy. A profound impression has been made upon the students of the impelling force of true expository preaching, which is true preaching.... [42]

Early Writings

In 1916 Chafer moved to East Orange, New Jersey. Working from this base, he gave lectures at Philadelphia College of the Bible and worked at the Fulton Street Mission in New York City. Also, he wrote copiously. His first published work, *Satan*, written in 1909, is replete with dispensational divisions and references to eschatological themes. He understands Satan to be a literal figure, and Chafer scripturally supports his conclusions concerning Satan's career:

Satan thus is revealed as having been created perfect in all his ways, mighty in power, and full of beauty and wisdom. While thus privileged, he purposed in his heart a stupendous project — to make himself like the Most High. Though remaining in heaven and having access to God, he is seen wrestling the world scepter from man. He is ruling as the god of this world until the judgment of the cross, and after that he still rules as a usurper. At the end of the age he is cast out of heaven into the earth, with further access to heaven denied. From there he is sent to the pit, and finally is banished to the lake of fire forever.[43]

Chafer speaks of the dispensation of law, grace, and kingdom in *Satan*.[44] Of the latter period Chafer writes: "There is a still more extensive body of Scripture which anticipates a literal kingdom of righteousness and peace upon the earth. This theme was the burden of the Old Testament prophets, and was announced by John the Baptist, by Christ, and His disciples."[45] Chafer in this first book is emphatic that the present age will not witness the kingdom:

> Again, this age is not the coming earthly kingdom for nowhere are the promised conditions of that kingdom now to be found. The Old Testament prophecies contain long and detailed descriptions of that glorious time. God's ancient people shall become the chosen nation, restored to their own land; the enemy shall be banished; the earth shall be purified, and blossom as a rose.[46]

It is obvious, then, that Chafer was a dispensational premillenialist by the time of the writing of this book. Why did Chafer begin his writing career with a book concerning Satan? He does not give a definite answer but only hints at a need for greater victory in the Christian life. Chafer believed in a literal Satan who commands authority over innumerable fallen angels. These angels possess immeasurable power. Satanic forces constantly bombard the Christian, but Chafer always emphasizes that the Christian can have victory. In addition to Satan, two other sources of sin

Chafer's Life and Career

are the *cosmos*, or the world system, and the fleshly nature which everyone possesses throughout his earthly life.

True Evangelism appeared in 1911, though written in 1901, and *The Kingdom in History and Prophecy* was published in 1915. In the latter, Chafer set forth what he considered a great problem in contemporary theology:

> A clear and thoroughly Biblical book on the kingdom in the Scriptures has long been a *desideratum*. Perhaps no truth of divine revelation has suffered more at the hands of interpreters than that concerning the Kingdom. Following the Roman Catholic interpretation, Protestant theology has very generally taught that all the kingdom promises, and even the great Davidic covenant itself, are to be fulfilled in and through the church.[47]

He continues:

> It stands to reason, since one-fourth of the Bible is in prophetic form, and five-sixths of the Bible is addressed to one nation to whom the kingdom promises are given, that any plan of study which avoids prophecy and ignores or "spiritualizes" God's covenants with His chosen earthly people will be incomplete, misleading and subject to mere human assumptions.[48]

By this time in Chafer's life, he had already formed his basic presuppositions concerning premillennialism and dispensationalism.

His next book, *Salvation*, was written in 1916. Chafer states concerning the subject of salvation: "Salvation is not a human undertaking. It did not originate in this sin-cursed world. It is of God and unto God, and hence moves along lines and under conditions and necessities which are of a higher realm."[49]

The subject of personal salvation was perhaps Chafer's most important life theme. He experienced God's saving grace as a child. Chafer rarely spoke without mentioning God's saving grace.

Chafer speaks much of the love of God in *Salvation* :

> Every moment of the earth life of Jesus was a manifestation of God's love, but one event in the ministry of Jesus is especially designated as the means by which the bosom of God was unveiled.... In the cross of Christ, therefore, God hath declared His love, and this declaration is addressed as a personal message to every individual.[50]

Chafer's work, *Salvation*, does not speak to the issue of eschatology, and there is virtually no discussion concerning dispensationalism.

In 1918 Chafer wrote *He That Is Spiritual*. In the preface the author writes:

> The importance of the subject of this book is beyond estimation. True spirituality is that quality of life in the child of God which satisfies and glorifies the Father. It brings celestial joy and peace to the believer's own heart. Upon it all Christian service depends. Since God purposes to work through human means, the fitness of the instrument determines the progress made.
>
> There is general agreement that the daily life of Christians should be improved; but improvement cannot be had other than in God's way.[51]

He makes many delightful statements such as: "Spirit filled Christians are quite apt to be physically exhausted at the close of the day. They are weary *in* the work, but not weary *of* the work." Or, "spirituality hinders sin, but should never hinder the friendship and confidence of sinners." He sees spirituality as "an inward adorning. It is most simple and natural and should be a delight and attraction to all."[52] Chafer also discusses in this book the work of the Spirit in various dispensations. He writes concerning the role of the Holy Spirit in the period of the Old Testament, the Gospels, the book of Acts, and the Epistles.

In 1922 Chafer wrote *Grace*, and many see this work as his finest. The book begins:

Chafer's Life and Career

> The exact and discriminate meaning of the word *grace* should be crystal clear to every child of God. With such insight only can he feed his own soul on the inexhaustible riches which it unfolds, and with such understanding only can he be enabled clearly to pass on to others its marvelous, transforming theme. Here is a striking illustration of the fact that very much may be represented by one word. When used in the Bible to set forth the grace of God in salvation of sinners, the word *grace* discloses not only the boundless goodness and kindness of God toward man, but reaches far beyond and indicates the supreme motive which actuated God in the creation, preservation and consummation of the universe. What greater fact could be expressed by one word?[53]

Grace to Chafer is the motivating force which empowers one to serve:

> When the essential message of Christianity is seen to be the measureless, transforming grace of God with all of its eternal glories in the new creation in Christ, it is a challenge to the deepest impulses of the heart, and offers a ministry for which one may well sacrifice all.[54]

Chafer's work, *Grace*, was written with dispensational distinctions emphasized through the work. Primarily he distinguishes among the dispensations of law, grace, and kingdom and portrays the operations of grace in each age. Chafer's premillenial eschatological views are also apparent in this work:

> The Bible affords no basis for the supposition that the Lord will come to a perfected social order. At His coming He will gather the saved to Himself, but the wicked He will judge in righteousness. The transcendent glory of this age is that grace which will have been either accepted or rejected.[55]

The theme of grace characterized Chafer's entire life.

Founding of Dallas Theological Seminary

By the early 1920s, Chafer, then in his fifties, looked for rest from his strenuous ministry of Bible conference activities. However, constantly in his thinking was the need for a school to train ministers. Since the Northfield days when he taught boys at the Mount Hermon School, he remembered his students' pleas that he might himself start a school for the purpose of training ministers. Chafer writes: "The vision of this specific type of seminary was given to me at least fifteen years before definite steps were taken to found this work."[56]

Concerning the genesis of the desire to begin a school, Chafer states: "The vision of a new and needed type of theological training came to me in the year 1912 and developed during the following twelve years."[57] Why was he so concerned about beginning a school? He believed that many of the seminaries of the day had failed to teach

> ... a knowledge of the Bible itself with a system of study which when followed in the later years, would be ceaselessly unfolding the riches of divine grace.... It is apparent that such a study as they had ... failed ... to give them any satisfactory knowledge of doctrine.... They had learned practically nothing of the spiritual life ... resulting in personal piety and divine power.[58]

Chafer gives added insight into the fervency created by the Bible conference movement and how this movement caused an increased desire on the part of many for a Bible study:

> There is abundant evidence that God is doing a new thing which cannot fail to arrest the attention of every spiritually minded person. His people are being quickened into a new interest in Bible study not unlike the great revivals and spiritual awakenings of the past....Being usually nondenominational, it unites believers of all branches into one common fellowship in the Lord. It is supplying a heart-felt need....The Bible conference movement is a challenge to ministers. It demands of them a tireless study of the Scriptures that they may keep abreast with this onsweeping tide of Bible study and knowledge.[59]

Chafer's Life and Career

Chafer saw a great hunger in the churches for more Bible teaching and preaching, but because he was also aware of the lack of Bible preparation in many seminaries for prospective ministers, Chafer gradually developed plans for the establishing of a school which would meet this great need. Years later he wrote that the seminary "follows a true dispensational and premillennial interpretation."[60]

At this period in American religion there was a great controversy between modernism and fundamentalism. In the early twenties, Clarence Macartney wrote:

> The Protestant Churches of America are being shaken as they have not been shaken for half a century. From every Protestant communion there come tidings of commotion. What is this all about? The man in the pew and the man in the street hear of "Modernism" and "Rationalism" and "Progressivism," of "Fundamentalists" and "Conservatives," and of how the different groups are arrayed against one another. He is anxious to know what lies back of these terms and what issue is at stake in the controversy.[61]

This was a period of great agitation and misunderstanding essentially between two groups. Kenneth Cauthen writes:

> It was not until about 1850 that the liberalism which was destined to overcome orthodoxy began to emerge in this country ... However, it was during the first thirty-five years of this century [twentieth century] that liberalism achieved its most pervasive influence among the leading thinkers of the day.[62]

The controversy continued and crescendoed in the Scopes Trials in 1925, and this event is understood as the culminating victory for liberalism. Cauthen's analysis, however, is limited to the leadership of denominations and seminaries. He does not speak of the great masses within the denominations who were concerned for orthodoxy.

Although Chafer had firm theological convictions, he rarely, if ever, descended to spewing venom or castigating those who differed with him. Chafer's ministry was characterized by a gracious and positive spirit. He wrote in the late 1920s, concerning the need for a new kind of theological training:

> During the last few years a large number of pastors and Bible teachers have voiced their conviction that there is a demand for a vital and extended course of study for ministerial students who seriously desire to "preach the Word." This verdict did not carry with it a criticism of the foundational courses of the present standard training which is being given by time-honored ... seminaries. It rather suggested that to these foundational courses which have long been proven of inestimable value some important material might be added with resultant profit.[63]

What was the great need in seminary training according to Chafer? He offers the following information:

> For more than thirty years it has been my lot to travel extensively, first as an evangelist and later as a Bible teacher. When thus brought into close intimacy with hundreds of pastors and many teachers, naturally such technical subjects as the preacher's training, his sermonic material, and his methods of study, came up for my discussion. In connection with these conversations it was my aim to secure the preacher's innermost conviction as to the value of certain possible courses which he did not receive. These conversations have disclosed a universal agreement that certain additional courses of study might be offered which would more fully qualify the minister as an expository preacher making him more accurate in doctrinal interpretation and equipping him more thoroughly as a spiritual guide.[64]

Chafer envisioned a seminary which would provide four essential elements for effective ministerial training:

1. a careful selection of those students only who are evidently

called of God to preach;
2. thorough and exhaustive treatment of the basic and approved theological subjects;
3. extensive and intensive introductory study of the Bible;
4. the painstaking development of the spiritual life of each individual student.[65]

These basic principles, then, became the guiding concerns for the new seminary.

Plans for the New Seminary

In November 1921 the first meeting occurred concerning the establishment of a new seminary. Those who cooperated in this initial meeting were Lewis Sperry Chafer, A. B. Winchester, B. B. Sutcliffe, and W. P. White. During the conference, the need for a seminary became one of the primary topics. During a prayer meeting, Chafer disclosed his concern for the establishing of a seminary, and his suggestion was taken with great seriousness and anticipation by those present.[66]

Chafer then went to Seattle, Washington, and spent three months filling the pulpit at the University Presbyterian Church, a welcomed change for Chafer after having spent years as an evangelist. During this brief period in Seattle, Chafer wrote to W. H. Griffith Thomas concerning the discussions in Portland about the interest in establishing a seminary. Thomas' reply was very favorable.[67]

On March 7, 1922 Chafer, A. B. Winchester, and W. H. Griffith Thomas met in the Piedmont Hotel in Atlanta, Georgia, to discuss the founding of the new seminary. Chafer was designated to find a suitable location for the school, to organize the school, and to write its doctrinal statement. Griffith Thomas, reflecting his English background, suggested the name Evangelical Theological College, and the name was accepted.[68]

Initially, there was much discussion as to the location of the new school. The locations suggested were Pittsburgh, Wheaton, Denver, and Dallas. Also considered was the establishment of two schools, one in the eastern section at Philadelphia and one in the western section of the United States at Seattle. By 1922 the two-school proposal was dropped, and a location for one school was sought. Chafer initially favored Pittsburgh

The Promise of Dawn

and Wheaton, but toward the end of the year these two proposals were not pursued.

Chafer was invited early in 1922 to hold a Bible conference in Pastor William M. Anderson's church, the First Presbyterian Church of Dallas. When Chafer related to the pastor the plans for a seminary, Anderson immediately declared Dallas must be the location. Renfer writes: "The concentration of Chafer's activities in Dallas and the resultant friendship with Anderson became major factors in locating the seminary in that city."[69] In November 1923, a committee comprised of six ministers and fifteen laymen initiated formal plans for the establishing of a seminary. The members of this committee were composed of two Dallas churches, the First Presbyterian Church and the First Congregational Church.[70]

The year 1923 proved to be not only an important one for Chafer but also an extremely busy and challenging one. On April 9, 1923, Chafer received a call to pastor the First Congregational Church of Dallas. Chafer wrote an acceptance letter on April 11, 1923, on a train between Dallas and St. Louis:

> Greetings! Your call for me to become your minister was duly delivered to me, at your appointment, by Mr. George Latham.
>
> I am deeply moved by this evidence of your confidence in me as one whom you deem, under God, to be fitted for this high service. Since you have known my doctrine, method and manner of life, through the past months in which it has been my privilege to occupy your pulpit, I am assured that you are prepared to stand with me by fellowship in prayer and service in the realization of the ideals which you know are mine.
>
> The honor of succeeding my great friend the late Dr. C. I. Scofield has moved me deeply, and it is with the thought that his prayers and ideals for you, in which I fully participate, may be realized; and with the thought that God has a very great service for you to render as a church with a peculiar spiritual witness for Him in these last days; and with the hope that I may have some share with you in this ministry, that I give my hearty consent to your request that I become your minister. This I do

Chafer's Life and Career

depending on the energizing power of God which I am assured will be mine through your prayers.[71]

One of Chafer's first suggestions was to change the name of the church since it had not been affiliated with the Congregational denomination for several years. In honor of their former pastor, C. I. Scofield, Chafer suggested the name be changed to the Scofield Memorial Church, and his suggestion was heartily accepted.[72] Today Scofield Memorial Church is located in Dallas, Texas, and has a large membership and several ministers.

The Central American Mission was also an integral part of the ministry of the church, and Chafer, during his pastorate, was appointed the secretary of the mission. Actually his responsibilities with the Central American Mission took precedence over that of pastor. Though Chafer had pastoral responsibilities and duties with the mission, foremost in his thinking was the establishing of a seminary.

Lewis Sperry Chafer's brother, Rollin Chafer, also had a significant role in the school because he was instrumental in the initial organization of the school. The new institution opened in the fall of 1924, and thirteen students enrolled. The resident faculty included Dr. William Anderson, Professor A. H. Perpetuo, and President Chafer. Visiting faculty included Dr. A. B. Winchester, Dr. A. C. Gaebelein, Dr. B. B. Sutcliffe, and Dr. H. A. Ironside. All of the faculty members, resident and visiting, were devoted dispensational premillennialists, and on the whole were in agreement with one another concerning eschatology. Dr. W. H. Griffith Thomas was to teach systematic theology, but he died in June of that year; thus, Chafer was chosen to teach in this area. The thrusting of the responsibility to teach systematic theology upon Chafer was an event which shaped the rest of his life as he immersed himself in the study of theology.[73]

Chafer recalled the first year of the seminary four years later:

> Though the new institution was to be in no wise local in its interests, it was by evident Divine leading established at Dallas. It was chartered under the laws of the state of Texas in 1924 with the name The Evangelical Theological College, and

in October of that year opened its doors to students.... At the present time the full complement of teachers ... are serving the college and the regular three-year course leading to the degree of Th.B. and additional courses leading to the degrees of Th.M. and Th.D. are being pursued by a student body numbering thirty-three.[74]

What was the school's relationship to and opinion of denominations?

Though not denominationally governed, the Evangelical Theological College is in no way opposed to spiritual and Biblical work being done by denominational organizations. Its faculty is composed of men who have standing in their respective communions, and a welcome is being accorded to the members of the present graduating class on the ground of their merit by the various denominations to which they belong.[75]

Chafer constantly refers to his desire for a nondenominational school:

Contrary to many predictions made when the college was being planned, its undenominational character has been an asset. ... Its student body is from the major denominational groups of this country and other countries, and upon graduation these students return for ministry almost invariably in their own fellowships. It is really a thrilling experience to hear from widely separated parts of our country, and from many different ecclesiastical bodies.[76]

Even though the school was conservative theologically, Chafer was determined from the beginning not to link the institution with fundamentalism. The actions of the Fundamentals Association's leaders were a constant source of concern for Chafer. Since the new school would be viewed as a fundamentalist institution, Chafer believed the policies of

Chafer's Life and Career

the Association would control the reputation of the seminary. Chafer wrote to A. C. Gaebelein: "Just what these ... men will do before they are checked remains to be seen. But it certainly is a great embarrassment to the rest of us, because of the accurate meaning of the name, we are coupled with all they do in the public eye."[77] Gaebelein concurred with Chafer by stating: "It would be too bad if the new school were linked in any way with Fundamentalism."[78] Renfer writes that Chafer contacted Robert Dick Wilson of Princeton Seminary to consider teaching as a visiting professor at Dallas Seminary. Chafer explains to Wilson:

> As a culmination of several years of prayer and preparation which seems to have been under the leading of the Spirit of God, a number of the best known Bible teachers of this country, quite independent of the Fundamentalist Movement, are establishing a new theological seminary here in Dallas ... and the aim is to make it of the very highest class in every particular.[79]

Chafer and other leaders were disturbed over the bitterness and defensive character of many of the leaders of the Association. By temperament, Chafer was a warm and positive individual, and he believed the atmosphere created by the leadership of the Fundamentals Association was not consonant with the policies and directions of the new school.

Chafer indeed was the driving force behind the establishment of the new seminary, and his distinct personality molded and characterized the school. Especially in the early years, the seminary was characterized by dispensational premillennialism, biblicism, modified calvinism, and moderate fundamentalism. At the commencement of the first classes in 1924, Chafer was fifty-three. His career until this period had been broad and intense, encompassing a ministry of evangelistic singer and preacher, writer, author, pastor, and mission's secretary. However, the next twenty-eight years were to be most productive for Chafer as seminary professor and president. Had he not lived these years, his name might not be significant. His vast well of experiences served as a catalyst for the arduous work which lay ahead.

The Latter Years

From 1924 - 1952 Chafer combined the responsibilities of seminary professor and president. Although enrollment grew steadily, the first years especially were financially difficult.

Chafer undertook the professorship of theology with little formal training in theology. He had, of course, heard and associated for many years with several of the leading Bible teachers of his day and no doubt acquired much knowledge in this capacity. Lincoln says of Chafer:

> When he undertook the professorship of Systematic theology in the seminary in Dallas, Texas, he at once gave himself to ceaseless study and reading in that division of ministerial training. He secured and became familiar with an exceedingly large library on Systematic Theology. The exercise of teaching this vast field of truth for many years required him to answer practically every question which students of serious mind could ask.[80]

He became recognized by his colleagues as capable, determined and thorough. Dr. Wilbur M. Smith, formerly a professor at Fuller Theological Seminary, describes Chafer:

> I do not believe there is a man in America today, who, in the last ten years, has made such a profound contribution to the theological education of young men, especially in equipping them with a love for the Word of God, and a knowledge of how to properly expound it, as Dr. Lewis Sperry Chafer.... We have in this beloved man of God ... a master teacher and pioneer in theological education.... I do hope and pray that God will spare our dear friend for ten more years of vigorous activity, that he may give to the Christian Church the theological work which he alone is able to produce.[81]

Because of his heavy schedule, in 1926 Chafer resigned his pastorate at the Scofield Memorial Church after three and a half years and never pastored again. Chafer had no children, and the lack of parental responsibilities allowed him to more fully devote his energies to the ministry.

At the very inception of the seminary, Chafer was concerned about a doctrinal foundation for the institution. In April 1924, Chafer asked a designated committee of the Board of Trustees of the Evangelical Theological College to assist in the formation of a doctrinal statement. Nevertheless, the bulk of the statement was Chafer's work. It was officially accepted by the Board of Trustees on March 5, 1925. Reprinted in *The Sunday School Times*, the primary emphases of the doctrinal statement were as follows: the Scripture, the Godhead, man created and fallen, the first advent, the extent of salvation, the Christian's walk, the great commission, the blessed hope, the second coming of Christ, and the eternal state.[82] Inherent to the doctrinal statement was a dispensational, premillennial interpretation. It was later expanded by Chafer to twenty-one articles and accepted by the Board of Incorporate Members on January 3, 1952.

One of the most significant steps for the school and Chafer was the acquisition of publication rights to *Bibliotheca Sacra*, America's oldest theological journal, in October 1933. The journal had been the literary voice of Andover, Oberlin, and Pittsburgh-Xenia with Marvin Grove Kyle as its last editor. The Evangelical Theological College began publishing articles through this vehicle in January 1934. Chafer became the editor of the *Bibliotheca Sacra* in 1940, and since that time the journal has been the voice of scholarly dispensational premillennialism.

Because the name Evangelical Theological College inferred an undergraduate institution, many students and alumni requested a change of name. From the beginning, the institution was unofficially known as "Dallas." A desire for a change in the name grew steadily, and on January 7, 1933, Chafer wrote the Board suggesting the name be changed to Dallas Theological Seminary. During the 1935 - 36 school year, the new name was announced at the commencement on May 12, 1936 and was legally consummated in July 1936.[83]

The seminary continued to prosper under Chafer's leadership, and by the time of his death in 1952, the enrollment was 257. At the founding of the school in 1924, Chafer wished to keep the enrollment small, around one hundred, but he gradually became aware of the need for expansion. In the 1990 - 91 academic year Dallas Theological Seminary is the largest nondenominational seminary in the world, and with its extension schools in Philadelphia and San Antonio, the seminary has approximately 2,000 students. Dallas Theological Seminary offers master's and doctor's degrees and is fully accredited with the Southern Association of Colleges and Schools and the Association of Theological Schools.

During his presidency at Dallas, Chafer remained active in Bible conference ministry. However, in 1935 while in California, Chafer suffered a heart attack which demanded him to live a more regimented life. Even though he was not as active as in previous years, he was remembered with affection by his students. Dr. Willard Aldrich, President Emeritus of Multnomah School of the Bible, recalls:

> At the time he was working on his theology, and we had mimeographed notes of the material he presented. Then there were about 2,500 questions he asked about his theology, and as I recall I was the first one to answer all of those questions and turn them in for his approval. This in itself was quite an exercise. These questions were in printed form in small booklets and covered every phase of his developing theology.[84]

Dr. Haddon Robinson, President of Denver Conservative Baptist Theological Seminary, who studied under Chafer, recalls the distinct impression Chafer made on him:

> His [Chafer's] last year on earth was my first year at the seminary. He was old. His voice was weak.... What came through to me as a member of his class on the spiritual life, was his concern for the student and his emphasis that before you could speak to men for God, you had to speak to God for men.[85]

Dr. Edwin Deibler, Professor Emeritus of Historical Theology at Dallas, writes of the compassion Chafer displayed: "He [Chafer] devoted entire chapel services to singing and teaching the great hymns to his 'boys.' He could not bring himself to give a low grade to any of his 'boys' — they had no children of their own."[86]

The succession of presidency of the seminary was granted to Dr. John F. Walvoord who served as president from 1952 - 1986. Dr. Donald K. Campbell was appointed the third president in 1986.

Chafer's wife, Ella Loraine, suffered a stroke in 1941 which left her an invalid until her death in 1944. A second heart attack afflicted Chafer in 1945, and a third attack occurred in 1948. In May of 1952, after finishing his spring semester responsibilities at the seminary, he visited various Pennsylvania cities that were on the Harrisburg Circuit of Bible Conferences. In June, 1952, he traveled alone to Seattle and there died on August 22 in the home of personal friends, Mr. and Mrs. Robert O. Fleming. Two months later, Walvoord wrote in *The Sunday School Times:*

> In the span of one short life was gathered the amazing career of musician, evangelist, Bible teacher, theologian, writer, editor, educator, man of faith, man of prayer, and man of deep spiritual understanding of the Scriptures. Like John Calvin, with frail body but keen mind and spiritual vision, Lewis Sperry Chafer left an indelible mark upon his generation. The monuments of his labor continue, and we trust will continue.[87]

The Systematic Theology

In 1926, Chafer wrote *Major Bible Themes*. These forty-six chapters express what Chafer believed are key emphases in the Scriptures. He wrote the *Ephesian Letter* in 1935. His last work, *Dispensationalism*, was completed in 1951. Also, during the academic period of Chafer's life, he wrote articles for *The Sunday School Times, Our Hope, Moody Monthly* and *The King's Business*. However, the most prominent vehicle through which Chafer expressed his theological and doctrinal views was the *Bibliotheca Sacra*.

The crowning literary accomplishment, and in many respects the primary achievement of Lewis Sperry Chafer's life, was his eight-volume *Systematic Theology*. The first systematic theology written from a dispensational, premillennial position, his *Systematic Theology* was the culminating work of many years of writing and organizing themes and doctrines. The initial step toward the completion of his *Systematic Theology* entailed the systematizing of his lectures in theology into outlines. He then published for his students three analytical questionnaires; the first two contained Chafer's theological divisions while the third was a study of 180 biblical doctrines. The third booklet was expanded into his final volume (VIII) of the *Systematic Theology* and was entitled *Doctrinal Summarization*.[88] The task was initially undertaken in 1937 and some of the material appeared in *Bibliotheca Sacra*. Walvoord writes: "Most sections were laboriously written in longhand twice before being committed to his faithful secretary, Mr. A. H. D. Duncan for typing."[89]

Chafer, in 1934, wrote of the need for a theology written from a dispensational, premillennial position in an article entitled "Unabridged Systematic Theology," which was published in *Bibliotheca Sacra*. Soon after the publication of the *Systematic Theology*, in 1948, Clarence Mason wrote:

> To those of us who hold a dispensational position this theology is greeted with enthusiasm and gratefulness. At last we have something codified, knit together in a logical unit, and in full enough compass to state adequately the Scriptural basis of our position. Many fine things have been said, scattered through many fine books; many fine sermons have been preached; but very little of this has been available to the average reader and, certainly, nothing as satisfying as this in codified form."[90]

Walvoord writes in a similar vein: "The appearance of the eight-volume work in *Systematic Theology* by President Lewis Sperry Chafer of Dallas Theological Seminary is without question an epoch in the history of Christian doctrine. Never before has a work similar in content, purpose, and scope been produced."[91]

Need for a New Systematic Theology

In the latter nineteenth and early twentieth centuries, several theologies were produced from a Reformed and Arminian theological perspective. Virtually, none of these theologies were sympathetic toward dispensational premillennialism. The Bible conference movement of this period primarily stressed premillennialism; thus, many were educated and instructed in this method of biblical interpretation. From this movement sprang Bible institutes and faith missions. Fundamentalism's beginnings were rooted in Bible conferences, Bible schools, and Bible study groups, and not in seminaries.[92] There was, then, a waiting constituency for the *Scofield Reference Bible* when it appeared in 1909. The latter, however, was never taken seriously in many academic circles, and the need for a systematic theology to synthesize Reformed theology and the Bible conference movement became increasingly apparent.

Three years before the commencement of the writing of the *Systematic Theology*, Chafer stated that a systematic theology was needed to cover the following areas: bibliology, theology proper, angelology, anthropology, soteriology, ecclesiology, and eschatology.[93] According to Chafer, seven essential aspects deficient in the theologies include: (1) the divine program of the ages; (2) the Church; (3) human conduct and the spiritual life; (4) angelology; (5) typology; (6) prophecy; and (7) the present session of Christ in heaven.[94] Chafer, then, perceived a need for a theology which was dispensational, premillennial and unabridged. Concerning the potential Chafer possessed in meeting the need, Wilbur Smith states:

> If Dr. Lewis Sperry Chafer would find time to build up a work based upon and answering the six thousand questions of his remarkable *Analytical Questionnaire*, he would give to ministers of this generation a work to which they would be constantly referring, resulting in an ever firmer grasp of the profound truths of the Word of God and in an ever richer preaching.[95]

The Construction of the Systematic Theology

Chafer constructed a theological course for the seminary which was required for the student's first two years, and this course of study was followed by a doctrinal summarization course in the third year of study.[96] During 1925, Chafer wrote forty-nine articles about Bible themes for *The Sunday School Times*.[97] Chafer's theology apparently was formed by

1926 as the theology curriculum of the seminary and *Major Bible Themes* follow the essential pattern later found in the *Systematic Theology*. Chafer, after stating in 1934 what he believed was the great need for a particular systematic theology, began to publish articles in *Bibliotheca Sacra* about future subjects to be contained in the *Systematic Theology*. Having as a goal of completing one volume each year, Chafer wrote in detail about various subjects in this order from 1937 - 1948: bibliology, theology proper, angelology, anthropology, hamartiology, soteriology, ecclesiology, eschatology, christology, and pneumatology. In 1936 a fourth year was added to the seminary requirements. However, the students were required to study christology and pneumatology during the third year.[98] Chafer's *Systematic Theology* was structured after the curriculum of the school.

Chafer finished his work in 1948; his eight volumes consisted of 2,700 pages. The author wrote them out by hand twice, and with the help of various faculty, his work was printed by the Dallas Seminary Press. In 1988 Dr. Donald K. Campbell, Dr. John F. Walvoord and Dr. Roy B. Zuck revised Chafer's *Systematic Theology*, and the abbreviated work consists of 930 pages, or one-third of the length of the original work.

Chafer states his reason for the writing of his *Systematic Theology*:

> It is therefore contended that an unabridged treatment of theology is needed. To cover the ground completely, a doctrinal summarization has been added to this work in which more than a hundred doctrines not found in a systematic treatment of theology are analyzed.
>
> Why premillennial? So far as the author knows the present work is the only one approaching theology from an orderly and logical premillennial interpretation of the Scriptures. The supreme value of this interpretation will be observed, it is believed, as one pursues this work.
>
> Why dispensational? Apart from a sane recognition of the great purposes and time-periods of God, no true understanding of the Bible has ever been received.
>
> When Systematic Theology includes the premillennial and

dispensational interpretations of the Bible, much added material is discovered and the work is greatly extended.[99]

Conclusion

The life and career of Lewis Sperry Chafer is remarkable. Without doubt, he had his human frailties and shortcomings. He did not graduate from a standard seminary curriculum; his doctorates were honorary. But Chafer had unusual ability as a systematizer, theologian and writer. He was also an articulate speaker. Chafer in a sense was a "self-made" theologian. No doubt he would wince at that description since he loved to ascribe any human virtue and merit to the grace of God. Nevertheless, in his eighty-one years, Chafer accomplished significant achievements in a variety of roles. His goals did not vacillate; he knew his theological position, which motivated him to surge ahead to minister in accordance with his unusual capacity for labor.

He gradually became aware of the need for a seminary to meet the needs of individuals desiring to understand the Bible more clearly. Had W. H. Griffith Thomas not died the year the seminary opened, Chafer perhaps would not be remembered as a theologian since the death of Thomas forced him to delve more deeply into all areas of theology. He was the president of the seminary for twenty-eight years, and his guidance and influence shaped the direction undertaken by the institution.

His crowning work, the *Systematic Theology*, was the product of years of experience in all facets of ministry. He saw the great need for a systematic theology written from a dispensational, premillennial perspective and produced a theology reflecting his life experiences and biblical interpretations.

Notes: Chapter 1

1. C. F. Lincoln, "Biographical Sketch of the Author," in *Systematic Theology*, by Lewis Sperry Chafer, vol. 8: *Biographical Sketch and Indexes* (Dallas: Dallas Seminary Press, 1948), p. 4.

2. C. F. Lincoln, "Lewis Sperry Chafer," *Bibliotheca Sacra* 109 (October 1952):332.

3. Edwin C. Deibler, Professor Emeritus of Historical Theology, Dallas Theological Seminary, personal letter, 17 January 1984.

4. John F. Walvoord, "Lewis Sperry Chafer," *The Sunday School Times* 94 (11 October 1952):855.

5. Mr. and Mrs. Lewis Sperry Chafer, *Selected Hymns* (New York: Biglow & Main Co., n.d.)

6. Edwin C. Deibler, personal letter, 17 January 1984.

7. John Bernard, *From Evangelicalism to Progressivism at Oberlin College, 1866-1917* (Columbus: Ohio State University Press, 1969), p. 106.

8. Sydney E. Ahlstrom, *A Religious History of the American People*, 2 vols. (Garden City, New York: Doubleday & Co., Image Books, 1975), 1:558.

9. John A. Witmer, "What Hath God Wrought — Fifty Years of Dallas Theological Seminary," *Bibliotheca Sacra* 130 (October 1973):292

10. Wally Howard, "Accident Man," *Sunday School Promoter* 6 (June 1944):19.

11. Lewis Sperry Chafer, *Systematic Theology*, vol. 3: *Soteriology* (Dallas: Dallas Seminary Press, 1948), p. 284.

12. Ibid. p. 7.

13. Lewis Sperry Chafer, *Systematic Theology*, vol. 4: *Ecclesiology-Eschatology* (Dallas: Dallas Seminary Press, 1948), p. 438.

14. Rudolph A. Renfer, "A History of Dallas Theological Seminary" (Ph.D. dissertation, University of Texas, 1959), p. 85.

15. Lewis Sperry Chafer, "Why Music Reaches Souls," *The Sunday School Times* 60 (23 February 1918):108.

16. Witmer, "What Hath God Wrought," p. 293.

17. Lewis Sperry Chafer, *True Evangelism* (n.p., 1919; rev. ed. Grand Rapids: Zondervan Publishing House, 1967). In chapter one, "False Forces in Evangelism" (pp. 3-23), Chafer outlines the three false forces of men, methods, and messages.

18. Ibid., p. 21.

19. Howard, "Accident Man," pp. 20, 54.

20. Chafer, *True Evangelism*, p. iii.

21. Ibid, p. 9.

22. Lewis Sperry Chafer, "An Attack upon a Book," *Bibliotheca Sacra* 104 (April 1947):130.

23. Deibler, personal letter, 17 January 1984.

24. Samuel H. Kellogg, "Premillennialism: Its Relations to Doctrine and Practice," *Bibliotheca Sacra* 45 (April 1888):270.

25. Ernest Sandeen, *The Roots of Fundamentalism* (Grand Rapids: Baker book House, 1978), p. 175.

26. Ibid., p. 176

27. Lincoln, "Biographical Sketch of the Author," p. 4.

28. Lewis Sperry Chafer, "Twenty Years of Experience," *Bulletin of Dallas Theological Seminary* 29 (July-September 1943).

29. Lewis Sperry Chafer, "Summer Bible Conferences: Their Meaning," *The Sunday School Times* 62 (24 April 1920):235; A substantial history and analysis of the Northfield Bible Conferences is contained in *James F. Findlay, Dwight L. Moody: American Evangelist, 1837-1899* (Grand Rapids: Baker Book House, 1969), pp. 339-355.

30. Howard, "Accident Man," p. 54.

31. Mrs. Howard Taylor, *Empty Racks and How to Fill Them* (Dallas: Evangelical Theological College, n.d.), p. 8.

32. Ibid.

33. Witmer, "What Hath God Wrought," p. 294.

34. Lewis Sperry Chafer, "The Founding of Dallas Theological Seminary," a tape recorded by Dallas Theological Seminary, n.d.

35. Lewis Sperry Chafer, "What I Learned from Dr. Scofield," *The Sunday School Times* 64 (4 March 1922):120.

36. Walvoord, "Lewis Sperry Chafer," p. 868.

37. Renfer, "A History of Dallas Theological Seminary," p. 9.

38. "A True Theological Seminary," *The Sunday School Times* 66 (6 September 1924):525.

39. Lewis Sperry Chafer, "History of the Scofield Reference Bible," a tape recorded by Dallas Theological Seminary, n.d.

40. Ibid.

41. James Sprunt, Board Member of Union Theological Seminary, Richmond, Virginia, to P. S. Crane, 9 December 1912, Dallas Seminary Archives, quoted in Renfer, "History of Dallas Theological Seminary," p. 94.

42. P. S. Crane, T. C. Bales and H. McQ. Shields to James Sprunt, 7 December 1912, Dallas Seminary Archives, quoted in Renfer, "History of Dallas Theological Seminary," p. 94.

43. Lewis Sperry Chafer, *Satan,* with a foreward by C. I. Scofield (n.p., 1919; rev. ed., Grand Rapids: Zondervan Publishing House, 1964), pp. 26-27.

44. Ibid., pp. 28-38.

45. Ibid., pp. 30-31.

46. Ibid., p. 36.

47. Lewis Sperry Chafer, *The Kingdom in History and Prophecy,* with an Introduction by C. I. Scofield (New York: Fleming H. Revell Co., 1915; reprint ed., Philadelphia: *The Sunday School Times,* 1926), p.5.

48. Ibid., p. 10.

49. Lewis Sperry Chafer, *Salvation* (rev. ed., Grand Rapids: Zondervan Publishing House, 1955), p. 10.

50. Ibid., p. 14.

51. Lewis Sperry Chafer, Original Author's Preface to *He That is Spiritual,* with a Foreword by John F. Walvoord (n.p., 1918; rev. ed., Grand Rapids: Zondervan Publishing House, 1967).

52. Ibid., pp. 140-141.

53. Lewis Sperry Chafer, *Grace* (n.p., 1922; rev. ed., Grand Rapids:

Zondervan Publishing House, 1950), p. 3.

54. Ibid., p. xiii.

55. Ibid., p. 149.

56. Chafer, "Twenty Years of Experience."

57. Lewis Sperry Chafer, "For the Glory of God," *Evangelical Theological College Bulletin* 7 (November 1930):4.

58. Chafer, "Twenty Years of Experience."

59. Lewis Sperry Chafer, "Is This the Era of the Teacher?" *The Sunday School Times* 61 (26 April 1919):228.

60. Lewis Sperry Chafer, "The Highest Standard," *Bulletin of the Dallas Theological Seminary* 19 (April-June 1943).

61. Clarence Edward Macartney, "The Crux of the Present Protestant Controversy," *The Sunday School Times* 65 (21 April 1923):247.

62. Kenneth Cauthen, *The Impact of American Religious Liberalism* (New York: Harper and Row, 1962), p. 3.

63. Lewis Sperry Chafer, "A New Departure in Theological Training," *Our Hope* 25 (January 1928):432.

64. Ibid., pp. 432-33.

65. Lewis Sperry Chafer, "Effective Ministerial Training," *Evangelical Theological College Bulletin* 1 (May 1925):11.

66. Renfer, "History of Dallas Theological Seminary," p. 119.

67. Ibid., pp. 119-20.

68. Witmer, "What Hath God Wrought," p. 296.

69. Renfer, "A History of Dallas Theological Seminary," pp. 133-34.

70. Ibid., p. 135.

71. Lewis Sperry Chafer to Scofield Memorial Church, Dallas, Texas, 11 April 1923.

72. Neil Ashcraft, present Senior Pastor of Scofield Memorial Church, Dallas, Texas, personal letter, 6 January 1984.

73. Walvoord, "Lewis Sperry Chafer," p. 855.

74. Chafer, "A New Departure in Theological Training," p. 433.

75. Ibid., p. 435.

76. Lewis Sperry Chafer, "The Evangelical College," *The Sunday School Times* 73 (6 June 1931):322.

77. Lewis Sperry Chafer to A. C. Gaebelein, 13 November 1923, Dallas Seminary Archives, quoted in Renfer, "A History of Dallas Theological Seminary," p. 139.

78. A. C. Gaebelein to Lewis Sperry Chafer, 21 December 1923, Dallas Seminary Archives, quoted in Renfer, "A History of Dallas Theological Seminary," p. 139.

79. Lewis Sperry Chafer to Robert Dick Wilson, Princeton Seminary, 20 December 1923, Dallas Seminary Archives, quoted in Renfer, "A History of Dallas Theological Seminary," p. 141.

80. C. F. Lincoln, "Biographical Sketch of the Author," p. 5.

81. Wilbur M. Smith to Archer E. Anderson, 6 July 1936, Dallas Seminary Archives, quoted in Renfer, "A History of Dallas Theolgicla Seminary," p. 102.

82. "A True Theological Seminary," p. 526.

83. Witmer, "What Hath God Wrought," p. 294.

84. Willard M. Aldrich, President Emeritus, Multnomah School of the Bible, personal letter, 9 January 1984.

85. Haddon Robinson, President, Denver Conservative Baptist Seminary, personal letter, 20 December 1983.

86. Deibler, personal letter, 28 December 1983.

87. Walvoord, "Lewis Sperry Chafer," p. 870. Cf. "Dr. Lewis Sperry Chafer, 81, Dies in Seattle,"*Dallas Morning News*, 23 August 1952, p. 4.

88. Witmer, "What Hath God Wrought," p. 302.

89. Walvoord, "Lewis Sperry Chafer," p. 869.

90. Clarence E. Mason, Jr., "A Readable and Thrilling Theology," *Our Hope* 55 (March 1949):535. Cf. Lynn Landrum, a popular journalist in the 40s and 50s, not only in Dallas but throughout the state of Texas, writes concerning the *Systematic Theology* after having received a set: "Think of it! Eight big volumes presented by the author as a gift to a working newspaperman — and every word of it about systematic theology. You do not need to be told that Lewis Sperry Chafer believes that systematic theology is the most important thing to which he could possibly devote his time. These eight volumes are his life work. Did you ever think about God, about His universe, about how sin and salvation got into this world and about what goes on in the next world? Stop now, just for an experiment, and ask yourself where is the starting point in thinking of that sort. The chances are you will give up before you get started. Well, Lewis Sperry Chafer didn't give up. And this unabridged work is a monument to his industry, to his analytical powers, to his amazing facility in fitting passages together, so that one throws light on the other.... But when you stop to savor what Dr. Chafer is saying, you come to realize that we have here one of the outstanding stylists among religious writers of the day. Dr. Chafer's sentences neither strut nor stumble. They march with orderly purpose and yet not without grace. In writing, he is "a workman that

needeth not to be ashamed." (Lynn Landrum, "Thinking Out Loud," *Dallas Morning News*, 13 July 1948). Cf. Dale Moody, "Present Theological Trends," *Review and Expositor* 47 (1950):9-11.

91. John F. Walvoord, "A Review of Dr. Chafer's Systematic Theology," *Bibliotheca Sacra* 105 (January 1948):115.

92. George M. Marsden, *Fundamentalism and American Culture* (New York: Oxford University Press, 1980), p. 62.

93. Lewis Sperry Chafer, "Ünabridged Systematic Theology," *Bibliotheca Sacra* 91 (January 1934):8-23.

94. Lewis Sperry Chafer, "Evils Resulting from an Abridged Systematic Theology," *Bibliotheca Sacra* 91 (April 1934):138-39.

95. Wilbur M. Smith, "Some Much Needed Books," *Bibliotheca Sacra* 91 (April 1934):193.

96. "Description of Courses," *Evangelical Theological Bulletin* 3 (June 1927):14-21.

97. Lewis Sperry Chafer, *Major Bible Themes* (Dallas: Dallas Theological Seminary, 1926; rev. ed., Grand Rapids: Dunham Publications, 1964), p. vii.

98. "Description of Courses," *Bulletin of Dallas Theological Seminary* 28 (September-October 1952).

99. Lewis Sperry Chafer, *Systematic Theology*, vol. 1: *Prolegomena-Bibliology-Theology Proper* (Dallas: Dallas Seminary Press, 1947), pp. xxxvii-xxxviii.

Chapter II
The Sources of Chafer's Eschatological Thought

In attempting to arrive at a conclusion concerning the wellspring of Lewis Sperry Chafer's eschatological thought, one quickly realizes that no one source explains his mature theology; he drew from a multiplicity of sources. While some sources clearly are definable and predominant, there are others which are subtle, and one must be aware of Chafer's background and experiences in order to understand his eschatological thinking.

Chafer coupled a certain "folksiness" with an urbanity of character. He had experienced the "sawdust trail" and apparently to the end of his life had an affection for such an atmosphere. Throughout his life, he retained some of the traits of revivalism which characterized the J. Wilbur Chapman evangelistic team. But conversely, the man was comfortable associating with the leading theologians and ministers of his time. He never tired of leading the seminary students in hymns of the faith and apparently was considered very approachable by his students. Howard writes of Chafer:

> "Dr. L. S.," as he is known to his students at Dallas, toys with his watch as he lectures, . . . students laugh at his wide assortment of jokes, of which he boasts more than 3,000. Typical is his reference to the college professor who dreamed he was teaching a class, woke up to find it was true. His humor is dry and subtle. He tells his stories with a wheezy chuckle, and is greeted with the laughter of the class who react as much to his own laughter as to the stories. Theology lectures are interspersed with sage advice — admonitions to always buy tailor-made suits, eat whole wheat bread and avoid coffee.[1]

Chafer was totally absorbed in his life's calling, but his human qualities and balanced lifestyle are obvious.

Chafer lived from 1871 - 1952, and throughout these years he witnessed vast changes in American religion. His life coincided with the era of controversy between modernism and fundamentalism, the reign of liberalism and the rise of neo-orthodoxy. A statement in the preface to his *Systematic Theology* displays his concern for a balanced approach to eschatology:

> Eschatology, as treated by authors on systematic theology, has included little more than a brief reference to the resurrection of the body, the intermediate state, a future judgment, a restricted treatment of the second advent of Christ, and an equally restricted reference to heaven and hell. Over against this, it it here insisted that since no given moment of time is a final point of division between things past and things future, eschatology, being the orderly arrangement of "things to come," should include *all* in the Bible which was predictive at the time it was uttered. When eschatology is thus expanded, the science of systematic theology fulfills its purpose.[2]

One of his interpreters, Daniel Fuller, missed the full import of the vast influences upon Chafer's eschatology by merely dismissing the latter as the recipient of the teachings of a Darby-Brooks-Scofield tradition.[3] Such an error characterizes many assessments. Rather, one must endeavor to obtain a more complete understanding of how Chafer came to his eschatological conclusions.

Chafer, of course, was reared in a religious home, the son and grandson of ministers, but his grandfather's eschatological views are not known. Boles cites an interview with C. F. Lincoln concerning the eschatology of Lewis's father: "Basically his [Thomas Franklin Chafer's] theology was typical of the traditional beliefs of the day. He preached views on prophecy that were not in accord with the later prekingdom teachings of his son."[4] But Boles and others have not shed light on the actual sources of Chafer's eschatology; the issue has been ignored. There

The Sources of Chafer's Eschatological Thought

are several sources of Lewis Sperry Chafer's eschatological thought. These include the Northfield Conferences, C. I. Scofield, and Chafer's personal study. It is not possible to point to specifics as the definite source of his eschatological thought since Chafer simply did not spell out these sources; thus, systematic investigation, estimation, and determination are involved in the process of forming a conclusion concerning his sources.

Chafer's Involvement with the Northfield Conferences

From 1903 - 1909, Chafer left his work as an evangelist and settled at East Northfield, Massachusetts where he was associated with the Mount Hermon School for Boys. Northfield brought new influences, emphases, and meaning into the life, experience, and thinking of Chafer. Walvoord writes of the influence of Northfield: "During the summer he mingled with the world's greatest preachers such as Moody, Scofield, Morgan, and Griffith Thomas....It was a stimulating and enriching experience associating with the greatest Christian leaders of the English-speaking world."[5]

Some of the speakers at Northfield around the turn of the century were Samuel Chadwick of Leeds, England; Charles Gordon of Winnipeg, Manitoba; John Kelman of Edinburgh, Scotland; Robert E. Speer; Henry G. Weston, and even Woodrow Wilson who spoke concerning religion and patriotism. The great majority of their messages concerned deeper life, or Christian spiritual growth, themes as evidenced by the titles of their sermons: "The Character of Holiness," "Christ's Promise of the Spirit," "The Struggle with Doubt," "The Consequences of Selfishness," "The New Testament Basis for the Spiritual Life," "The Temptations of Christ," and "A Life in the Will of God."[6]

One can readily see the influence of these themes upon Chafer in his work written in 1918, *He That is Spiritual*. He writes:

> Spiritually is not a future ideal: it is to be experienced *now*, The vital question is, "Am I walking in the Spirit *now?"* Answer to this question should not depend on the presence or absence of some unusual manifestation of the supernatural. Much of life

will be lived in the uneventful commonplace; but, even there, we should have the conviction that we are right with God and in His unbroken fellowship.[7]

Nothing indicates that Chafer thought eschatology of primary importance until his coming to Northfield. His work was that of an evangelist; he was concerned about such subjects as repentance, salvation, and grace. Perhaps his greatest concern during these years was a burning ambition to correct what he believed were abuses in evangelism. However, the seed for his latter eschatological views can be seen at Northfield.

D. L. Moody was associated with the Northfield Conferences beginning in the 1880s. Sandeen writes:

> During the last two decades of the nineteenth century the unordained Dwight L. Moody was the most influential "clergyman" in America....From 1880 until his death Moody brought speakers to Northfield, Massachusetts for the summer conference sessions that attracted men of all persuasions and changed the character of American Protestantism....With Moody as ally and convert, and with Northfield as a sounding board for their views, the millenarians had an unparalleled opportunity to impress their own view of the world and next upon evangelical Christianity.[8]

Northfield by the time of Chafer's arrival was a center of premillennial and dispensational teaching and preaching.

H. W. Webb-Peploe

One of the speakers Chafer heard, and with whom he associated, was H. W. Webb-Peploe. The latter was well known, especially in Great Britain since he was head of the Low Church party in the Anglican Church. He was one of the chief promoters of the Keswick movement, which emphasized the "victorious life" of the believer. A. T. Pierson, a speaker at Northfield, quoted an English visitor to Northfield as stating, "There is not need of any one's going to Keswick who was at Northfield in August last; for the cream of Keswick teaching was to be found there."⁹ Webb-Peploe writes concerning the subject of prophecy:

> Have you ever considered why the subject of prophecy should engage our attention? Is there any intelligent being capable of carrying on a Christian life without reference to prophecy? Are not all of God's promises concerning our future really prophecies? A man who calculates with reference to the future is accounted a wise man; so should a man be considered wise who studies the field of prophecy concerning the future, which should guide us as to the present. Moreover if Christ is the center of my life, how can I abstain from the study of the prophetic utterances which pertain to His kingdom. The world's future is wrapped up in prophecy, and through this we can study the destiny of the kingdom, the Church, the world, or of ourselves. To refuse to study prophecy, therefore, is to be wanting in the spiritual intelligence and hope of the Christian.[10]

Webb-Peploe outlines three means of viewing eschatology. The pretorists hold the view that all that was written by the Old and New Testament writers was written from their own understanding and is prophetic only insofar as any keen-sighted politician might foresee coming events. Second, the historicists claim that all of Revelation from the fourth chapter to the end of the book has been fulfilled. Webb-Peploe holds to the third, the futurist view of prophecy. He sees Revelation chapters 4 - 22 as a vision of future events, and the Old Testament prophecies, he claims, allude to the same period. But he is open enough to believe all three views have en element of truth.[11] Concerning a secret rapture of the saints, Webb-Peploe claims that those who are vibrantly serving the Lord upon the earth will be taken, while for a variety of reasons those who suffer lethargy will have to go through a seven-year period of tribulation before they are finally brought into the presence of God.[12] He obtains his theological justification by citing the parable of the virgins in Matthew 25:1-13. Only five of them had sufficient oil, representative of the Holy Spirit. The remaining five had no oil, even though they were waiting for the bridegroom. As the Lord in the end will not exclude the five foolish virgins, so those who are burdened with temporal matters will at the end of the tribulation period be restored to their Lord. Chafer heard Webb-Peploe while affiliated with the Mount Hermon School for boys and while serving as song leader and speaker at the Northfield Conferences.

Chafer in later years alluded to Webb-Peploe and his positive impact upon this thinking.[13] Chafer, like Webb-Peploe, viewed the book of Revelation as containing a division between the third and fourth chapters; chapters one through three have been fulfilled in church history, while chapters four through twenty-two allude to a future period.[14] The book of Revelation was of vital importance to Chafer, as he believed the book contained a thoroughly eschatological scheme. Chafer found in the book of Revelation the tribulation period, the resurrection, the millennium, the Great White Throne judgment, and the commencement of the eternal estate.

In fact, Chafer understood the vast majority of the book of Revelation as referring to the future seven-year period of tribulation of earth. Webb-Peploe and Chafer both held to a secret translation, or rapture of the saints. Chafer, however, was not convinced this occurrence is only for a select few, as did Webb-Peploe, but he believed all who belong to the Lord will experience it.

Dwight L. Moody

While not an intimate friend with Dwight L. Moody, Chafer recounted having had many conversations with him. Moody, until his death in 1899, remained associated with the Northfield Conferences. Findlay is correct in stating that while Moody was a premillennialist he was "not an outright advocate of dispensationalism as he only uses the term twice in his writings."[15] But Findlay believes that "through the years Moody remained firm in his advocacy of premillennialism and the verbally inspired Bible."[16] Findlay admits it is difficult to pinpoint exactly when Moody adopted premillennialism, but that it occurred sometime in the 1870s under the influence of the Plymouth Brethren. In a pamphlet, *Heaven,* Moody does not give any kind of eschatological scheme but speaks solely of such a place. The work, like his preaching, is filled with personal illustrations aimed at distinguishing between the eternal and the

The Sources of Chafer's Eschatological Thought

temporal.

Of course, Moody's primary concern was that of evangelism. Mabie recounts the evangelist's words:

> "Now when you Christians go home from here," he said at the closing of the meeting of the 1881 Conference, "don't go getting up in prayer meeting every chance you find, to tell people about what you heard at Northfield. If you do, everyone will just be sick of the sound of the place. No, when you get back home, talk about Jesus Christ. Tell what He has done for you. Remember, my friends, the world never has, it never will, get tired of that name."[17]

Moody established the tone for the Northfield Conferences. Though there was apparently much latitude concerning dispensationalism and the precise ordering of events to occur prophetically in the future, it is apparent that the claim of premillennialism was a constantly recurring theme at the Northfield Conferences. Moody, however, did display a more open-minded approach than the majority of his colleagues; he was severely criticized for inviting such theologians as Henry Drummond, W. R. Harper, and John A. Broadus to the Northfield Conferences. But the teachings at the Northfield Conferences were twofold: dispensational premillennialism and deeper life teachings.

A. T. Pierson

A. T. Pierson was well known in Northfield circles, and in his address, "Some Hints on Bible Study," he speaks of "prophetic prediction." According to Pierson:

> As every single prediction may or may not prove true, it has at most only half a chance of fulfillment. Consequently the moment a prophecy embraces two particulars, we enter the realm of compound probability, and the chance of both proving accurate is one fourth, and so every additional item reduces the fraction by one half. What shall be said of the prophecies of

Nineveh, Babylon, Moab, Egypt, Tyre, etc. which embrace from twenty to forty particulars? And above all, how can we account for the vast mass of Messianic prophecy which embraces three hundred and thirty-three particulars? To estimate the fraction of probability that all these minutiae will meet in one person at one time, we must raise one-half to its three hundred and thirty-second power. In other words, there is but one chance in eighty-five followed by ninety-seven ciphers![18]

Pierson in this address portrays the Scriptures as from God, and claims, along with prophetic prediction, there are six other indications that attest to the Scripture's divine source. These are philosophical history, supernatural works, structural unity, general accuracy, ethical perfection, and the practical benefit.[19] Sandeen stresses that A. T. Pierson was one of the most popular evangelical clergymen of the day. A graduate of Union Theological Seminary, he adopted premillennialism under the influence of George Müller, the Bristol minister and orphan-master.

Chafer frequently spoke of A. T. Pierson with great respect. Chafer, as Pierson, was concerned with displaying the supernatural origin of the Scriptures. Under a major section, "The Supernatural Origin of the Bible," Chafer enumerates fifteen reasons which point to the supernatural character of the Scriptures. His tenth point is "Prophecy and Its Fulfillment," and his argument is very similar to Pierson's.[20] Chafer, then begins his *Systematic Theology* with the intention of testifying to the divine origin of the Scriptures, and this desire was also predominant in the ministry of A. T. Pierson.

G. Campbell Morgan

Another individual with whom Chafer was well acquainted was G. Campbell Morgan, the prince of pulpiteers. According to Sandeen, he was a regular preacher at Northfield in the years following 1897.[21] In Morgan's "The Character of Holiness," there is not a definable eschatological scheme. However, there are pertinent statements such as:

> Look within! Christ in you the hope of glory. It is wonderful how blind some of us are. We do not see Him there at all; it is

a great mistake. Grant that you are the worst person in America, if you are His, Christ is in you, and He is able to conquer all the evils within you. You are complete in Him. Then what do you see when you look on? The shadow of the land of death? Then you do not lift your eyes quite far and high enough. The horizon is filled with the glory of Himself. He is coming. When? Oh, you can't measure the doings of God by calendars and almanacs. He is coming. But you may die. No Christians never die, never. "He that liveth and believeth in me shall never die." Jesus abolished death. There may be a falling asleep but it will be only to wake with Him.[22]

In this sermon, "The Character of Holiness," Campbell gives several illustrations of individuals who were "waiting for the coming of the Lord."[23]

Perhaps G. Campbell Morgan's most extensive address at Northfield was "The Messages of the Minor Prophets." In outline form, he gives what he believes to be the prophetic message of the books of Hosea, Joel, Amos, Obadiah, Jonah, and Micah. In his analysis of the book of Joel, Morgan speaks of a future event known as the "day of the Lord":

> This outlook and interpretation is made the basis of a larger message. The prophet's mind is burdened with the fact of the Divine government, and the certainty that beyond all the failure resulting from human administration, the time will come when God will administer His own affairs. This period he speaks of as the day of the Lord.... The burden is that of the day of the Lord, which is declared to be a day of judgment and destruction, issuing in a reign of order and restoration of all things.[24]

He continues: "The ending of the day will be ushered in by signs and portents mysterious and supernatural. During its course 'whosoever shall call upon the name of the Lord shall be saved.' "[25] Further he comments:

> It is for us to declare that the day of the Lord must come, but that we are living in the dispensation of the ... Spirit. We must urge

men to call on the name of Jehovah, for only thus may they be saved from the perils, the judgments, of His coming day.[26]

Chafer cites in his *Systematic Theology*, G. Campbell Morgan's *The Spirit of God*. But more significantly, Chafer alludes to the "Day of the Lord" several times. There is a great similarity of thought between Morgan and Chafer concerning the "Day of the Lord." Chafer explains:

> The greatest exposition of the Old Testament was that of the Day of the Lord, yet ... it has not come to the present time. It is still future (cf. I Thess. 5:1-2). It is related to Christ's second advent and not to His first advent. This period extends from Christ's coming "as a thief in the night" (Matt. 24:43; Luke 12:39-40; I Thess. 5:2; 2 Peter 3:10; Rev. 16:15) to the passing of the heavens and the earth that now are and the melting of the elements with fervent heat. It seems highly significant that, in the same context and under the same theme in which those outmost boundaries of the Day of the Lord are given (2 Pet. 3:8-12), it is declared that one day with the Lord is as a thousand years and a thousand years as one day with the Lord.[27]

Clearly then, many of the messages which Chafer heard at Northfield dealt with the end times, although the primary emphasis was that of the Christian's spiritual life. Nevertheless, the spiritual life was nurtured and encouraged under the teachings of the imminent rapture of the Church and the premillennial return of the Lord.

George F. Pentecost

George F. Pentecost was a frequent speaker at Northfield, and Sandeen claims he was active as a millenarian until 1915.[28] In his sermon entitled "The Imperialism of Christ," Pentecost clearly preaches an eschatological message. He states:

> In the eyes of the Hebrew, Jesus was but a provincial Galilean prophet and preacher.... He lifted up His eyes, and gazing into the far future and seeing the ends of the earth, spoke of great

The Sources of Chafer's Eschatological Thought

> tribulations coming down upon the world, of nations rising against nations, of vast political changes, of cosmic disturbances and the end of the world.... The conception of the world-wide dominion of Christ is no new thought. It is as old as the revelation of God. From the beginning the Bible foretold the failure of the human race in every department of human world power.... Nebuchadnessar's image was the picture of the supremest human efforts in the direction of world empire, and the prophecy of the stone cut out of the mountain, breaking in pieces the image of iron and brass, silver and gold, is the prophecy of that heavenly kingdom which shall be universal and never destroyed.[29]

Chafer also speaks of the image which represents world empires and the smiting of the stone which represents the power of the Lord.[30] In Pentecost's message, as in Chafer's writings, one finds the usual dispensational, premillennial motifs such as the seed of Abraham and the covenants which were granted to Abraham, the gospel of the kingdom, and Christ as the completion of the line of David.

Chafer clearly came in contact at Northfield with many of the best-known expositors of his time. He cut his theological teeth as he actively listened and participated at the Northfield Conferences and taught at the Mount Hermon School for Boys. He was exposed primarily to premillennialism, some dispensationalism, and much deeper life teaching. These teachings continued to be characteristic of his own ministry. Northfield was truly an interdenominational enterprise since the speakers represented a variety of seminaries and denominations. However, there was a fairly unified language; thus, theological differences were minimized. The Northfield Conference was related to the entire Bible conference movement which commenced at Niagara. One cannot specifically point to any single individual at Northfield as an influence upon Chafer; rather, the atmosphere, speakers, and his associates as a whole became ingrained in his theological and eschatological development.

Reflecting on the great impact the Northfield days had upon his development, Chafer wrote in 1943: "Early association and close acquaintance with some of the world's greatest expositors ... placed before me ideals of expository preaching based on extended knowledge and familiarity with the Scriptures of Truth."[31] Chafer in this article also credited his personal theological views to H. W. Webb-Peploe, G. Campbell Morgan, A. T. Pierson, A. C. Gaebelein, H. A. Ironside, C. I. Scofield, and F. B. Meyer, all of whom were affiliated with the Northfield Conference.

C. I. Scofield

Without a doubt, the man who had the most significant influence and impact upon the theological and, more specifically, the eschatological thinking of Lewis Sperry Chafer was C. I. Scofield. Chafer met the latter in 1902 when Chafer moved to Northfield for the purpose of acquiring a center for his evangelistic work. At that time, Scofield was the pastor of the Northfield Congregational Church and director of the Northfield Bible Training School. Chafer recalls the first time he heard Scofield:

> Until that time I had never heard a real Bible teacher. True to my ministerial training, I had gathered sufficient material of a most unscriptural character in the usual series of meetings. Naturally these sermons were prized exceedingly. My first learning of Dr. Scofield was at a morning Bible class at the Bible school. He was teaching the sixth chapter of Romans. I am free to confess that it seemed to me at the close that I had seen more vital truth in God's Word in that one hour than I had seen in all my life before. It was a crisis for me. I was captured for life.[32]

Chafer and Scofield apparently developed a father-son relationship.[33] The closeness of the two became even more evident in following years, and Chafer indeed became known as Scofield's successor.[34]

C. I. Scofield was born in Michigan in 1843. His mother died soon after his birth, and the family moved to Tennessee. Scofield did not pursue a formal education but was a voracious reader even as a child. He had planned to enter the University of Virginia, but the Civil War required that he join the forces of the Confederacy, for whom he fought for four years and was awarded the Confederate Cross of Honor.

Following the Civil War, he moved to St. Louis to study law and finished his studies in 1869. He became involved in politics, and twice he was elected as a representative to the Kansas State Legislature, and then he served as the U. S. District Attorney for Kansas. In 1874, Scofield returned to St. Louis and again practiced law. He began to drink heavily, and the quality of his law practice began to lapse.

Thomas McPheeters confronted Scofield with the gospel in 1879, and the latter accepted God's grace and had a conversion experience. Scofield immediately placed himself under the teaching of Dr. James H. Brookes, pastor of the Washington and Compton Avenues Presbyterian Church. Scofield says of Brookes:

> James H. Brookes was the greatest Bible student I have ever known....Dr. Brookes was an amazing blessing to me, but never more than in telling me this, "There is no such thing in the Bible as an abstract proposition. Everything in the Bible is meant to be turned into life."[35]

In 1882 Scofield became the pastor of a Congregational church in Dallas, Texas, and served there until 1887.

After 1886, Scofield traveled extensively conducting Bible conferences. Trumbull claims the Niagara Bible Conference was very influential upon the thinking of Scofield:

> Among the mighty formative influences of Pastor Scofield's life during these years was the far-famed Niagara Bible Conference....Under Dr. W. J. Eerdman, James H. Brookes, Nathaniel West, H. M. Parsons, and others, the Bible was taught with the highest scholarly and spiritual power. Dr. Scofield was welcomed into this fellowship and became a favorite teacher.[36]

In 1895, Scofield was called to be pastor of the Trinitarian Congregational Church of Northfield, Massachusetts and concurrently to the presidency of the two Northfield preparatory schools, the East Northfield and Mount Hermon Schools, founded by D. L. Moody. He continued in those positions until 1902 when he resigned to return to Dallas to again pastor where he had served from 1882 - 1887. During his second pastorate in Dallas, Scofield founded the Central American Mission.[37]

By the turn of the century, Scofield had commenced to work on his reference Bible. The undertaking literally became a marathon project for him as it consumed most of his time until the actual publication on January 12, 1909. There were many consulting editors, including Henry G. Weston of Crozer Theological Seminary; James M. Gray, dean of Moody Bible Institute; William J. Eerdman; W. G. Morehead, professor at Xenia Seminary; Elmore Harris; Arthur T. Pierson; A. C. Gaebelein; and W. L. Pettingill.[38]

In 1910 Scofield resigned from his pastorate and went to Europe. He returned in 1914 to establish the Philadelphia School of the Bible, an institution with which Chafer was briefly affiliated. Suffering from declining health, Scofield's activities were limited, and on July 24, 1921, he died.

The Influence of Scofield on the Life and Ministry of Chafer

Chafer, from the onset of his introduction to Scofield, was impressed with him. Apparently Chafer immediately sensed Scofield's patience with him:

> Dr. Scofield seemed to fathom my ignorance and to be able to tell me the next truth I needed to know. He seemed never to dream of displaying his knowledge, or of teaching merely to refresh his own soul in the truth. He was absorbed in the work of imparting to others and with incomparable skill he was able to select from what seemed a limitless storehouse the truth they needed. Though he had explained a Bible question a thousand times, his dogged patience was unimpaired if he found one to whom it had not been explained before. This was not cultivated

patience; it came from the heart. It was the normal working of the teacher's gift when enriched by the enabling power of the Spirit of God. This absorbing interest in the exact need of others characterized all his public teaching and preaching.[39]

During Scofield's tenure as pastor of Northfield, he taught his knowledge of the Word to his younger student. By 1909, Scofield began to commend Chafer to the reading public as a clear expositor of the biblical and dispensational aspects of the doctrine of Satan. Scofield writes of Chafer's work: "I know of no other book on Satan in which the dispensational aspects of the subject are so clearly stated, nor any other so severely biblical.[40]

Scofield also influenced Chafer's idea of the spiritual life. Chafer describes this influence:

> Dr. Scofield knew God personally as his own Father with more reality than any other person I have ever known. That living consciousness of God was no doubt the key to his freedom from every superficial pose and counterfeit in the spiritual life. It too, was as great a corrective as human resources could provide for the spoiling of the spirit of pride and vain show to another.[41]

Scofield taught Chafer that spirituality is the fruit of the Spirit, and Chafer comments: "There is a Scriptural spirituality which is the natural manifestation and fruit of the indwelling Spirit."[42] Thus, developing what he had been taught by Scofield, Chafer, in 1918, published his work on the spiritual life, *He That Is Spiritual*.

During Scofield's second term as pastor of the Congregational Church in Dallas, he invited Chafer to hold evangelistic meetings there. This event had to occur sometime between 1902 - 1910 while Chafer was living at Northfield. Chafer recollects that Scofield was at the church two years before he resigned to give more time to the writing of the notes for his reference Bible.[43] Therefore, in Chafer's thinking, Scofield's second tenure as pastor of the Dallas church was from 1902 - 1904.

A significant event occurred at the close of these meetings in

The Promise of Dawn

Scofield's church. Scofield remarked to Chafer that he had seen Dr. George Truett, pastor of the large First Baptist Church of Dallas, on a streetcar that day. Truett asked Scofield if the latter had a good evangelist at his church, but Scofield replied he saw in the evangelist one who had great potential as a Bible teacher.[44]

The following morning Scofield invited Chafer to his study, and Chafer describes this event as the second great crisis of his life (the first was his yielding to God to preach). Chafer recollects:

> Perhaps my doctrine was not as bad as it might have been; but I am now aware that my preaching for those two weeks was, of necessity, a peculiar torture to him. I know now that there are few things more painful to one who knows the truth and is jealous for it than to hear it distorted and mangled. Those meetings were counted a success because of the goodly number who accepted Christ; but in spite of all that, Dr. Scofield invited me to meet him alone in his study the day following the close of the meetings. He had a duty to perform.
>
> We both suffered under his unveiling of my ignorance of the fundamental truths of the Bible; but he, like a skillful surgeon, was true to my deepest need. The operation was a success. I left that fellowship, not disheartened with my too evident failure, but with a new, unbounded ambition and ideal which was no less than a purpose to be a life-student of God's Word, and to prepare for the ministry of a Bible teacher.... Who can estimate the value of one hour of such surgery?[45]

What new truth did Chafer learn from Scofield at this critical meeting? He learned of the shallowness of his entire approach to theology and to ministry. Until this time of meeting with Scofield, he was confident that through the medium of music the gospel could be presented clearly and that his sermons were the result of correct interpretation. Why did he call this time with Scofield the second crisis of his life? Because he had to admit to himself that he had been woefully inadequate as a preacher and teacher. He had given himself to the Lord for ministry several years previously, yet that commitment had been a failure. Yes, he had been

The Sources of Chafer's Eschatological Thought

preaching, but Chafer at this time in his life did not understand the basic mechanics of putting together a sermon. He had not studied the original languages of the Scriptures, and therefore was not able to perform exacting exegesis upon passages. He had heard the great preachers, but he himself lacked the training, experience, and insight at this period in his life. Scofield helped Chafer to see he was not extraordinarily gifted as an evangelist, and that he could make a far greater contribution in the area of Bible teaching. Thus, Chafer's entire life took on a totally new orientation after this encounter with Scofield. Chafer called it "spiritual surgery," that is, there was a cutting away of the former modes of thought and the acceptance of his role as a Bible teacher.

Another dimension to this time with Scofield was Chafer's identification with Scofield. Chafer literally saw himself as walking in the footsteps of his mentor, and from all indications, the great admiration for Scofield on Chafer's part stemmed from this momentous event. Since Scofield held to dispensationalism and premillennialism, these topics came to be of great importance in Chafer's eschatological scheme. Scofield was greatly respected as a Bible teacher, so Chafer determined to excel in this area of ministry. Three years after Scofield's death, Chafer was chosen pastor of Scofield's church, and Chafer suggested it be named after Scofield.

In 1911, Chafer left Mount Hermon to join Scofield as a Bible teacher at Scofield's New York City school. Scofield was responsible for the correspondence aspect of the school while Chafer aided in the teaching. From New York, Chafer began to hold meetings along the east coast and became known as the evangelist-teacher. Eventually the title "evangelist" was dropped and he became known as a Bible teacher only. From 1911 - 1916, Chafer traveled during the winters and springs conducting meetings and teaching with Scofield. Summers and falls were spent in East Northfield where he tended to his farm and grew apples.

In 1916, Chafer moved from East Northfield to East Orange, New Jersey and taught for some time at the Philadelphia College of the Bible, which had been founded by Scofield.[46] Chafer's book, *Grace*, published in 1922, was dedicated to Scofield, who died the year before the publication of the book.[47]

Scofield revised his reference Bible in 1917, and finally in 1967 a committee of nine scholars, after ten years of readjustments, produced the *New Scofield Reference Bible*. Since the publication of the original reference Bible, there has been much appreciation but also much misunderstanding of the *Scofield Reference Bible*. In 1952, the year he died, Chafer wrote:

> A common criticism of the Scofield Bible is the assertion that there is no scholarship back of it. The way it was published is a perfect answer to this notion. The writer [Chafer], for many years a close associate of C. I. Scofield, heard from his lips the following facts:
> As Dr. Scofield returned from Switzerland where he had completed the notes on his Bible, he passed through England and was urged there to present his manuscript to the Oxford University Press, which he did with some hesitation because of the tradition upheld by the Oxford Press not to publish any other Bible than the Authorized Version and the English Revised Version.... On the first vote all were in favor of publishing the Bible excepting one man, and he made a single vote negative because of his decision to stand by the tradition respecting publication of other editions of the Bible. But when he saw that he stood alone on this, he changed his first vote and made it unanimous. There has never been any ground for regret respecting this action. Thus the question of so-called scholarship is answered forever in the publication of the Scofield Bible by the Oxford University Press.[48]

This assertion, however, must be countered by the fact that there are some inadequacies in the reference Bible; thus, in 1967 the 1917 edition was revamped by a committee of nine. Nevertheless, since the publication of the original work, literally millions have been either directly or indirectly influenced by the work. On a popular level, a dispensational, premillennial method of interpreting and understanding the Scriptures was available.

The Sources of Chafer's Eschatological Thought

C. I. Scofield's Influence upon the Eschatology of Chafer

In the early 1920s, Chafer, while speaking at Moody Bible Institute, told the audience:

> One of the first interviews I ever had with the late Dr. Scofield ... was when he asked me if under God, I would be a life student of the Bible, not just to get a few things, but rather to purpose to be a life student. Very little understanding what I was undertaking, I acknowledged that that would be my purpose. I meant it.... We prayed together, and under God, and through His grace, to some extent I have been able to keep that resolution.[49]

One can safely say that of all the people with whom Chafer associated throughout his life, Scofield exerted the greatest impact upon his ministry. However, it is not possible to point to specific borrowing from Scofield's eschatology. As the two men's works are compared, one can see a definite correspondence, and it is primarily from a comparison that a judgment of Scofield's influence upon Chafer's eschatology is made.

Scofield's first work was published in 1896 and was entitled *Rightly Dividing The Word Of Truth*. Scofield begins this work by distinguishing among three groups: the Jew, the Gentile, and the Church of God. Scofield believes that Israel began with the call of Abram, whereas the Church's initiation is recorded in Acts 2 and its termination is portrayed in I Thessalonians 4. The Gentiles are a third major division, and Scofield believes this group is rarely alluded to in the Scriptures.[50]

Scofield strongly insists that Israel and the Church must always remain distinct. He describes the differences among the Church, Israel, and the Gentiles:

> It should be needless to say that, in this dispensation, neither Jew nor Gentile can be saved otherwise than by the exercise of that faith on the Lord Jesus Christ whereby both are born again (John 3:3, 16) and are baptized into that "one body" (I Cor. 12:13) which is the "Church" (Eph. 1:22, 23). In the Church the distinction of Jew and Gentile disappears (I Cor. 12:13; Gal.

3:28; Eph. 2:14). So in writing to the Ephesians the Apostle speaks of them as "in time past Gentiles" (Eph. 2:11; I Cor. 12:2).[51]

Scofield holds to a seven-dispensational scheme. He believes:

> The Scriptures divide time (by which is meant the entire period from the creation of Adam to the "new heaven and new earth" of Revelation 21:1) into seven unequal periods, usually called "Dispensations" (Eph. 3:2), although these periods are also called "ages" (Eph. 2:7) and "days" — as, "day of the Lord," etc.
>
> These periods are marked off in Scripture by some change in God's method of dealing with mankind, in respect of two questions: of sin, and of man's responsibility. Each of the dispensations may be regarded as a new test of the natural man, and each ends in judgment — marking his utter failure in every dispensation.
>
> Five of these dispensations, or periods of time, have been fulfilled; we are living in the sixth, probably toward its close, and have before us the seventh, and last — the millennium.[52]

These seven dispensations include innocence, conscience, government, promise, law, grace, and kingdom.

Scofield holds that the present time is the period of grace. He claims that Jesus' death introduced this period and the law is no longer binding. But like all dispensations, or specific periods of time, this age too will end in failure; there will be a judgment upon an unbelieving world and an apostate church. The divine event which will close this present dispensation, according to Scofield, will be the descent of the Lord from heaven to take up the Church with Himself into the heavens, and this event he calls the "rapture of the Church." A period of seven years called the tribulation will occur, and after this time the personal return of the Lord, or the second coming of Christ, will take place. With the commencement of the millennium, Israel will be restored and the Lord will reign over the earth for one thousand years. The seat of authority will be at Jerusalem, and the

The Sources of Chafer's Eschatological Thought

Church along with the saints of the period of grace will be associated with Him. At the end of the thousand-year reign, Satan who has been bound will be loosed, and because of him, nations will gather to battle against the Lord and His saints. This battle will end in victory for the Lord and His armies. The Great White Throne judgment will take place, and all the wicked dead will be raised and judged. After this event, the eternal state will commence.

Scofield holds to two advents. The first is Christ's birth and is consummated in His death and resurrection. Scofield does not divide the second coming into a coming for the saints and a coming with the saints. He apparently only designated a general second coming; the taking up of the saints and a return with them are both included in the "second coming."[53]

Scofield believes that the Scriptures teach two resurrections:

> Two resurrections, differing in respect of time and of those who are the subjects of the resurrection, are yet future. These are variously distinguished as "the resurrection of life" and "the resurrection of damnation"; as the resurrection of the just and the unjust.[54]

Scofield alludes to Revelation 20:4-6 as teaching two resurrections. The first resurrection according to Scofield does not involve all the dead but only those which "sleep in Christ." He understands I Thessalonians 4:13-16 as teaching the first resurrection. He summarizes his thinking concerning the resurrection by stating:

> The testimony of Scripture, then, is clear that believers' bodies are raised from among the bodies of unbelievers, and caught up to meet the Lord in the air a thousand years before the resurrection of the latter. It should be firmly held that the doctrine of the resurrection concerns only the *bodies* of the dead. Their disembodied spirits are instantly in conscious bliss or woe.[55]

Scofield claims that the Scriptures do not teach one general judgment but instead there are five. "The expression 'general judgment', of such frequent occurrence in religious literature, is not found in the Scriptures, and, what is of more importance, the idea intended to be conveyed by that expression is not found in the Scriptures."[56] According to Scofield, these five judgments are as follows: (1) the judgment of the believer which took place on the cross; (2) the judgment of sin in the believer which can take place anytime; (3) the judgment of the works of believers which will occur when Christ comes again. The results of this judgment will be reward or loss of reward; (4) the judgment of nations which happens at the close of the tribulation and takes place along the Valley of Jehoshaphat; (5) the judgment of the wicked dead, or the Great White Throne judgment. The latter judgment according to Scofield occurs sometime after the millennium, and the result is eternal separation from God.[57]

Central to Scofield's eschatology is his adamant belief of the distinction between the periods of law and grace:

> It is, however, of the most vital moment to observe that Scripture never, in any dispensation, mingles these two principles. Law always has a place and work distinct and wholly diverse from that of grace. Law is God prohibiting and requiring. Grace is God beseeching and bestowing. Law is a ministry of condemnation; grace, of forgiveness. Law curses, grace redeems from that curse. Law kills; grace makes alive....
>
> Everywhere the Scriptures present law and grace in sharply contrasted spheres.
>
> The mingling of them in much of current teaching of the day spoils both; for law is robbed of its terror, and grace of its freeness.[58]

Scofield emphasizes that the law by itself cannot justify an individual. Law began at Sinai and extended to Calvary. The law only displays one's helplessness. Scofield sees the person who has faith in Christ in a special grace relationship during this present age.

Essential to this period of grace is the Church, which is not found in any other dispensation. "The Church, apart from the prophetic word, 'I

The Sources of Chafer's Eschatological Thought

will build my church' (Matt. 16:18), remained a 'mystery hid in God' (Eph. 3:9,10). The unfolding of that mystery was reserved to the Apostle Paul, to whom was also entrusted the exposition of the doctrine of grace (Eph. 3:1-10)."[59] Scofield in his *Addresses on Prophecy* says the Church is found only in the New Testament since its beginning is seen in Acts 2 and its consummation is portrayed in the fourth chapter of First Thessalonians.[60] Scofield habitually counters the Reformed doctrine of the Church in the Old Testament. "Why should we suppose then that all good people through all ages, were members, and are members of the Church? As a matter of fact, they were nothing of the kind."[61] To Scofield, the Church was unknown to Old Testament prophets. It is a period of indeterminate time. The Gospels, according to Scofield, do not pertain to the Church.[62] Scofield believes:

> Christ is never called King of the Church. "The King" is indeed one of the divine titles, and the Church in her worship joins Israel in exalting "the King, eternal, immortal, invisible" (Ps. 10:16; I Tim. 1:17). But the Church is to reign with Him. The Holy Spirit is now calling out, not the subjects, but the co-heirs and co-rulers of the kingdom.[62]

Scofield constantly stresses that the true Church is a pilgrim in a world which is not consonant with the purposes of God. "What in a word, is the relation of the church to the world? Briefly this: to pass through it a pilgrim body of witnesses."[63]

Central to Scofield's eschatological thinking is his strong adherence to prophecy and its fulfillment:

> Fulfilled prophecy is a proof of inspiration because the Scripture predictions of future events were uttered so long before the events transpired that no merely human sagacity or foresight could have anticipated them, and these predictions are so detailed, minute, and specific as to exclude the possibility that they were mere fortunate guesses.[64]

Prophecy, then, according to Scofield, is one means of determining that the Scriptures are from God. According to Scofield, there must be a literal fulfillment to prophecy.

What is the purpose of prophecy; is it some pretentious claim to augury? Scofield sees prophecy and the belief in its fulfillment as instilling confidence in the one who waits for the Lord.[65] According to Scofield the understanding of prophecy is a systematic procedure: "My task is to gather into orderly sequence the testimony of the Holy Spirit, through the prophets."[66]

Scofield believes 2 Peter 1:21 teaches that the prophetic message which men articulated came from God. The primary prediction in the Bible, he believes, is found in Daniel 9 since this passage speaks of the seventy weeks in the prophetic calendar and only sixty-nine of them have been fulfilled. The seventieth week, according to Scofield, is the period of the tribulation, and it has yet to be fulfilled.[67] Scofield interprets the seventy weeks into three segments: (1) seven weeks which in prophetical calculations is equal to forty-nine years, (2) sixty-two weeks which corresponds to 434 years, and (3) the week which is to be a seven-year period. Scofield claims the first seven weeks or forty-nine years were fulfilled from the decree to the actual rebuilding of Jerusalem. This decree, which is found in Nehemiah 2, is understood to be during the twentieth year of the reign of Artaxerxes, or in 445 B.C. The decree is understood to be the initial point of calculating the sixty-nine weeks as they relate to the cutting off of the Messiah. The last week, or the seventieth week, Scofield believes, is still future and alludes to the tribulation period on the earth while the Church will be in the presence of God. Scofield writes of the seventieth week of Daniel: "When the Church-age will end, and the seventieth week begin, is nowhere revealed. Its duration can be but seven years. To make it more violates the principle of interpretation already confirmed by fulfillment."[68] Between the sixty-ninth and seventieth week is the present age of grace.

The central person during this seven-year period, or the seventieth week, will be an individual whose career is contrary to the Lord's; he is known as the Antichrist.

> The "he" of verse 27 (Daniel 9) is the "prince that shall come" of verse 26, whose people (Rome) destroyed the temple, A.D.

The Sources of Chafer's Eschatological Thought

70. He is the same with the "little horn" of chapter 7. He will covenant with the Jews to restore their temple sacrifices for one week (seven years), but in the middle of that time he will break the covenant and fulfill Daniel 12:11 and 2 Thessalonians 2:3,4.[69]

Scofield claims this Antichrist and his work are depicted also in 2 Thessalonians 2:3,4 and in Matthew 24:15. He will be energized supposedly by Satan, and his purpose is to destroy the Church and establish his personal evil empire.

Scofield believes much biblical prophecy pertains to the seventh dispensation, the millennium, or also termed the kingdom. He emphatically claims:

> ... the kingdom was no mystery. The kingdom is the great theme of the prophets. From Isaiah to Malachi the burden of the prophetic testimony is the kingdom to be set up by the Messiah, David's great Son, but who was to be also "the mighty God, the Everlasting Father."[70]

He repeatedly describes the millennial period as not one of grace but of righteousness.[71] The King will be reigning during this period, as Satan has been bound. He alludes to this reign as the time when the Davidic dynasty will be reestablished.[72] He is definite concerning the initiation of the millennial period. Repeatedly he claims this period will begin immediately after the seven-year period of tribulation. Scofield claims the form of government will be a theocracy.[73] Jesus Christ will reign as King during this thousand year period.

Scofield distinguishes between the phrases "kingdom of God" and "kingdom of heaven."

> The "kingdom of God" is a great inclusive expression, which takes in the whole sphere where God rules. The "kingdom of heaven" is the establishment, through Christ, of God's righteous reign on the earth, it is always limited to the earth ... though glorified saints of this and past ages are concerned with it.[74]

The Promise of Dawn

The disciples preached the kingdom of heaven but this gospel was rejected; therefore, according to Scofield, there has been a postponement of the kingdom and God is calling out His own through the Church. He sees Matthew chapter eleven as a pivotal chapter in this rejection on the part of the Jews toward the gospel of the kingdom.[75] Scofield believes the phrase "kingdom of heaven" is found only in Matthew.[76] The principles of the kingdom are specified, Scofield says, in the Sermon on the Mount. This passage, therefore, has only a secondary reference to the present Church age. Many of the parables relate to the kingdom of heaven and the kingdom of God, but Scofield emphasizes they refer primarily to the former.

It is not possible nor necessary to look more deeply into the eschatology of C. I. Scofield. The above analysis includes the essentials of his eschatology, and this investigation is sufficient to understand much of the eschatological position of his protégé, Lewis Sperry Chafer.

As one views Chafer's eschatology, it is readily apparent there are only minor differences from the eschatology of C. I. Scofield. In chapter one, it was seen that Chafer's opinion of Scofield the first time he heard him teach was summed up in the words, "I was captured for life." Chafer was the successor of Scofield's eschatology. Chapters three and four will probe more deeply into Chafer's dispensationalism and millennialism; however, some comments concerning Chafer's indebtedness to Scofield at this time are pertinent.

Scofield sees three classifications of humanity: the Jews, the Gentiles, and the Church of God. Chafer refers to four major divisions of beings: the angels, the Jews, the Gentiles, and the Christians. Both views are identical with the exception of the inclusion of angels in Chafer's division. Chafer perhaps does not use "Church of God" because of his controversy with Calvinists who believe the Church can also be found in the Old Testament. The designation "Christians," Chafer believes, helps avoid misunderstanding.

Chafer and Scofield both see the importance of distinguishing between Israel and the Church.[77] Chafer understands the Church as commencing at Pentecost "through the new ministries of the Spirit."[78]

Scofield and Chafer's seven dispensational scheme is identical.

The Sources of Chafer's Eschatological Thought

The differences between Scofield and Chafer are only a matter of emphases. Scofield continually depicts the differences between law and grace.[79] Chafer, however, places more emphasis upon the designation of the future kingdom age.

Both Scofield and Chafer hold to a second coming of the Lord which has two parts: first, a taking out of the saints, and second, a returning with the saints. Thus, both Scofield and Chafer have a similar understanding concerning the second coming.

Scofield's doctrine of the resurrection is not as complicated as Chafer's. The former holds to only two resurrections while the latter to three resurrections. Chafer stresses that at the end of the bloody seven-year period, a resurrection of the saints will take place. Again, it is noted, the differences are slight in regard to their view of the resurrection.

Chafer believes the Scriptures teach eight judgments, though he himself emphasizes only three: the Judgment Seat of Christ, the judgment of the nations, and the Great White Throne judgment.[80] All true believers who have died between the death of Christ and the rapture of the saints will be present at the Judgment Seat of Christ. Raptured saints will also be present at this judgment. The Judgment Seat of Christ will not be a time of dread, but each will receive commendation from Christ. The second judgment, the judgment of nations, is found in Matthew 25:31-46. This judgment will determine who will enter the millennial kingdom. The third judgment, the Great White Throne judgment, Chafer believes, is found in Revelation 20:11-15, and this judgment is only for those outside of God's grace. Scofield also emphasizes the same three.

Chafer, like Scofield, held to the primacy of prophecy. Chafer claims there must be literal fulfillment of the prophetic utterance. Chafer understands the seventieth week of Daniel to be future and the present period is the age of grace. This age began with Christ's death and continues in the present time. The Church will be taken out before the commencement of this seventieth week. Both Scofield and Chafer, then, are pretribulational in reference to the translation of the Church, since both see believers being taken out before the time of tribulation begins.

The distinction between the kingdom of heaven and the kingdom of God is important to Scofield and Chafer's thought.[81] The phrase "kingdom of heaven" is found in the gospels, and Chafer believes it speaks of the millennial rule of Christ, while the phrase "kingdom of God" alludes to the new birth itself and is concerned with the authority of God over the entire universe.

Chafer and Scofield's eschatologies are almost identical. A few areas exist in which there are contrasts, but on the whole, they approach, interpret, and conclude their eschatological schemes in similar fashion.

In order to come to a fuller understanding of Chafer's eschatology, it is necessary to understand the importance of his personal study of the Scriptures and various theologians' works. Such an endeavor will help to reveal the setting in which he developed his eschatology.

Chafer's Eschatological Conclusions as Derived from His Personal Study

In attempting to analyze the personal sources from which Chafer drew, one has difficulty ascertaining precisely which writers were definitely crucial to his thinking and development. He was familiar with such a variety of theologians and Bible scholars. Of course, the common belief is that Chafer's eschatological though is but a mere rubber stamp of John Nelson Darby. But John Witmer, who knew Chafer personally, writes:

> John Nelson Darby had no direct theological influence on Dr. Chafer. ... But he and his theological position undoubtedly had an indirect influence to the extent that they influenced the entire theologically conservative movement in North America and the British Isles in the last quarter of the nineteenth century and the first quarter of the twentieth century.[82]

Outside of his *Systematic Theology*, Chafer never mentions Darby. Chafer was always candid about his sources; thus, there does not appear to be a deliberate omission on his part by not quoting J. N. Darby. The obvious conclusion is that Darby had no direct substantial influence upon Chafer. The only reference to J. N. Darby in Chafer's *Systematic Theology* is from Darby's *Synopsis of the Books of the Bible*. Chafer used a

The Sources of Chafer's Eschatological Thought

quotation from this work, but it does not even pertain to eschatology, but instead to the doctrine of salvation. This is Chafer's sole mention of Darby! How then can one claim Darby exerted a powerful influence upon the eschatological development and thinking of Chafer? Witmer supplies the correct answer by stating this influence was only "indirect." Since Chafer does not quote Darby, it is best not to read into Chafer's eschatology a source which does not significantly involve him.

In determining Chafer's sources and the manner in which he approached his eschatology, an understanding of his personal methodology is essential. Joseph Boles, however, claims Chafer had no methodology.[83] Boles also makes a dubious statement that "Chafer's scheme is more rationalistic that biblical."[84] However, Boles does make a keen observation in stating that "Chafer's system is a combination of Calvinism, pietism and dispensationalism."[85]

Though there were vast influences upon Chafer's eschatological thought, one can conclude that Chafer reached his conclusions concerning eschatology by rigorous personal study. By stating that Chafer was influenced by personal study, the writer is claiming that by independently studying the Scriptures and various theologians, Chafer came to his conclusions. He was convinced that through prayer and study the truth would be revealed to him. Although Chafer associated with many dispensationalists, read hundreds of theologians who held to this system, and was the successor of C. I. Scofield, he came to his eschatological conclusions by independent study. Chafer interpreted the Bible according to what he believed is a historical-grammatical and literal method of interpretation. Such a method led him to dispensational premillennialism.

Donald K. Campbell, the third president of Dallas Theological Seminary, and appointed to the faculty by Chafer, believes that Chafer's personal study of George N. H. Peters had a considerable influence upon Chafer.[86] But Campbell also states: "His [Chafer's] convictions regarding dispensationalism and premillennialism derive, I believe, from his determination to have a theology that was informed by scriptural study. The long list of Scripture references in many sections of his theology preserve for us his original inductive studies."[87]

John F. Walvoord, Chancellor of Dallas Seminary, who knew Chafer perhaps better than any living individual, states that Chafer came to his personal views concerning premillennialism primarily through personal study: "Accordingly, his [Chafer] premillennial teachings largely were a result of his own Bible study and application of principles of literal interpretation of prophecy."[88]

Walvoord claims that Chafer was influenced by his contacts at Mount Hermon, but these were not as significant as the conclusions at which he arrived by personal inductive study. Walvoord also holds the same is true with Chafer's dispensationalism which, of course, is intimately connected with premillennialism. Walvoord says:

> Chafer drew his dispensationalism from the common view of dispensationalism held by Scofield and many others in the early part of the 20th century. It was almost the standard Bible teaching in the Bible conference ministry and in Bible schools, such as Moody Bible Institute, and many others of similar character that arose in America. No doubt his dispensationalism, however, was developed when he began writing his eight-volume *Systematic Theology* which was completed in 1948. He had previously written a separate pamphlet on dispensationalism, but there is no doubt that his thinking matured a great deal and he drew up his major work.[89]

Walvoord believes that Chafer considered dispensational premillennialism significant for the following reasons:

> Chafer held that premillennialism was important ... because it provides the key to the interpretation of about 25 percent of the Bible. Major sections of the Old Testament, if interpreted literally, lead to the premillennial conclusion.[90]

In Chafer's theological system, dispensational premillennialism could not be fused in any manner with either postmillennialism or amillennialism. Writing the foreword in 1936 to Charles L. Feinberg's work, *Millennialism: The Two Major Views*, Chafer offered substantial insight into why he believed premillennialism to be of such great importance. He does not see postmillennialism as a threat to his eschatological beliefs:

> There has been a millennial question among Biblical interpreters ever since speculative theologians began to take liberty with the Scriptures, either by a "spiritualizing" system of interpretation or by an utter neglect of the plain teaching of the Bible. Of the three contentions — postmillennialism, amillennialism and premillennialsim, or as the latter was known in the early centuries from the Greek designation, chiliasm — postmillennialism is dead. Whether the present insane, corrupt condition of the world killed the theory by the contradiction of its own developing character, or whether the more intensified study of prophetic truth in these latter times so magnified its inconsistencies that it died, future historians must determine.[91]

Chafer sometimes equates his understanding of premillennialism with the early Church's view. He perhaps should have been clearer in stating that the premillennialism of the early Church and dispensational premillennialism are not the same. For example, the premillennialism of the early Church did not speak of a secret rapture of the saints.

Why did Chafer believe so strongly in premillennialism? Chafer believes in approaching the Scriptures in a literal manner — understanding the words as they were written. Of course, this does not mean Chafer does not hold to figures of speech and symbolism as contained in the Scriptures, but their interpretation is subject to a historical-grammatical hermeneutic. One of Chafer's first books was *The Kingdom in History and Prophecy*, 1915, and he discloses even at this time, about twenty years before the commencement of his *Systematic Theology*, some insights into how he approached the writing of theology. He speaks of "rightly dividing" Scripture, a phrase common to C. I. Scofield:

> It has been said, "All Scripture is for us, but all Scripture is not about us." It all bears a message to us, but is not all our rule of life. It will not do for Gentile believers to read themselves into the great portion of the Bible which treats distinctly of a chosen nation, still a separate people in the earth, under the special

unbroken purpose of God and exactly where God intended them to be at this very hour.⁹²

He refers to one system of interpretation: "Either the divine revelation follows a definite order in the development of the kingdom in the earth, or it does not. If it does, there could hardly be two distinct programs coexisting in the mind and purpose of God."⁹³

In his last work, *Dispensationalism*, published in 1951, Chafer continues to stress the need for organization, categorization, and biblical interpretation:

> The Bible is God's one and only Book. In it He discloses facts of eternity as well as of time, of heaven and hell as well as of earth, of Himself as well as of His creatures, and of His purposes in all creation.... The Bible presents the origin, present estate, and destiny of our major classes of rational beings in the universe: the angels, the Gentiles, the Jews, and the Christians.⁹⁴

Chafer in his early writings endeavors to find themes, categories and methods of dividing his material. Such a methodology encompasses both the Old and New Testaments. Chafer sees the need for "expounding the Scriptures of the Old and New Testaments clearly, convincingly, from a thoroughly conservative and premillennial viewpoint."⁹⁵ Further he believes that "no progress can be made in kingdom studies unless plain words are taken in their obviously plain meaning. In the Bible 'Israel' is not the 'Church,' 'Zion' is not the body of saints of this dispensation; the 'throne of David' is not heaven, nor will it ever be."⁹⁶

Chafer did not study theology in a rigorous and intensive manner until he was chosen to teach theology in the Evangelical Theological College. Lincoln records that Chafer secured at this time a large library on systematic theology.⁹⁷ However, Chafer was ever aware of his deficiency in theology at this period in his life as the following self-revelation portrays, written five years after the opening of the seminary:

> I have burned the midnight oil for five years attempting to beat

myself into some little recognition of those vast subjects which enter into the field of systematic theology. What in the world have I been doing for five years, if our courses of study are the same as those offered in Bible institutes?[98]

Chafer worked diligently to master his field because he was concerned that the school for whose existence he had been largely responsible develop a reputation for solid scholarship.

Throughout his life, Chafer was pietistic, and he constantly stressed the need to depend upon the teaching ministry of the Holy Spirit. He firmly believed that "apart from the teaching of the Spirit you will not understand what you read in those great spiritual portions of the Scriptures."[99] Speaking to a gathering of students at Moody Bible Institute, Chafer advised the graduating class:

> God save you young people from being anything because any man says so. Every bit of sectarianism in the world, every modern cult is made possible because people are willing to accept some person's statement in place of a first-hand investigation of the truth itself. Do not believe anything because anyone says so. Let that person lead you to the Word of God.[100]

To better understand God's revelation, Chafer sees the use of original languages, specifically Greek and Hebrew, as essential. He speaks of studying the Bible book by book for both analysis and spiritual content.[101] He believes "no substitute will ever be found for the knowledge of the Word of God. That Word alone deals with things eternal and infinite, and it alone has power to convert the soul and to develop a God-honoring life."[102]

Speaking of the purpose of the theological seminary, Chafer offers insight into his personal theological method:

> Exegesis belongs to the department of original languages and its importance cannot be overestimated, nor should its prosecution cease with the student's graduation. It is the province of exegetical research to aid in the study of doctrinal, devotional,

historical, prophetical, and practical aspects of divine revelation. ... Studies in theology, original languages, and history should contribute to one ideal, namely, *the knowledge of the Scriptures.*[103]

To Chafer, systematic theology "is the collecting, scientifically arranging, comparing, exhibiting, and defending of all facts from any and every source concerning God and His works."[104] But concerning eschatology, Chafer assumes a dispensational division. "The dispensational study of the Bible consists in the identification of certain well-defined time periods...."[105] Central to his entire theology and specifically to his eschatology is his view that eschatology is built upon specific time periods which are disclosed in many biblical passages.

Chafer understands prophecy as inherent in eschatology, and divides the former into fulfilled and unfulfilled prophecy. There are seven major themes of prophecy in the Old Testament, and these include prophecy concerning the Gentiles, Israel's early history, the nation itself, Israel's last dispersion and regathering, the advent of the Messiah, the Great Tribulation, and Messiah's kingdom. The New Testament also has themes concerning prophecy, namely prophecy concerning the present age, which is unannounced, the divine purpose in the calling out of the Church from both Jews and Gentiles, the Great Tribulation, Satan and the forces of evil, the second coming of Christ, the Messianic Kingdom, and the eternal estate. Chafer speaks of ten major highways of prophecy traced through the Bible. These are the Lord Jesus Christ, the Church, the resurrection and translation of the saints, the Great Tribulation, Satan and evil, the Antichrist, the course and end of apostate Christendom, the beginning, extenuation and end of Gentile times, the second coming of Christ, and Israel's covenants.[106] Chafer was convinced if he could categorize, he would be an effective preacher.

> How many even sincere men can preach an uncomplicated gospel sermon? No man can be trusted to do this until he is dispensationally instructed. ... The great expositors of this and past generations are such because they are thoroughly established in these essential distinctions.[107]

The Sources of Chafer's Eschatological Thought

How did Chafer approach his personal study? He was thoroughly biblical; he went to the text and through an inductive method came to his conclusions. He was systematic and longed to discover themes which he found in both testaments. He believed in the use of the original languages in ascertaining the clearest meaning of a given passage. Central to his understanding of the end time was Chafer's belief in the premillennial return of the Lord. Why did he believe Jesus would return to establish His kingdom? Through the principle of a literal, historical-grammatical interpretation, Chafer came to his conclusions. With his natural analytical and systematizing ability, Chafer categorized by searching for themes and patterns. He had heard the rudiments of dispensational premillennialism at Northfield. He also was heavily indebted to C. I. Scofield for a fuller understanding of his eschatology. These sources, however, were solidified by his personal study.

Since this book is concerned with the eschatology of Chafer, attention will not be given to doctrines other than eschatology. His entire *Systematic Theology* is written from a dispensational, premillennial perspective. Chafer believes "when systematic theology includes the premillennial and dispensational interpretations of the Bible, much added material is discovered and the work is greatly extended."[108]

Even though Chafer, through an inductive study of the Scriptures, came to definite conclusions, one cannot discount the great influence of other theologians upon his understanding of how the end will come. From the early 1920s, he read many theologians, and some of these without doubt had a great impact upon his thinking and development of the *Systematic Theology*.

Chafer alludes to George N. H. Peter's work, *The Theocratic Kingdom*, published in 1884, repeatedly throughout his volume on *Eschatology*. Chafer derived much of the material for this volume from an article he wrote for the *Bibliotheca Sacra* in 1943, "An Introduction to the Study of Prophecy." Chafer refers constantly to George N. H. Peters in this article. It is important to note that Chafer quotes Peters and Scofield about equally in his volume on eschatology.

Chafer had great respect for the three-volume work by Peters, *The Theocratic Kingdom*, referring to this work as "unsurpassed either for

89

completeness or for scholarship."[109] Perhaps the greatest impact Peters had upon the eschatological thinking of Chafer is portrayed in the following, which stresses the importance of giving to language its literal and grammatical meaning:

> We unhesitatingly plant ourselves upon the famous maxim (Eccl. Polity, B. 2.) of the able Hooker: 'I hold for a most infallible rule in exposition of the Sacred Scriptures, that where a literal construction will stand, the furtherest from the latter is commonly the worst. There is nothing more dangerous than this licentious and deluding art, which changes the meaning of words, as alchemy doth, or would do, the substance of metals, making of anything what it pleases, and bringing in the end all truth to nothing.' ...[110]

Wilbur M. Smith, during his professorship at Fuller Theological Seminary, wrote the preface to a reprint edition of *The Theocratic Kingdom*. Smith refers to Peters' work as "the most important single work on Biblical predictive prophecy to appear in this country at any time during the nineteenth century."[111] Peters quotes almost four thousand authors from the Church Fathers to his own day. Smith believes Peters' impact upon Chafer's development was intense.[112]

George N. H. Peters is obscure. It is known that he graduated from Wittenberg College in 1850, and held pastorates in Lutheran churches in the state of Ohio. Smith says:

> He [Peters] wrote at a time when many were about to conclude that the millennium was at hand, but his knowledge of the Word told him otherwise; and the deep shadows which have fallen across the earth since that bright day our author clearly foresaw on the horizon through the prayerful use of the binocular telescope of Biblical prediction.[113]

This work of Peters, then is premillennial and discusses what the author believes will be the thousand-year reign of Christ upon the earth. He

The Sources of Chafer's Eschatological Thought

grounds his belief in the kingdom upon the Scriptures. He found prophecies in the Old Testament which point to the time of the kingdom, and also John the Baptist preached of this kingdom. This kingdom, according to Peters, will be Jewish. It was offered to the Jewish nation but was rejected. The Church is not the kingdom, but is the preparatory stage for it. Peters believes the kingdom, if it is to be established, will demand national restoration of the Jews to their land. This kingdom will be visible, external, and exist upon the earth. Jesus, as the Son of David, will inherit the throne and will reign with an iron hand. However, the kingdom cannot be established until the Antichrist is overthrown, and the kingdom age will be preceded by a great battle known as Armageddon. This kingdom will end the "times of the Gentile," or Gentile domination, and a true theocracy will be established upon the earth.

Without a doubt, Chafer read and quoted Peters' *The Theocratic Kingdom*. Though others of the caliber of Wilbur M. Smith extol the work, it remains shrouded in obscurity. Smith suggests it was not reviewed because "perhaps reviewers did not think themselves competent to adequately survey and appraise such a monumental work."[114] But perhaps the real reason seems to be the spirit of the period in which it was written. The period was a time of extreme optimism; thus, Peters' work seemed out of place. Nevertheless, Chafer was most impressed with the work and agreed wholeheartedly, especially with the hermeneutical approach employed by Peters. This approach is characterized by its literalness and emphasis upon the grammatical significance of interpretation.

Chafer read many of the standard Reformed works such as A. A. Hodge's *Outline of Theology*, Charles A. Hodge's *Systematic Theology*, and B. B. Warfield's *Studies in Theology*. These sources will be discussed in chapter four. Chafer's system is on the whole Reformed. While he does not hold to limited atonement, or the view that Jesus died for only a select few, and though he does not accept an all-encompassing covenant of grace spanning both the Old and New Testaments, Chafer is strongly in the Reformed tradition. Therefore, as Chafer read the standard Reformed works, he as an ordained Presbyterian minister concurred with these works. He disagreed, however, strongly in how and when the end will come. Chafer alludes to the fact that many of the standard theologies minimized eschatology or even admitted their inadequacy concerning eschatology. Charles Hodge, the Princeton theologian, readily admits his own inadequacy concerning the subject.[115]

Chafer also read extensively the following: W. Lindsay Alexander's *A System of Biblical Theology*; E. V. Gerhard's *Institutes of the Christian Religion*; C. H. Mackintosh's *Notes on Leviticus*; John Miley's *Systematic Theology*; W. G. T. Shedd's *Dogmatic Theology*; A. H. Strong's *Systematic Theology*; and Richard Watson's *Theological Institutes*. But none of these authors are quoted in his works on eschatology.

H. A. Ironside and Chafer became acquainted during the latter's ministry at Northfield. Ironside was one of the first visiting professors at the Evangelical Theological College, and remained actively involved with the institution the years after it officially became known as Dallas Theological Seminary. A prolific writer, Ironside wrote over forty works; nevertheless, Chafer in his writings on eschatology quoted only from Ironside's *Lectures on Daniel* and *Lectures on Revelation*. Marsden honors Ironside by mentioning the latter as pastor of Moody Church in Chicago.[116] Chafer quotes Ironside on the latter's interpretation of the four beasts in Daniel seven. Ironside writes concerning the beasts:

> In Daniel's visions he was given to see the course of each of the empires which these wild beasts figure. That is, each wild beast is of such a character as to picture the leading features in the entire history of the empire which it represents. For instance, the whole course of Babylon is set forth in the winged lion.... The whole course of Medo-Persia is pictured in the vision of the bear with three ribs in its mouth....The entire history of the Grecian empire and its four-fold division is set forth in the four-headed and winged leopard. And the course of the Roman empire right on down to the Time of the End (a condition which has not yet been reached) is depicted in the beast, dreadful and terrible, with the great iron teeth and ten horns....But now, for a moment look at the 17th verse. There the four beasts are said to be "four kings which shall arise out of the earth."[117]

Ironside believed that this fourth kingdom is still future and refers to the power which will arise as depicted in Revelation thirteen.

The Sources of Chafer's Eschatological Thought

Chafer chose Ironside to be visiting professor of English Bible at the seminary in Dallas. Chafer was familiar with Ironside's works concerning eschatology. In Ironside's *Not Wrath but Rapture*, he argues for the rapture of the saints before the commencement of the tribulation period. Ironside, as do Scofield and Chafer, believes that there are two parts of the second coming, Christ coming for the saints and with the saints.[118]

This work by Ironside, on the whole, is identical with Chafer's. Through the study and interpretation of Bible passages according to their plain meaning, both came independently to similar conclusions. The Church will not be present during this time of trial, according to Ironside. He sees this period not as present or past but as a distinctly future event.

Ironside also wrote *Wrongly Dividing the Word of Truth;* and of course, one can readily see the influence of Scofield in this work. This work, published in 1938, is a plea for correctly understanding the significance of dispensational distinctions. Specifically, Ironside writes against those who hold to ultra-dispensationalism. This doctrine, according to Ironside, states that the book of Acts covers a transition period between the dispensation of law and the dispensation of the Church. Thus, in the book of Acts the Church, the Body of Christ, is not found. The Greek word *ekklesia* (church, assembly) as found in the book of Acts alludes to a different church altogether and is not the same as is found in Paul's prison epistles. This earlier church, then, was simply an aspect of the kingdom and was not the same as the Body of Christ. Also, ultra-dispensationalists claim the Christian ordinances, baptism and the Lord's Supper, are not for this age but are in error carried over from the past. They may again have a place in the Great Tribulation.[119] Most ultra-dispensationalists claim E. W. Bullinger, a minister of the Church of England, as their source for this teaching. Ironside rebuked the ultra-dispensational position.

> Having had most intimate acquaintance with Bullingerism as taught for the last forty years, I have no hesitancy in saying that its fruits are evil. ... So true are these things of this system that I have no hesitancy in saying it is an absolutely Satanic perversion of the truth.[120]

Chafer in his *Ecclesiology* also takes issue with Bullinger; however, he is more gracious than is Ironside in denouncing ultra-dispensationalism.[121]

Ironside's work, *Lectures on Revelation*, published in 1920, is a standard dispensational interpretation of this book of the Bible. Ironside claims the first three chapters of Revelation refer to this present dispensation, the age of grace, but from chapters four through the end of the book the subject concerns future events, and pertains primarily to the seven-year tribulation period.

> As we turn from chapter 3 to chapter 4, ... we are no longer occupied with the professing church in the place of testimony, nor with events on the earth at all.... From the close of chapter 3, we never see the church on earth again through all the rest of this solemn book.[122]

Chafer and Ironside were colleagues for almost fifty years, and they died within one year of each other. They were aware of one another's writings, and upon comparison of the two, it is apparent they possessed a common understanding of eschatology.

A. C. Gaebelein and Chafer were also close acquaintances, and the former was chosen by Chafer to serve in the capacity as visiting professor at the seminary. Chafer and Gaebelein were associates until the latter's death in 1945. Commemorating the life of A. C. Gaebelein, Chafer writes:

> Only the scale of measurement which the Lord himself will use at the *bema* — His judgment seat — could declare the value to his generation of the ministry of Dr. A. C. Gaebelein of New York City, editor of *Our Hope*....His two most dominant themes were, first the glory of Christ, and second, His imminent return to receive His own....Such a life, apart from the written ministry he left behind, cannot be measured by earthly values. We glory in God who raised up and sustained Dr. Gaebelein....[123]

In Chafer's old age, he often spoke of the great respect he had for A. C.

Gaebelin.[124]

Gaebelein is one of the sixty-four authors of the *Fundamentals*, the series of pamphlets which greatly promoted the fundamentalist movement. He was editor of the millenarian periodical, *Our Hope*, and was a consulting editor of the *Scofield Reference Bible*. He convened a large Bible conference in Carnegie Hall, New York City, during November 25 - 28, 1919 which attracted large crowds.[125] Sandeen devotes much attention to Gaebelein and describes him as "ambitious and conscientious, providing the spark for the millenarian movement during the first two decades of the twentieth century."[126] Gaebelein was a pretribulationist and of course a premillennialist, and found himself in heavy contention with Robert Cameron who held to postribulationism, which view claims the Church will have to go through the time of tribulation on earth.

Gaebelein wrote *The Revelation* and describes the book of Revelation as "the capstone of the entire revelation of God, without which the Bible would be an unfinished book. We find in its pages the consummation of the great prophecies which were given by the Prophets of God in the Old Testament times."[127] *The Revelation* in general is a dispensational, premillennial approach to the interpretation of this book of the Bible. Both Chafer and Gaebelein understand Revelation four through twenty-two as alluding to a future time. Gaebelein states:

> The future things, things after the removal of the true Church from the earth, occupy the greater part of this Book. It is of the greatest importance to see that nothing whatever after the third chapter of Revelation has yet taken place.... No seal can be broken as long as this event has not been. But after the Rapture, the Seals of the Book, which the Lamb received, are broken by Him, the trumpet and the vial judgments fall upon the earth. All this takes place after the homegoing of the true Church and before the glorious appearing of our Lord Jesus Christ (xix:11, etc).[128]

Gaebelein speaks of the second coming of Christ, the overthrow of the Beast and the kings and armies of the earth, the binding of Satan, and the reign of Christ for a thousand years. He also writes of the Great White Throne judgment and the eternal destiny of the redeemed.[129]

Gaebelein wrote *The Prophet Daniel* and understands the book of Daniel as being intimately connected with the book of Revelation. "The last Book of the Bible, the Book of Revelation, the only prophetic Book of the New Testament, would ever be a sealed Book, if we had not the prophecies of Daniel, and the prophecies of Daniel would in part remain sealed if we had not Revelation."[130]

In his book, *The Conflict of the Ages*, he speaks of the certainty of the fulfillment of prophecy:

> The Bible forecasts the future. Its forecasts are sure and certain beyond the shadow of even the remotest doubt. History proves it. Hundreds of years before certain empires came into existence, the Bible predicted their coming and what should come to pass. This we find in the prophecies of Daniel.... Still more striking is the prewritten history of the people of Israel. This fact no infidel has ever been able, nor will be able, to answer. Fulfilled prophecy demonstrates the Bible as the infallible Word of God.[131]

Gaebelein divides the work into three sections and relates each section to either the people of Israel, the Gentiles, or the Church. This division, of course, reminds one of Scofield's and Chafer's identical divisions. The book covers the usual dispensational, premillennial topics and does not diverge from the essential teachings of this system. Chafer, Gaebelein, and Ironside are of one mind in matters relating to eschatology.

Chafer also thought very highly of Sir Robert Anderson's work, *The Coming Prince*, published in 1909. Sandeen tells us that Anderson was a pretribulationist who was in opposition to Cameron.[132] Chafer writes concerning *The Coming Prince*: "A careful reading of that treatise is suggested for every student of prophecy."[133] Chafer, then, was familiar with this classic in prophetic fulfillment and wholeheartedly endorsed its conclusions.

Conclusion

What conclusions can be drawn concerning the sources of Chafer's eschatological thought? It is apparent that one cannot make a generalized statement and claim his thinking on eschatology is simply drawn from one source or individual. Chafer apparently was very objective, yet definite, in his final writing concerning eschatology. He had heard and been associated with many of the leading dispensational premillennialists of his time during his tenure at Northfield. He was especially influenced through his intimate acquaintance with C. I. Scofield. However, it was primarily through his personal study of the Scriptures, aided by the study of select theologians' works, that Chafer came to his eschatological conclusions. George N. H. Peters exerted a great impact upon Chafer's eschatological thought. But one must always be cognizant of the fierce independency of thought which Chafer displayed throughout his life; he was personally convinced that the Scriptures themselves taught dispensational premillennialism.

Notes: Chapter 2

1. Wally Howard, "Accident Man," Sunday School Promoter 6 (June 1944):55.

2. Lewis Sperry Chafer, *Systematic Theology*, vol. 1: *Prolegomena-Bibliology-Theology Proper* (Dallas: Dallas Seminary Press, 1947), p. xxxiv.

3. Daniel P. Fuller, "The Hermeneutics of Dispensationalism," (Th.D. dissertation, Northern Baptist Seminary, 1957), p. 379.

4. Joseph Boles, "The Theology of Lewis Sperry Chafer in the Light of His Theological Method," (Th.D. dissertation, Southwestern Baptist Seminary, 1963), p. 2.

5. John F. Walvoord, "Lewis Sperry Chafer," *The Sunday School Times* 94 (11 October 1952):855. Cf. Lewis Sperry Chafer, "Summer Bible Conferences: Their Meaning," *The Sunday School Times* 62 (24 April 1920):235. In this article Chafer spoke of the "spiritual change," understanding and vitality which occurred in his thinking at Northfield.

6. Delevan L. Pierson, ed., *Northfield Echoes, Northfield Conference Address for 1902* (East Northfield, Massachusetts: The Northfield Bookstore, 1902), pp. 13-420. Cf. *Bible Studies at Northfield* (Terre Haute, Indiana: Ambassadors for Christ, n.d.)

7. Lewis Sperry Chafer, *He That Is Spiritual*, with a foreward by John F. Walvoord (n.p., 1918; rev. ed., Grand Rapids: Zondervan Publishing House, 1967), p. 139.

8. Ernest Sandeen, *The Roots of Fundamentalism* (Grand Rapids: Baker Book House, 1970), p. 172-73.

9. Delevan L. Pierson, ed., *The Victorious Life, the Post Conference Addresses Delivered at East Northfield, Massachusetts,. August 17-25, 1895* (New York: Baker & Taylor Co., 1896), p. iii.

10. H. W. Webb-Peploe, "The Victorious Life," in *The Victorious Life, the Post Conference Addresses Delivered at East Northfiled*, p. 40.

11. Ibid., p. 42.

12. Ibid., pp. 43-46. Webb-Peploe apparently holds to a dispensational, premillennial interpretation of eschatology. He is not entirely systematic in his presentation of eschatology, but it appears he holds to a taking out of the saints before the tribulation period, a millennial period, the defeat of Satan and his hosts, the judgment of the unregenerate, and the eternal estate, pp. 46-51. The great majority of Webb-Peploe's messages, however, concern the subject of the "victorious life." Some of the titles of his messages are "The Way of Blessing," "How to Meet Temptation," and "The Spirit and the Believer." Cf. Janet Mabie, *The Years Beyond, The Story of Northfield, D. L. Moody and the Schools* (East Northfield, Massachusetts: The Northfield Bookstore, 1960). The author relates the deeper life emphasis at Northfield: "The Conference phase of Northfield began to be spoke of as 'an American Keswick.' One common denominator certainly was that, in both placaes, the primary objective of main platform meetings was the deepening of the spiritual life." p. 78.

13. Lewis Sperry Chafer, "Twenty Years of Experience," *Bulletin of Dallas Theological Seminary* 19 (September 1943).

14. Lewis Sperry Chafer, *The Kingdom in History and Prophecy*, with an Introduction by C. I. Scofield (New York: Fleming H. Revell Co., 1915; reprint ed., Philadelphia: The Sunday School Times, 1926), p. 117.

15. Findlay, *Dwight L. Moody*, p. 408.

16. Ibid., p. 409.

17. Mabie, *The Years Beyond*, p. 80.

The Sources of Chafer's Eschatological Thought

18. Pierson, "Some Hints on Bible Study," in *Northfield Echoes, Northfield Conference Addresses for 1902*, p. 296.

19. Ibid., pp. 296-300.

20. Chafer, *Prolegomena-Bibliology-Theology Proper*, pp. 22-36.

21. Sandeen, *The Roots of Fundamentalism*, p. 180.

22. G. Campbell Morgan, "The Character of Holiness," in *Northfield Echoes, Northfield Conference Addresses for 1902*, p. 33.

23. Ibid., p. 35.

24. Ibid., pp. 388-89.

25. Ibid., pp. 391-92.

26. Ibid., p. 392.

27. Lewis Sperry Chafer, *Systematic Theology*, vol. 7: *Doctrinal Summarization* (Dallas: Dallas Seminary Press, 1948), p. 110.

28. Sandeeen, *The Roots of Fundamentalism*, p. 174.

29. George F. Pentecost, "The Imperialism of Christ," in *Northfield Echoes, Northfield Conference Addresses for 1902*, pp. 362-63.

30. Lewis Sperry Chafer, *Systematic Theology*, vol. 4: *Ecclesiology-Eschatology* (Dallas: Dallas Seminary Press, 1948), p. 333.

31. Chafer, "Twenty Years of Experience."

32. Lewis Sperry Chafer, "When I Learned from Dr. Scofield," *The Sunday School Times* 64 (4 March 1922):120.

33. Ibid.

34. Fuller, "The Hermeneutics of Dispensationalism," pp. 131-34. Cf.

Sydney Ahlstrom, *A Religious History of the American People*, 2 vols. (Garden City, New York: Doubleday & Company Image Books, 1975), 2:279. Ahlstrom makes reference to Scofield's school which continued as Dallas Theological Seminary; thus, this mistake by Ahlstrom displays how many historians realize the closeness which exists between Chafer and Scofield. Ahlstrom's mistake is stating Scofield's Correspondence School continued as Dallas Seminary. There was no relationship between the two schools.

35. C. G. Trumbull, *The Life Story of C. I. Scofield* (New York: Oxford University Press, 1920), p. 36.

36. Ibid., p. 53.

37. A. C. Gaebelein, "The Story of the Scofield Reference Bible," *Moody Monthly* 43 (October 1942):97.

38. A. C. Gaebelein, "The Story of the Scofield Reference Bible," *Moody Monthly* 43 (November 1942):135.

39. Chafer, "When I Learned from Dr. Scofield," p. 120.

40. C. I. Scofield, Foreward to *Satan*, by Lewis Sperry Chafer (n.p., 1919; rev. ed., Grand Rapids: Zondervan Publishing House, 1964).

41. Chafer, "When I Learned from Dr. Scofield," p. 120.

42. Ibid.

43. Lewis Sperry Chafer, "Cyrus Ingerson Scofield, D.D.," in *And in Samaria*, Midlred W. Spain (Dallas: Central American Mission, 1940). p. 4. Scofield did not resign as pastor of the Congregational church in Dallas until November 4, 1909. Cf. Rudolph Renfer, "A History of Dallas Theological Seminary" (Ph.D. dissertation, University of Texas, 1959), pp. 90-91. But Scofield did take a hiatus from the church to go to Europe to work on his reference Bible. Cf. *Trumbull, The Life Story of C. I. Scofield*, pp. 80-100. After 1904 Scofield was rarely in Dallas, and in 1909 he officially resigned the pastorate of the

Congregational church in Dallas. This was after the completion of the reference Bible.

44. Walvoord, "Lewis Sperry Chafer," p. 868.

45. Chafer, "When I Learned from Dr. Scofield," p. 120.

46. Renfer, "A History of Dallas Theological Seminary," p. 93.

47. Lewis Sperry Chafer, *Grace* (n.p., rev. ed., Grand Rapids: Zondervan Publishing House, 1950).

48. Lewis Sperry Chafer, "The Scofield Reference Bible," *Bibliotheca Sacra* 109 (April 1952):98.; Cf. Sandeen, *Roots of Fundamentalism*, p. 22. The author claims that Scofield "never demonstrated great ability as a biblical scholar, apologist, or organizer." However, Ahlstrom, *A Religious History of the American People*, 2:279-80, has a general positive tone about Scofield and his work.

49. Lewis Sperry Chafer, "Preaching and Teaching a Supernatural Work," *Moody Montly* 24 (September 1923):8.

50. C. I. Scofield, *Rightly Dividing the Word of Truth* (Neptune, New Jersey: Loizeaux Bros., [1896]), p. 6.

51. Ibid., p. 8.

52. Ibid., p. 12.

53. Ibid., p. 20.

54. Ibid., p. 26.

55. Ibid., p. 28.

56. Ibid.

57. Ibid., pp. 28-33.

58. Ibid., pp. 34-45.

59. C. I. Scofield, *What Do The Prophets Say?* (Philadelphia: Sunday School Times Co., 1918), pp. 102-03.

60. Scofield, *Addresses on Prophecy*, p. 21.

61. Ibid., p. 32.

62. C. I. Scofield, ed., *The Scofield Reference Bible* (New York: Oxford University Press, 1909), p. 990.

63. Scofield, *Addresses on Prophecy*, p. 25.

64. *Scofield Reference Bible*, p. 1318.

65. Scofield, *Addresses on Prophecy*, p. 90.

66. Ibid., p. 56.

67. *Scofield Reference Bible*, pp. 914-15.

68. Ibid., p. 914.

69. Ibid., pp. 914-15.

70. Scofield, *Addresses on Prophecy*, p. 17.

71. Ibid., p. 378.

72. Ibid., p. 66.

73. Ibid., p. 113.

74. Ibid., p. 105.

75. *Scofield Reference Bible*, p. 1011.

76. Ibid., p. 998.

77. Lewis Sperry Chafer, *The Kingdom in History and Prophecy*, with an Introduction by C. I. Scofield (New York: Fleming H. Revell Co., 1915; reprint ed., Philadelphia: Sunday School Times, 1926), pp. 15, 74, 78, 87.

78. Ibid., p. 79.

79. Scofield, *Rightly Dividing the Word of Truth*, pp. 34-44.

80. Lewis Sperry Chafer, *Major Bible Themes* (Dallas: Dallas Theological Seminary, 1926; rev. ed., Grand Rapids: Dunham Publications, 1964), pp. 283-300.

81. Chafer, *Ecclesiology-Eschatology*, pp. 26-27.

82. John A. Witmer, Professor Systematic Theology, Emeritus, Dallas Theological Seminary, personal letter, 3 June 1983.

83. Boles, "The Theology of Lewis Sperry Chafer in the Light of His Theological Method," p. 2.

84. Ibid., p. 67

85. Ibid.

86. Donald K. Campbell, President, Dallas Theological Seminary, personal letter, 28 December 1983.

87. Ibid.

88. John F. Walvoord, Chancellor, Dallas Theological Seminary, personal letter, 30 December 1983.

89. Ibid.

90. Ibid.

91. Lewis Sperry Chafer, Foreward to the First Edition in *Millennialism: The Two Major Views*, by Charles L. Feinberg (Chicago: Moody

Bible Institute, 1936; 3rd ed. rev. & enl., Chicago: Moody Press, 1982), p. 9.

92. Chafer, *The Kingdom in History and Prophecy*, p. 16.

93. Ibid., p. 17.

94. Lewis Sperry Chafer, *Dispensationalism* (Dallas: Dallas Theological Seminary, 1936; rev. ed., Dallas: Dallas Seminary Press, 1951), p. 19.

95. Lewis Sperry Chafer, "The Evangelical Theological College," *The Sunday School Times* 73 (6 June 1931):322.

96. Chafer, *The Kingdom in History and Prophecy*, pp. 15-16.

97. C. F. Lincoln, "Biographical Skech of the Author" in *Systematic Theology*, by Lewis Sperry Chafer, vol. 8: *Biographical Sketch and Indexes* (Dallas: Dallas Seminary Press, 1948), p. 5.

98. Lewis Sperry Chafer, to A. B. Winchester, 2 October 1929, Mosher Library Archives, quoted in Renfer, "A History of Dallas Theological Seminary," p. 101.

99. Lewis Sperry Chafer, "Preaching and Teaching a Supernatural Work," *Moody Monthly* 24 (September 1923):8.

100. Ibid.

101. Lewis Sperry Chafer, "Expository Preaching," *Bibliotheca Sacra* 104 (October 1947): 386.

102. Lewis Sperry Chafer, "Evils Resulting from an Abridged Systematic Theology," *Bibliotheca Sacra* 91 (April 1934): 135.

103. Chafer, *Prolegomena-Bibliology-Theology Proper*, p. vii.

104. Ibid., p. x.

105. Ibid., p. xi.

106. Lewis Sperry Chafer, "Unabridged Systematic Theology," *Bibliotheca Sacra* 91 (January 1934):21-22.

107. Lewis Sperry Chafer, "Gospel Preaching," *Bibliotheca Sacra* 95 (July 1938):343.

108. Chafer, *Prologomena-Bibliology-Theology Proper*, p. xxxviii.

109. Chafer, *Ecclesiology-Eschatology*, p. 283.

110. George N. H. Peters, *The Theocratic Kingdom*, 3 vols. (New York: Funk & Wagnalls Co., 1884), 1:13, quoted in Chafer, *Ecclesiology-Eschatology*, pp. 259-60.

111. Wilbur M. Smith, Preface to *The Theocratic Kingdom*, by George N. H. Peters (New York: Funk & Wagnalls Co., 1884; reprint ed., Grand Rapids: Kregel Publications, 1952). p. 129.

112. Ibid.

113. Ibid.

114. Ibid.

115. Charles Hodge, *Systematic Theology*, vol. 3: *Soteriology* (Grand Rapids: Wm. B. Eerdmans Publishing Co., 1940). p. 790, quoted in Chafer, *Ecclesiology-Eschatology*, p. 255.

116. George Marsden, *Fundamentalism and American Culture* (New York: Oxford University Press, 1980), p. 95.

117. H. A. Ironside, *Lectures on Daniel* (New York: Loizeaux Bros., 192-0), pp. 118-20, quoted in Chafer, *Ecclesiology-Eschatology*, pp. 335-36.

118. H. A. Ironside, *Not Wrath but Rapture* (Neptune, New Jersey: Loizeaux Bros., n.d.), p. 43.

119. H. A. Ironside, *Wrongly Dividing the Word of Truth* (Neptune,

New Jersey: Loizeaux Bros., 1938), p. 9-10.

120. Ibid., p. 11.

121. Chafer, *Ecclesioology-Eschatology*, pp. 127-31.

122. H. A. Ironside, *Lectures on Revelation* (Neptune, New Jersey: Loizeaux Bros., 1938), pp. 9-10.

123. Lewis Sperry Chafer, "Dr. A. C. Gaebelein," *Bibliotheca Sacra* 102 (January 1946):1.

124. Chafer, "Twenty Years of Experience."

125. Sandeen, *The Roots of Fundamentalism*, p. 235.

126. Ibid., p. 221.

127. A. C. Gaebelein, *The Revelation* (New York: Our Hope Press, n.d.; reprint ed., Neptune, New Jersey: Loizeaux Bros., 1961), p. 10.

128. Ibid., pp. 17-18.

129. Ibid., p. 19.

130. A. C. Gaebelein, *The Prophet Daniel* (n.p.; rev. ed., Grand Rapids: Kregel Publications, 1955), p. 5.

131. A. C. Gaebelein, *The Conflict of the Ages* (n.p.: Arno C. Gaebelein, 1933; reprint ed., Neptune, New Jersey: Loizeaux Bros., 1983), p. 161.

132. Sandeen, *The Roots of Fundamentalism*, pp. 218-19.

133. Chafer, *Ecclesiology-Eschatology*, p. 289.

Lewis Sperry Chafer at the age of three

Chafer as a young man in 1893

Lewis Chafer and Ella Chase Chafer at the time of their marriage

The Chafers as a team ministering in evangelism and Bible Teaching

Lewis and Ella Chafer with C. I. Scofield

Lewis Sperry Chafer (on right) with W. H. Griffith Thomas (bearded man in rear center) with a group at a Bible Conference

The Chafers relaxing on a porch in Tacoma, Washington, in 1925 during ministry in that city

Lewis Sperry Chafer (on right) with H. A. Ironside (beside Chafer on left) and unidentified men at a Bible Conference

Chafer chopping wood in 1925

Lewis Chafer leading the faculty and student body in singing in a chapel service

Dr. Chafer teaching a class at Dallas Theological Seminary in 1944

A photograph of Dr. Chafer that he used for several years for publicity purposes in his Bible teaching ministry

Chapter III
Chafer's Dispensationalism

Chafer knew that the study of systematic theology during his day was no longer a priority for most ministers.

> It is no secret that the average minister is not now reading Systematic Theology, nor will such writings be found to occupy a prominent place in his library. Shocking indeed this condition would have been to ministers of two generations ago — men whose position was respected in their day because of their deep knowledge of the doctrinal portions of the Bible and whose spoken ministries and writings have gone far toward the upbuilding of the Church of Christ.[1]

Chafer understands the Bible as the wellspring for systematic theology.

The Dispensational Organization of the *Systematic Theology*

Chafer's eight-volume *Systematic Theology* consists of the following: volume one, *Prolegomena-Bibliology-Theology Proper*; volume two, *Angelology-Anthropology-Hamartiology*; volume three, *Soteriology;* volume four, *Ecclesiology-Eschatology*; volume five, *Christology;* volume six, *Pneumatology*; volume seven, *Doctrinal Summarization*; and volume eight, *Biographical Sketch and Indexes*. His entire *Systematic Theology* is written from a dispensational, premillennial perspective. He believes that "the message of the Bible is complete. It incorporates its very chapter and verse into its perfect unity, and all its parts are interdependent. The mastery of any part necessitates the mastery of the whole."[2]

In his *Prolegomena*, Chafer expresses strongly his belief that a systematic theology must be unabridged:

> Like every true science, Systematic Theology is interdependent and interrelated in all its parts. The astronomer or chemist would not attempt to organize his materials or to reach dependable conclusions with a third of the elements or facts pertaining to his science unaccounted for. Nor should the theologian expect to reach any true estimation of his various doctrines when vast fields of the divine revelation have been eliminated from his consideration. Theologians, more than any other scientists, are apt to be bound by tradition or by sectarian prejudice. The field of investigation is no less than the entire Bible, which field extends beyond the boundaries of creeds and that limited body of truth which was recovered in the Reformation.[3]

Chafer constantly emphasizes a "dispensational program of God." In his thinking, this program spans the entire Bible, Old and New Testaments. The seven dispensations are a key to understanding and interpreting this entire program.

In volume one, Chafer divides created beings into angels, Gentiles, Jews, and Christians. In the present age, which he believes to be bounded by two advents, the first and second advent of Christ,

> all progress in the national and earthly program for Israel is in abeyance and individual Jews are given the same privilege as the individual Gentiles of the exercise of personal faith in Christ as Saviour and out of those thus redeemed, both Jews and Gentiles, the heavenly people are being called.[4]

Chafer believes that in the future when the present purpose of God is complete, God will fulfill His promises to Israel. In volume one, Chafer discusses the general divisions of the Bible. He initiates this section by offering a helpful analysis of the entire Bible:

The books of the Old Testament are classified as *historical* — Genesis to Esther —, *poetical* — Job to Solomon —, and *prophetical* — Isaiah to Malachi. The New Testament books are classified as *historical* — Matthew to Acts —, *epistolary* — Romans to Jude —, *prophetical* — Revelation. As bearing on the Person of Christ — He who is the central theme of all Scriptures — the Old Testament is classified as *preparation*; the four gospels as *manifestation*; the Acts as *propagation*, the epistles as *explanation*; and the Revelation as *consummation*.[5]

He speaks concerning "the time periods of the Bible," and under this category outlines divisions related to humanity, the dispensations, the covenants, the prophetic periods, the earthly kingdom, the history of Israel in the land, the Gentiles, and the Church. Concerning the covenants, Chafer understands these as totaling eight: the Edenic, Adamic, Noahic, Abrahamic, Mosaic, Palestinian, Davidic, and New Covenants. In volume one, Chafer articulates a strong dispensational beginning, which he expounds in all volumes.

In volume two, a full treatment is given to angels and Satan. Concerning the latter, his entire career is portrayed, including his final judgment. Chafer believes the judgment of Satan has already occurred, and this event happened at the cross.[6] His final judgment is still future, and this judgment is portrayed in Revelation 20:7-10 when Satan is thrown into the lake of burning sulfur.

The section on anthropology is introduced with an examination of humanity's original state and the Fall. Chafer also speaks extensively of the future of the human body and the resurrection body.

> The Word of God is uncomplicated in its testimony to the truth that the believer's body is as eternal in character as the soul and spirit. As has been observed, the term immortality refers only to the future of the redeemed body and not at all to the soul, and whatever reality this great word asserts applies only to the body.[7]

Chafer speaks in a negative and positive manner of the condition of humanity by stating that outside of Christ there is no hope.[8]

Hamartiology, the doctrine of sin, is a subject which Chafer takes seriously, and in his *Systematic Theology*, he understands it as theologically identified with anthropology.

Chafer writes:

> The worthy approach to the doctrine of *sin* is to discover all that is revealed about the sinfulness of sin and then to recognize that God's provided Saviour is equal to every demand which sin imposes....It is too often assumed that it is wiser to leave this loathsome monster called *sin* to lurk in the dark, and to dwell on the more attractive virtues of human life.[9]

Chafer discusses the essential problems dealing with hamartiology. His final chapter is entitled, "The Final Triumph Over All Sin." Chafer believes:

> Revelation and reason unite in one testimony that evil is a temporary thing in the universe of God. Reason declares that since God is infinitely holy and the Designer and Creator of the Universe, evil must have begun its manifestation subsequent to creation by His permission and is to serve a purpose compatible with his righteousness. Reason also anticipates that, when that purpose is accomplished, evil will be dismissed from the universe of God....[10]

Chafer, then, views sin as an important doctrine. In fact, Chafer claims the future holds a wonderful promise — the absence of sin. He claims the Fall in Genesis three introduces the principle of sin into the lives of every human being; thus, Chafer claims all are sinners by nature. But consistently in his messages and writings, he emphasizes the Christian does not need to be conquered by sin.

Volume three is divided into five sections and is concerned with such subjects as Christ as Saviour, Christ's sufferings and what He accomplished, election, the eternal security of the believer, and the terms of salvation. In this volume, Chafer's dispensational concern is readily apparent.

He also writes a section entitled, "Scripture Dispensationally Misapplied." Chafer constantly encourages his readers to beware of the time scheme to which particular passages allude. To fail to do so "is a root of (doctrinal) evil."[11]

Though Chafer explained the value of the death of Christ during the present age of grace, he is somewhat cloudy on the means of salvation in the age of law. Chafer enjoys discussing the grace of God, and the dispensation of grace is viewed by him in a most favorable manner. Chafer writes:

> The law provided no enablement for its observance. No more was expected or secured in return from its commands than the natural man in his environment could provide. Therefore, whatever is undertaken in the energy of the flesh is legal in its nature....For the child of God under grace, every aspect of the law is now done away.[12]

The first section of Chafer's fourth volume is concerned with ecclesiology, the doctrine of the Church. The volume is organized under three divisions: the Church as an organism, the Church as an organization, and the rule of life for the believer. His discussion of the Church is replete with dispensational distinctions. Of particular importance to Chafer is the sharp distinction between Israel and the Church: "The distinction between the purpose for Israel and the purpose for the Church is about as important as that which exists between the two Testaments."[13]

He gives twenty-four distinct contrasts between Israel and the Church in order to give clout to his argument of their disparity. He claims that Israel occupies nearly four-fifths of the text of the Bible while the Church occupies about one-fifth. Chafer articulates this distinction by stating:

> The earthly people, though their estate may vary, are present in the earth in all ages from their beginning in Abraham on into eternity to come, while, as stated before, the Church is re-

stricted to the present dispensation. The dispensation now operative itself is characterized by her presence in the world.[14]

Why is Chafer concerned that Israel and the Church must be distinguished? His dispensational, premillennial interpretation concludes that such a distinction is inherent in the Scriptures. He believes God has a separate program for both Israel and the Church. The Church is found only in the dispensation of grace, or since the time of Pentecost, as recorded in the book of Acts. The prophets of the Old Testament spoke to God's covenant people, Israel, and the promise to them is a millennial reign upon the earth with their King.

Chafer speaks of the vanquishing of the sin nature and the final transformation of the child of God:

> At the end of his pilgrim journey, there is for the believer a release from the lifelong conflict with the sin nature. He will have sustained a warfare with the *cosmos* world and with Satan; but these are forces from without whose pressure will be withdrawn forever.[15]

He believes the child of God will have a transformed body. "He may go the way of death and resurrection, or he may go by translation; yet a standardized reality awaits him. He will have a body like unto Christ's glorious body (Phil. 3:20-21)."[16]

One must constantly recognize that Chafer emphasizes primarily three dispensations: law, grace and kingdom. In his *Ecclesiology*, under the third section, "The Believer's Rule of Life," Chafer draws contrasts among these three:

> Since there is so wide a difference in the character of these ages — of law, of grace, and of the kingdom — and in the peoples of the earth — the Jews, the Gentiles, and the Church — as they stand related to God throughout the ages, it is to be expected that there will be a variation in the divine government according to the essential character of the seven ages. This is not only reasonable, it is the precise teaching of the Bible.[17]

Chafer's Dispensationalism

According to Chafer, Jesus lived within the age of law, but He spoke concerning the three dispensations of law, grace and kingdom:

> The fact is forgotten that Christ, while living under, keeping, and applying the law of Moses, also taught the principles of His future kingdom, and, at the end of His ministry and in relation to the cross, He also anticipated the teaching of grace. If this threefold division of the teaching of Christ is not recognized, there can be nothing but confusion of mind and consequent contradiction of truth.[18]

Why did Chafer emphasize primarily the three dispensations of law, grace and kingdom? First, these three make up the vast majority of the Bible; thus, by virtue of sheer bulk, the three are dominant. The first four dispensations — innocence, conscience, government, and promise — are found in only Genesis and Exodus. Second, Chafer believes Jesus spoke of the three dispensations and did not in a significant manner allude to the other four. Third, Chafer understands the three dispensations of law, grace and kingdom to be contained in the New Testament. In a legitimate sense Chafer holds to a three-part dispensational scheme. This fact, at least in number, is similar to the Reformed theologians' division of a two or three covenant scheme. They speak of the covenants of works and grace, and some theologians add a third, the covenant of redemption. Thus, there is a similar divisional scheme in both a Reformed and a dispensational scheme.

Chafer draws distinctions between law and grace, but also between grace and kingdom:

> If it be accepted that the Messianic, earthly kingdom, with Israel restored to her land in the full realization of all her covenants, under the reign of Christ sitting on the throne of David, has not been established ... then it follows that the laws and principles which are to govern in the kingdom, and which could apply only to conditions within that kingdom, are not yet applied by God to the affairs of men in the earth. It is not a question, as in the case of the Law of Moses, of discontinuing

that which has once been in force under the sanction of God; it is rather a question of whether the kingdom laws, which have their application of necessity in the future earthly kingdom of Messiah, should be imposed now on the children of God under grace.[19]

Chafer's eschatology comprises the second division of volume four. Under "General Features of Eschatology," he discusses the offer and rejection of the kingdom, as well as chiliastic beliefs of the early Church, the Reformation, and subsequent years. Here he presents his understanding concerning the subject of biblical prophecy. Under the second division, "The Major Highways of Prophecy," he discusses prophecy as it relates to the Lord Jesus, Israel's covenants, the Gentiles, Satan, the course and end of apostate Christendom, the Great Tribulation, and the Church. He also discusses major themes of the Old and New Testaments, predicted events in their order, the judgments, and the eternal estate.

Chafer begins his volume on eschatology in the following way:

The time word *now* is ever moving and things yet future at the present time will soon have passed into history. A worthy eschatology must embrace all prediction whether fulfilled or unfulfilled at a given time. In other words, a true eschatology attempts to account for all the prophecy set forth in the Bible.[20]

Chafer, then, believes the prophetic element is a necessary component in understanding how God has revealed His program for the ages. Chafer realized through study of the original languages and through a literal method of interpretation, one can begin to comprehend what God planned in past ages, the present, and what He will perform in the future age.

Chafer's *The Kingdom in History and Prophecy* was published in 1915. As one compares this work with the *Systematic Theology*, specifically his fourth volume, which concerns eschatology, one sees that Chafer's essential eschatological position was formed by 1915. C. I. Scofield wrote in the introduction to the work: "I welcome therefore this present book on these fundamental truths."[21] Scofield, then, put his approval upon the work, and in it one finds many of the themes which

Chafer's Dispensationalism

Scofield articulates. Chafer begins the book with the following thoughts:

> The Bible revelation concerning the kingdom presents the purpose, process, and final realization of a divine government in the earth. This objective is the heart of the prayer: "Thy kingdom come. Thy will be done *in earth*, as it is in heaven." The kingdom revelation is a distinct body of Scripture running through both the Old Testament and New and its study, of necessity, leads to some definite conclusions touching the meaning of much unfulfilled prophecy, the two advents of Christ, the present age of Grace and the future of both Jews and Gentiles.[22]

Analyzing this statement by Chafer, written about thirty years before the completion of his *Systematic Theology*, one can recognize that the basic themes of his eschatology are contained within this brief initial paragraph. He speaks of the kingdom, as revealed in both Old and New Testaments, which will be a divine rule. This government will be upon the earth; it is prophetic, and it is associated with the advent of Christ. Though a time of blessing for God's covenanted people, the kingdom will also be a blessing for select Gentiles.

In *The Kingdom in History and Prophecy*, Chafer gives in outline form many of the themes which were later seen in the *Systematic Theology*. He writes of the kingdom as prophesied in the Scriptures, the Kingdom offered and rejected, the present age of grace, the church, the succession of the kingdoms as predicted by Daniel, the Olivet discourse, the second advent, and the millennium itself. All of these themes are in essential agreement with his mature eschatology as contained in the *Systematic Theology*. Concerning the second advent, Chafer believes that attention to this doctrine from pastors will bring rejuvenation to a lethargic church:

> If the pastor is mourning over the cold, unspiritual condition of his church, let him consider the warm, glowing love and devoted service that has always accompanied the right understanding of the "blessed hope." If the church is given to

carelessness and worldliness, let him recall that for this there has been provided the "purifying hope." As under-shepherds shall we not go down on our faces before God and there question whether we have been giving these dependent ones their "meat in due season"?[23]

During his entire life, Chafer saw eschatology not as something mystical and shrouded in obscurity, but as a subject whose themes are lively, practical, and understandable.

The fifth volume, following the chronological pattern of Jesus' life, discusses the preincarnate person and work of Christ. Chafer devotes much attention to the incarnation. The last three chapters of his *Christology* are devoted specifically to eschatological subjects concerning Christ. Chafer describes what he believes the Scriptures teach concerning the second coming of Christ, the messianic kingdom, and the transition from the kingdom to the eternal estate. In this section, Chafer quotes extensively from George N. H. Peters.

Pneumatology is Chafer's sixth volume in the *Systematic Theology*. He speaks of the attributes and works of the Holy Spirit. Attention is given to the subject of the Spirit's work in the Old Testament as well as in the present age. Of particular interest, Chafer understands the Holy Spirit as the author of prophecy:

> The Holy Spirit is the Author of prophecy in its widest form and to its last and least detail. This is the doctrine of inspiration which is advanced in the Sacred Text itself and which has been defended in this theological work. The Holy Spirit is likewise the subject of prediction. His person and work are so extensive and so vital to the whole program of God that any scheme of prediction which essays to forecast the plan and purpose of God from its beginning would hardly fail to contemplate features which pertain to the Holy Spirit.[24]

The remainder of the volume contains material which generally is omitted from systematic theologies, as he discusses the Holy Spirit's relationship to the Christian and the latter's responsibility to live in accordance with the control of the Spirit of God. Chafer also contrasts the work of the Holy Spirit in the Old Testament and in the present age.

The seventh volume contains 312 pages, discussing 184 theological subjects and treats them in alphabetical order. In essence, it is an encyclopedia of scriptural doctrines.

The eighth and last volume of Chafer's *Systematic Theology* is his *Indexes*. The work contains a brief biographical sketch of the author by C. F. Lincoln and a table of contents for all volumes. The volume also has an author index citing every author Chafer uses, a Scripture index, and a subject index.

In brief form, then, it has been shown that Chafer's complete *Systematic Theology* is written from a dispensational, premillennial perspective. However, of course, the bulk of his eschatology is contained within the volume, *Eschatology*.

The subjects of bibliology, theology proper, angelology, anthropology, hamartiology, soteriology, ecclesiology, eschatology, christology, and pneumatology comprise the volumes of Chafer's *Systematic Theology*. Chafer neatly weaves within each volume his particular dispensational and premillennial interpretation. He sets the tone for the work in the *Prolegomena* by stating:

> Published systems of theology too often omit the dispensational program of God; the Pauline revelation concerning the Church which is Christ's Body; the entire field of truth; angelology with satanology and demonology; prophecy, which alone occupies more than one-fifth of the text of the Scriptures; typology; and the present ministry of Christ in heaven ... the theologian, having eliminated all or any part of this great field of revelation, cannot hope to hold truth in its right perspective or to give to it its right emphasis.[25]

Beginning, then, with the first volume, one can readily see the dispensational, premillennial interpretation, and this means of viewing and interpreting is found throughout the entire *Systematic Theology*.

One can find precursors to his *Systematic Theology* in many of his earlier works. This is especially true with *The Kingdom in History and*

Prophecy. In a sense it is a blueprint for the *Systematic Theology.*

The Dispensations

How does Chafer understand dispensationalism? He sees specific periods in the Bible, and these he calls "dispensations." In his work, *Dispensationalism*, which is an outgrowth of an article published in 1936 in the *Bibliotheca Sacra*, Chafer understands the word "dispensation" as a derivative from the Latin *dispensatio*, which is translated "economic management" or "superintendence." The Greek equivalent is *oikonomia*, which is generally translated "stewardship" or "economy."[26]

Chafer offers a definition of a dispensation as "a specific, divine economy, a commitment from God to man of a responsibility to discharge that which God has appointed him."[27] Chafer supports the definition offered by C. I. Scofield; namely, "a dispensation is a period of time during which man is tested in respect of obedience to some specific revelation of the will of God."[28]

Chafer believes there are seven distinct dispensations. The dispensation of innocence extended from the creation to the Fall. The dispensation of conscience spanned from the Fall to the flood. The dispensation of human government extended from the flood to the call of Abraham, while the dispensation of promise spanned from the call of Abraham to the giving and receiving of the Mosaic law. The fifth dispensation, law, continued from the giving and accepting of law until the death of Christ. Interestingly, Chafer understands that this age will again be reinstituted in the future. This period will be the 70th week of Daniel, according to Chafer, and is future to the present age. The sixth and present dispensation is that of grace, or the age which extends from the death of Christ until His return to receive his Bride. Chafer says:

> It is an age characterized by grace in the sense that in this age, God, who has always acted in grace toward any and all of the human family whom He has blessed, is now making a specific heavenly demonstration of His grace by and through the whole

company of Jews and Gentiles who are saved by grace through faith in Christ.[29]

The seventh and last dispensation, according to Chafer, will be that of the Kingdom. It will be a period of one thousand years and will end with the creation of a new heaven and a new earth. What will distinguish this period? "It is characterized by the facts that Satan is bound, the covenants of Israel are fulfilled, creation is delivered from its bondage, and the Lord Himself will reign over the earth and on the throne of His Father David."[30]

These seven dispensations comprise Chafer's dispensationalism. Chafer essentially emphasizes only law, grace, and kingdom; therefore, it is necessary to look more intently into his understanding of these three. Two of these dispensations pertain solely to Israel:

> Quite apart from the revealed will of God as recorded of earlier ages, the Bible sets forth at length three distinct and complete divine rulings which govern human action. None of these rulings are addressed to the angels or to the Gentiles as such. Two are addressed to Israel — one in that age that is past, known as the Mosaic law, and the other the setting forth of the terms of admission into, and the required conduct in, the Messianic kingdom when that kingdom is set up on the earth. The third is addressed to Christians and provides divine direction in this age for the heavenly people who are already perfected with respect to standing, in Christ Jesus.[31]

What is the Mosaic Law to Chafer? He believes it was specifically designed to govern Israel in the land and was an interim form of government, described in Exodus 19 to the coming of Christ. The Apostle Paul, Chafer believes, writes of the purpose of the law in Galatians 3. That purpose is to stress the insufficiency of human works and the need for God's grace through Christ. Chafer sees the law in three parts: (1) the commandments which governed Israel's moral life (Exodus 20:1-17); (2) the judgments which pertained to Israel's civic life (Exodus 21:1 - 24:11); and (3) the ordinances which governed Israel's religious life (Exodus

24:12 - 31:18).³² The law, however, cannot give spiritual life; it simply points out humankind's weaknesses and failures. Of course, in a sense there is grace in the law economy in that the law does serve as a *paidagogos*, literally a "child conductor," which leads the Israelite to an awareness of a knowledge of Christ as God revealed Himself through the sacrificial system. Chafer believes "Christ was foreshadowed in the sacrifices"³³ and the law was never ordained by God as a method of salvation. He writes, "Nor is the situation relieved for those who claim that the law has ceased as a means of justification; for it was never that, nor could it be (Gal. 3:11)."³⁴ Chafer carefully distinguishes between law and grace: "Under their works, Israel could not come unto God lest they die, but under grace, all come to God, and to Jesus, and to the blessed associations and glory of heaven itself."³⁵

The dispensation of grace is the second time period to which Chafer devotes much attention. In his volume concerning ecclesiology, Chafer writes extensively about this economy. But reading his book *Grace*, published in 1922, one quickly realizes many of the same divisions, and indeed words, were borrowed and found themselves in his *Systematic Theology* published twenty-six years later! This fact signifies that Chafer's theological foundation was on the whole established before the founding of the seminary. He did, however, during his lifetime read widely in all areas of theology, and of course, this included his eschatology.

Chafer realizes that "like the teachings of the law of Moses, the teachings of grace have not applied to men in all ages. These teachings were revealed from God through Christ and His apostles."³⁶ When Chafer writes of this present age of grace and its benefits, he is inclusive in his thinking:

> There is but one issue in this dispensation between God and the unregenerate man, and that is neither character nor conduct; it is the personal appeal of the gospel of the grace of God. Until the unsaved receive Christ, who is God's gift in grace, no other issue can be raised. Men may moralize among themselves, and establish their self-governments on principles of right conduct; but God is never presented in the unfoldings of grace as seeking

to *reform* sinners. Every word regarding the quality of life is reserved for those who are already related to Him on the greater issue of salvation.[37]

Chafer writes of three specific features of the age of grace. First, he speaks of the independent character of this age. The age of grace extends from the death of Christ until the translation of the Church. It is called grace because during this period God, as revealed in His Son, demonstrates His grace in bringing to salvation both Jew and Gentile.[38] This present age is a mystery, and Chafer defines this term as "some work or purpose of God hitherto unrevealed. It may be related to something which needs to be understood but must have a key."[39] The present age, then, was unanticipated by the Old Testament prophets. They saw the first and second comings of Christ but not the intervening age between these two events. Whereas the dispensations of law and kingdom are characteristically legal, the Church age is distinguished by grace. Thus, the age of grace is independent of law and kingdom. Under grace, it is recognized that Christ has died, is risen and ascended, and the Holy Spirit resides in the hearts of God's redeemed.

Second, Chafer speaks of the exalted requirements of this age. Chafer sees the standard of life under grace as actually higher than required under law or kingdom:

> It may be well stated again that the standard of conduct prescribed under the teachings of grace is immeasurably more difficult to maintain than that prescribed either by the Law of Moses, or the law of the kingdom.... Turning to the Scriptures which reveal the position and responsibility of the child of God under grace, it is found that a *superhuman* manner of life is proposed.[40]

But Chafer, thirdly, does speak of divine enablement. There is supernatural power for the child of God according to Chafer.

> Under grace, the all-powerful, abiding, indwelling and sufficient Holy Spirit of God is given to every saved person.... The

> superhuman manner of life under grace is not addressed to some spiritual company alone within the whole Body of Christ; it is addressed to all believers alike.⁴¹

Chafer's gracious nature constantly is apparent. Grace is for all who are in the Body of Christ, not a select few. Inherent in the age of grace is a compassionate God who, though not unmindful of sin in His own, lovingly showers His favor upon His recipients. There is hope for one to live a victorious life.

> If the manner of life under grace is superhuman, so, also, the provided enablement is supernatural, and is as limitless as the infinite power of God. Since God has proposed a humanly impossible manner of life, He has, in full consistency, provided the Spirit who giveth life.⁴²

The kingdom age is the third period to which Chafer devotes much thought. The elements of the dispensation of grace are not found in the kingdom age. He claims:

> The third administration which is contained in the Bible is that which is designed to govern the earthly people in relation to their coming earthly kingdom. It is explicit, also, with regard to the requirements that are to be imposed upon those who enter that kingdom. The body of Scripture is found in the Old Testament's portions which anticipate the Messianic Kingdom and in large portions of the Synoptic Gospels.⁴³

He strongly asserts that the Old Testament prophets knew nothing of the age of grace but only saw the kingdom age.⁴⁴ Where are the kingdom teachings to be found?

> Kingdom teachings will be found in those Psalms and prophecies of the Old Testament which anticipate the reign of Messiah in the earth, and in the kingdom portions of the Gospels. The teachings as found in the Old Testament and the

Chafer's Dispensationalism

New are purely legal in essence, both by the inherent character and by the explicit declaration of the Word of God. The legal requirements of the kingdom teachings are greatly advanced, both in severity and detail, beyond the requirements of the Law of Moses.... In the kingdom law, anger is condemned in the same connection where only murder had been prohibited in the Law of Moses, and the glance of the eye is condemned where only adultery had previously been forbidden.

The kingdom Scriptures of the Old Testament are occupied largely with the character and glory of Messiah's reign, the promises to Israel of restoration and earthly glory, the universal blessing to the Gentiles, and the deliverance of creation itself.[44]

There are several key passages in the Old Testament which pertain to the kingdom age, Chafer argues. Isaiah 2:1-2 speaks of a time of peace as nations beat their swords into plowshares and their spears into pruning-hooks; peace will finally be upon the earth. He claims that only when the Lord is ruling in a literal earthly kingdom will this occur. Isaiah 11:1-5 depicts the rule of righteousness upon the earth. Jeremiah 23:3-8 tells of a righteous king reigning, Israel no longer living under fear and trial, and perfect justice characterizing this period. Hosea 3:4-5 claims there will be a day when the children of Israel will seek the Lord their God and serve Him totally. At this point, one might ask if Chafer understands any portion of the New Testament as alluding to this kingdom age:

... there is to some extent, a commingling in the Gospels of the message of the kingdom and the teachings of grace. Moreover, these teachings were given while the Law of Moses was in full authority. In harmony with the demands of that dispensation, many recognitions of the Mosaic system are embedded in the teachings of Christ. The Gospels are complex almost beyond any other portion of Scripture, since they are a composite of the teachings of Moses, of grace, and of the kingdom.[45]

Chafer believes the kingdom teachings are crystallized in the first portion of the Gospel of Matthew. In this book is found the phrase, "the kingdom of heaven," and Chafer understands this phrase as alluding to the rule of Christ upon the earth. This phrase is to be distinguished from the similar phrase, "the kingdom of God," which, according to Chafer, is the rule of God throughout the bounds of the universe. Chafer states:

> The Messianic rule of God in the earth was the theme of the prophets; for the prophets only enlarged on the covenants which guaranteed a throne, a king, and a kingdom over regathered Israel, in that land which was sworn to Abraham. The term, *the kingdom of heaven*, was used by Christ to announce the fact that the covenanted kingdom blessings were "at hand." This good news to that nation was the "gospel of the kingdom," and should not be confused with the gospel of saving grace.[46]

Even though Israel did not accept the gospel of the kingdom, Chafer still claims it was a legitimate offer to them. But one may rightfully ask if Chafer believed the kingdom was currently occurring in some form since the forces of darkness had been defeated upon the cross. Chafer writes:

> There is a sense in which the kingdom of God, as the rule of God in the hearts of individuals, is present in the world today. This should not be confused with the Messianic kingdom which is to be set up all over a nation, and extended through them to all nations with the King ruling, not in the individual heart, but on the throne of David, in the city of Jerusalem.[47]

Although Chafer holds to a seven dispensational scheme, rarely does he speak of the seven as a unit. Rather he speaks primarily of the dispensations of law, grace, and kingdom. Each is a distinct time period, and each has specific conditions imposed upon it by God.

To clarify his thinking on dispensationalism, Chafer specifies what he believes a true dispensationalist is:

> What persons, then, according to these definitions, should be classified as dispensationalists? The answer to this question

may be stated in a variety of ways. Three of these may suffice: (1) Any person is a dispensationalist who trusts in the blood of Christ rather than bringing an animal sacrifice. (2) Any person is a dispensationalist who claims any right or title to the land which God covenanted to Israel for an everlasting inheritance. And (3) any person is a dispensationalist who observes the first day of the week rather than the seventh. To all this it would be replied that every Christian does these things, which is obviously true; and it is equally true that, to a very considerable degree, all Christians are dispensationalists.[48]

Select Dispensational, Premillennial Writers

At this point, it is necessary to view the eschatological views of other dispensationalists. Such an endeavor will help to understand more fully dispensational, premillennial thought.

C. H. Mackintosh

C. H. Mackintosh, primarily known as C. H. M., articulates a premillennial return of the Lord.[49] He speaks of a resurrection and a translation of the saints:

> All the saints of God, both those of Old Testament and New Testament times, who lie sleeping in our cemeteries and graveyards, or in the ocean's depths—all these would rise from their temporary sleep. All the living saints would be changed in a moment, and all would be caught up to meet their descending Lord, and return with Him to the Father's house (John 14:3; 1 Thess. 4:16-17; 1 Cor. 15:51-52).[49]

He claims there will be two resurrections, according to Revelation 20:5-6. One is before the thousand-year period, and the second is after this period of time.

Like most dispensational, premillennial writers, Mackintosh uses the word "rapture":

> Here, then, we have presented to us what is commonly spoken of against us as the rapture of the saints — a most glorious, soul-stirring, and enrapturing theme surely — the brightest hope of the Church of God, and of the individual believer. The Lord *Himself* shall descend from Heaven with a summons designed only for the ears and hearts of His own.... The dead in Christ, including, as we believe, the Old Testament saints, as well as those of the New, ... all those shall hear the blessed sound, and come forth from their sleeping places. All the living saints shall hear it, and be changed in a moment.[50]

Speaking of the Church's relationship to the tribulation period, Mackintosh says "The Church shall have met her Lord, and returned with Him to the Father's house, before that terrible day bursts upon the world."[51] Mackintosh claims there are three classes of people found in the Scriptures: the Jews, the Gentiles, and the Church of God.[52] He also holds to a judgment of the nations, and this judgment will determine who can enter the millennium.[53]

Clearly then, C. H. Mackintosh holds to dispensational premillennialism, and one can see little difference between his eschatology and Chafer's views. Chafer in his *Systematic Theology* cites several works by Mackintosh.

William L. Pettingill

Chafer in his pre-seminary years was affiliated with William L. Pettingill. The latter was a consulting editor of the 1909 edition of the *Scofield Reference Bible*, and Pettingill was thoroughly dispensational and premillennial in his eschatological stance. He writes that righteousness will be a key word in the dispensation of the kingdom.

> This word *righteousness* is a key word in Matthew, being found seven times in the book....In Matthew *righteousness* is the law of the kingdom of Heaven which is to be set up on the earth. In the present mystery form of the kingdom, during the king's absence from the earth, there is a mixture of good and evil in the kingdom, as shown in chapter 13, but when he shall

return and establish the kingdom in manifestation, only the *righteous* shall enter into that kingdom to reign with Him. This righteousness is an absolute thing, an inflexible requirement for entrance into that kingdom.[54]

Like Chafer, Pettingill is adamant that the Church and the kingdom cannot be identical.[55] Writing concerning Matthew 24, Pettingill believes:

> The twenty-fourth chapter of Matthew is the climax of the predictive teachings of the Lord Jesus. It is altogether a Jewish prophecy. It must ever be remembered, in the study of prophecy, that Jesus Christ was, first of all, "a minister of the *circumcision* for the truth of God, to confirm the promises made unto the father," and it is only afterwards that His ministry is toward the nations.... Therefore if we are to understand the chapter before us, we must eliminate the *Church* and the church *age* altogether from our calculations, and think only of the *kingdom*, which is to be manifest when the King comes back to earth again.[56]

Pettingill discusses the return of the Lord after the tribulation, the judgment of the nations, and the last judgment itself.[57] Pettingill's eschatological views are identical with those of Chafer's.

William Kelly

Chafer read several of the works of William Kelly, a Plymouth Brother. Kelly, a premillenarian who also holds to a pretribulational translation of the Church, writes concerning the abruptness of the establishment of the kingdom rather than the gradual appearance of the kingdom:

> It is irrational to talk of the fulfillment gradually growing more complete in life, but perfected only when the probation is over. Scripture reserves the mighty change for the appearing of the Lord, when we are manifested with Him in glory. Then at once, but not till then, shall the creation be delivered from the

bondage of corruption into the liberty of the glory of the children of God.[58]

Kelly speaks of the rule of the Messiah during the kingdom age: "In that day, when Israel is restored, and spiritually as well as literally in their land under Messiah and the new covenant, the nations shall be blessed, and bow before the Son of man."[59] Concerning the Jew, Kelly says:

> If a Jew were to believe now, he, baptized by the Holy Ghost, becomes a member of Christ's body; whereas what we find in the prophets is, that a godly Jew in the last days remains a Jew. The Lord will quicken his soul, no doubt; but he will be found in his own land, where, instead of suffering, he will be blessed in earthly things.[60]

Kelly stresses there will be a gospel of the Kingdom which will be preached in the time of tribulation. This gospel, he believes, is not identical with the gospel of grace, which is being preached during the present dispensation of grace.[61] Kelly also describes in detail the judgment of the nations and the conditions for entrance into the kingdom. He places great emphasis upon the Lordship of Christ during the kingdom reign:

> Satan's getting power over man was only a fearful interruption, but not one whose consequences the Lord could not overmaster and purge out: He means to do it; and to have this world the scene of incomparably greater blessedness than its present misery is through Satan's work. God means to give the kingdom of this world to His son — yea, He will have the universe put under Christ.[62]

About the only discernible difference between Kelly and Chafer is the style of writing. Both were in essential agreement with one another.

Erich Sauer

Erich Sauer, an evangelical German theologian, espouses a dispensational and premillennial eschatology. Unlike Chafer, he does not hold to eight judgments (Chafer actually stresses only three of the eight), but to two judgments, those of the Judgment Seat of Christ and the great White Throne judgment.[63] Sauer describes the present age of the Church as "full of power and activity."[64] He also gives more prominence to the position of the Church in its relationship to the millennium than does Chafer. Sauer writes:

> The kingdom of God in its form as the kingdom of glory will be the sphere of the active rule of the church: "Know ye not that the saints shall judge the world" (1 Cor. 6:2,3).... The church is thus the ruling aristocracy, the official administrative staff, of the coming kingdom of God.[65]

Sauer also places more of an emphasis on the kingdom as a victory of God:

> In the light of the enmity of man we proclaim the kingdom as the victory of God. The stone which shattered the colossus of Nebuchadnessar went on to fill the whole earth (Dan. 2:35, 44; Rev. 11:15; 19:11-21). Therefore it becomes the believer to have a confident spirit, an assurance of victory, and courage.[66]

E. Schuyler English

E. Schuyler English, though a dispensationalist and premillennialist, does not emphasize, as does Chafer, the significance of the covenants. The fact that Chafer does lay great stress upon the fulfillment of the covenants promised to Israel gives cohesiveness to his thought and establishes a thread of unity between the two testaments. English, however, does not, and his thought on Israel and the Church are not as cohesive as Chafer's. It must be kept in mind that the differences between the various premillanarians are slight, and we find that English espouses the traditional dispensational, premillennial interpretation.

> It is our conclusion, however, that the translation of the saints, the rapture of the Church will occur before any portion of the Tribulation, Daniel's seventieth week, takes place. And it is our

further conviction that once the truth of this is seen, all difficulties vanish and all Scriptures that pertain to the subject fall into place in such a way as to complete a perfectly clear and beautifully concise picture of God's dealing with His Church....[67]

H. A. Ironside

H. A. Ironside, a well-known dispensational premillennialist, describes in a more picturesque fashion than does Chafer the physical conditions of the millennium:

> All that is lovely, such as the grandeur of Lebanon, the beauties of Carmel and Sharon's plains will be retained in that new era, and to these will be added many additional testimonies to the Creator's joy in the world which He brought into being by the word of His power, but which has been so terribly marred as a result of man's sin. Every fruitful field or orchard, every lovely garden, presents a foretaste of what in Messiah's day will be every where prevalent, when the parched deserts will give place to verdant meadows....[68]

The differences between Chafer and Ironside are indeed few. One distinction is in their view of Matthew 24:36-41. Chafer claims this passage alludes to the separation which will occur at the end of the tribulation; some will be taken to judgment while other Jews will be allowed to enter the kingdom.[69] Ironside, however, believes that "this passage is often applied to the separation at the Rapture, and it is quite possible to so use it."[70] Chafer disagreed with this conclusion of Ironside's.

A. C. Gaebelein

A. C. Gaebelein and Chafer were in essential agreement concerning eschatology. However the former explains more clearly than Chafer does the remnant during the time of tribulation upon the earth. A. C. Gaebelein believes:

> The orthodox Jews, who have held on to the faith of their

fathers, who pray for the coming of the Messiah-King ... from them the veil will be removed. The Holy Spirit after having finished His work in connection with the body of Christ, begins His work with the remnant of Israel. Their eyes are opened. It dawns upon them that the long-expected King is about to come. They begin to pray prayers prewritten by the Spirit of God (see Psa. lxxx:17-19; Isa. lxiii:15 - lxiv:1-8). When the man of sin appears they refuse his lying signs and wonders, they refuse him worship, as Mordecai refused to bow the knee before Haman. They have to suffer persecution and many of them will be killed.[71]

Also, Gaebelein does not merely limit the significance of the second coming to a spiritual conquest, as Chafer had a tendency to do, but includes tangible results of the second coming. The coming Messiah will solve all the problems which plague humanity today.

Various Views of the Rapture

An issue which has divided and continues to promote controversy among dispensationalists is the view of the time of the translation of the saints. One who holds to a pretribulational rapture of the Church believes that the saints will be translated before the commencement of the time of tribulation upon the earth. A postribulational view claims that the Church must pass through the time of testing and will be translated only at the end of this period, and immediately after the translation the second coming of Christ will occur. Some notable postribulationists are: W. J. Eerdman, Robert Cameron, Oswald J. Smith, James R. Graham, and J. Barton Payne. The latter, though a premillennialist, writes:

> But more than this, the Book of Revelation, if taken seriously, leads to the final abandonment of the pretribulationist concept. Its chapters constitute the prime source for all New Testament eschatology, but they leave no room for a secret rapture, or for a pretribulational resurrection, or for any coming of the Lord

prior to His appearing in glory in chapter 19.... What is true of the Book of Revelation is also true of the rest of the Word. In fact, the greatest single objection to dispensational premillennialism is that the Bible simply does not teach it.[72]

Other writers and works that espouse a postribulationalist stance are Alexander Reese, *The Approaching Advent of Christ*; Norman McPherson, *Triumph Through Tribulation*; and George E. Ladd, *The Blessed Hope*. Ladd, though a premillennialist, does not believe in a rapture of the saints but speaks only of the second coming of Christ. The blessed hope, according to Ladd, "is the appearing of our great God and Saviour Jesus Christ."[73]

Walvoord summarizes the usual arguments for a postribulational view of the rapture of the Church: (1) the early Church fathers supposedly held to this view; (2) the Church will be divinely kept through the time of tribulation; (3) biblical passages allude to the saints being in the tribulation; and (4) Scriptures such as Matthew 24:31 allude to the rapture.[74]

There are two other views of the time of the translation of the Church. The midtribulational view claims that the Church will go through only three and a half years of the seven years of tribulation before she is raptured. The other is the partial-rapture view which claims only those saints who are spiritually qualified will be taken before the time of tribulation.

The Amillennial Position

Albertus Pieters is a classic amillennialist who believes there is not justification for a separation of Israel and the Church; this belief is a basic tenet of dispensational premillennialism. Pieters writes:

> I desire in this chapter to state and defend the faith of the Christian church at large as held from the beginning, to the effect that the prophecy of the New Covenant given through Jeremiah was fulfilled at the coming of Christ; that He did, before His death, inaugurate this New Covenant and announce

its inauguration; and that the Christian church which He founded is in very truth the New Covenant Israel.[75]

Pieters violently disagrees with the dispensationalist's claim that the Church began at Pentecost.[76] Pieters, then, is stating the the Abrahamic covenant was conditioned upon Israel's obedience. The resultant failure of that group transferred the promises to the Church. There is no promise of a future kingdom or millennial reign, as the power of Christ is currently manifested through the Church. Pieters even understands the new Jerusalem in Revelation 21 as alluding to the perfected state of the Church.[77] The premillennialist, of course, understands the passage literally, interpreting the new Jerusalem as heaven itself.

Anthony A. Hoekema

Crucial to understanding the amillennial approach is the belief that Satan was bound at the first coming of Christ. Anthony A. Hoekema claims that the only mention of the thousand-year reign is in Revelation 20, and this period does not refer to a literal thousand-year reign, but that through the first coming of Christ, Satan was bound. The kingdom exists now, according to Hoekema:

> The book of Revelation is full of symbolic numbers. Obviously the number "thousand" which is used here must not be interpreted in a literal sense. Since the number ten signifies completeness, and since a thousand is ten to the third power, we may think of the expression "a thousand years" as standing for a complete period, a very long period of indeterminate length.[78]

According to Hoekema, Revelation 20 speaks of two resurrections; the first is spiritual or a reigning with Christ, and the second resurrection is also not a physical raising from the dead.

> John is here speaking about the unbelieving dead — the "rest of the dead," in distinction from the believing dead whom he has just been describing. When he says that the rest of the dead did not live or come to life, he means the exact opposite of what

The Promise of Dawn

he had just said about the believing dead. The unbelieving dead, he is saying, did not live or reign with Christ during this thousand-year period. Whereas believers after death enjoy a kind of life in heaven with Christ in which they share in Christ's reign, unbelievers after death share nothing of either this life or this reign.[79]

Hoekema believes that Revelation 20 is not alluding to a literal earthly millennium, but to a heavenly reign.[80]

Hoekema stresses that the amillennial approach holds to two aspects of the kingdom: the kingdom as present and the kingdom as yet future. Concerning the former, the amillennialist claims the decisive victory over sin has been won:

> Amillennialists believe that the kingdom of God was founded by Christ at the time of his sojourn on earth, is operative in history now and is destined to be revealed in its fullness in the life to come.... The kingdom of God means nothing less than the reign of God in Christ over his entire created universe.[81]

Hoekema sees the Church as currently in the millennium. What is the binding of Satan?

> The fact that Satan is now bound does not mean that he is not active in the world today but that during this period he cannot deceive the nations — that is, cannot prevent the spread of the gospel. The binding of Satan during this era, in other words, makes missions and evangelism possible.[82]

Concerning a future eschatology, Hoekema states that the amillennialist believes the return of Christ will be preceded by various signs, such as the preaching of the gospel to every nation, the conversion of Israel, the great tribulation, and the appearance of Christ. These signs according to Hoekema, have been present from the beginning of the Christian era to the present period.[83] According to the amillennial position the second coming of Christ will be a single event, and at His coming there will be a general resurrection of both believers and unbelievers. Concerning the subject of judgment, Hoekema writes:

> Whereas dispensationalists commonly teach that there will be at least three separate judgments, amillennialists do not agree. The latter use scriptural evidence for only one Day of Judgment which will occur at the time of Christ's return. All men must then appear before the judgment seat of Christ.[84]

After this judgment the eternal estate will commence, according to the amillennial interpretation.

The Postmillennial Position

The postmillennial eschatological position, unlike the amillennial stance, typically posits the final realization of the millennium in the future, and in this respect is similar to the premillennial interpretation. Chapter four will speak more fully to the issue of postmillennialism because the eschatology of the Hodges and Warfield is discussed more extensively than at this point.

Charles Hodge

Hodge believes the Scriptures teach that the Church is powerful and that the message of the gospel will literally be brought to all nations before the coming of the Lord:

> Having imposed upon His Church the duty to preach the Gospel to every creature under heaven, he endowed it with all the gifts necessary for the proper discharge of this duty, and promised to send his Spirit to render their preaching effectual. ... The duties of the ministry, therefore, are to continue until all, that is all believers, the whole Church, or, as our Lord says, all the elect, are gathered in and brought to the stature of perfection in Christ.[85]

Hodge holds to a general resurrection, which is to occur at the last day.[86] Hodge also believes the Bible teaches one judgment. "This judgment is to take place at the second coming of Christ and at the general resurrection."[87]

What will be the nature of the future kingdom, according to Hodge?

> As to the nature of this kingdom, our Lord Himself teaches us that it is not of this world. It is not analogous to the kingdoms which exist among men. It is not a kingdom of earthly splendour, wealth, or power. It does not concern the civil or political affairs of men, except in their moral relations.... It is said to consist in "righteousness and peace, and joy in the Holy Ghost." (Rom. xiv.17) ... The condition of admission into that kingdom is regeneration (John iii.5), conversion (Matt. xviii.3), holiness of heart and life....[88]

Hodge believes "the seat of the Church, after the second coming, is not to be found in the earth, but a new heavens and a new earth."[89]

Hodge also describes the eternal estate itself:

> When Christ comes again it will be to be admired in all them that believe. Those who are then alive will be changed, in the twinkling of an eye; their corruptible shall put on incorruption, and their mortal shall put on immortality. Those who are in the graves shall hear the voice of the Son of Man and come forth to the resurrection of life, their bodies fashioned like unto the glorious body of the Son of God. Thus changed, both classes shall be ever with the Lord.[90]

Hodge, then, states that the millennium will gradually appear. The new heavens and the new earth will be created. The kingdom is to extend over the entire earth and all nations will serve the Lord their King.

Loraine Boettner

Loraine Boettner, another postmillennial theologian, articulates the same stance as does Hodge. Boettner says:

> Postmillennialism is that view of the last things which holds that the kingdom of God is now being extended in the world through the preaching of the gospel and the saving work of the Holy Spirit in the hearts of individuals, that the world eventually is to be Christianized and that the return of Christ is to occur at the close of a long period of righteousness and peace commonly called the millennium. It should be added that on postmillennial principles the Second Coming of Christ will be followed immediately by the general resurrection, the general judgment, and the introduction of heaven and hell in their fullness.[91]

What is the millennium according to Boettner?

> The millennium to which the postmillennialist looks forward is thus a golden age of spiritual prosperity during this present dispensation, that is, during the Church Age. This is to be brought about through forces now active in the world.
> This does not mean that there will be a time on this earth when every person will be a Christian or that all sin will be abolished. But it does mean that evil in all its many forms eventually will be reduced to negligible proportions....[92]

How will the millennium come in, according to Boettner? "The redemption of the world is a long, slow process, extending through the centuries, yet surely approaching an appointed goal."[93]

Thus, there is a great divergence of eschatological conclusions between amillennialists, postmillennialists, and premillennialists. These differences stem from the method of interpretation. Boettner believes the premillennialists are too literal. "Premillennialists often materialize and literalize the prophecies to such an extent that they keep them on an earthly level and miss their deeper meaning."[94]

Walvoord describes the postmillennial method of interpretation:

> The general features of postmillennialsim are not difficult to summarize. Postmillennialism is based on the figurative inter-

pretation of prophecy which permits wide freedom in defining the meaning of difficult passages.... The prophecies of the Old Testament relative to a righteous kingdom on earth are to be fulfilled in the kingdom of God in the interadvent period. The kingdom is spiritual and unseen rather than material and political.... The kingdom of God in the world will grow rapidly but with times of crisis.... The final coming of the Lord is climactic and is in the very remote future.[95]

Walvoord also depicts major differences between the premillennial and the amillennial views. "Premillenarians follow the so-called 'grammatical-historical' literal interpretation while amillenarians use a spiritualizing method."[96]

The amillennial and postmillennial views are at great variance with the premillennial argument. According to premillennialism, the kingdom is not part of the Body of Christ at this time and will only appear at the second coming of Christ.

Four Distinct Groups

Chafer sees biblical divisions as inherent in the Scriptures; Chafer appears concerned for order, literalism, and symmetry in his Scriptural interpretations. Chafer believes the division of rational beings is helpful in understanding dispensationalism. The four groups, consisting of angels, Gentiles, Jews, and Christians, will retain their separate identities throughout their history; they will not merge into another group or become nonentities. Rather, each group is distinct, individual, and perpetual.

A number of Old and New Testament passages are cited to shed light on the nature of angels. He writes of them as created beings whose activity is both on earth and in heaven. He cites Matthew 25:41 to prove his point that they are classified throughout time as angels.[97] In his *Systematic Theology* one gains insight into Chafer's opinion concerning angels:

Chafer's Dispensationalism

> The angels are reported to be present from creation and on into the eternity to come. Under a comprehensive fivefold division of God's finite creatures, as they now exist, the angels comprise two divisions, namely, the holy angels and the fallen angels. To these are added the Gentiles, the Jews, and the Christians. However, all classes of beings, regardless of the order or time or beginning, being originated and constituted as they are, go on in their group distinctions into eternity to come. There is no evidence that other orders of finite beings will be introduced in this age or future ages.[98]

Concerning their dispensational importance, Chafer does not dwell extensively on the subject of angels. His primary concern seemingly is to help others become aware of their existence, perpetuity, and biblical role.

The Gentiles are an important subject to Chafer, and to this group he devotes much attention. He summarizes this group by stating they had their origin in Adam, they have partaken of the Fall, and as subjects of prophecy, they will share with Israel, though subordinate to that people, in the coming kingdom. Chafer cites Acts 10, 11, and 13 to give credence to his claim that Gentiles are also a part of the elect group God is calling out during this present age. But he emphasizes that the mass of Gentiles will reject the offer of grace, and this group, also known as the nations in the Bible, will be present during the tribulation upon the earth. Also, they will be judged at the termination of the period, and in Matthew 35:31-46 the group is designated as the goats and are distinguished from the sheep. The latter are heirs of eternal life, while the former are not. Chafer stresses that this is not the last judgment but only will determine who will enter the kingdom, which is the thousand-year reign of Christ upon the earth. The final judgment will be an event which occurs at the termination of the kingdom period, according to Chafer. He summarizes the career of the Gentiles:

> Thus it is disclosed that—in spite of the fact that a dispensation of world-rule is committed to them, that in this age the gospel is preached unto them with its offers of heavenly glory, that in

the coming age they share the blessings of the kingdom with Israel, and that they appear in the future ages — they remain Gentiles, in contradistinction to the one nation Israel, to the end of the picture; and there is no defensible ground for diverting or misapplying this great body of Scripture bearing on the Gentiles.[99]

According to Chafer: "But to Daniel is given the complete review of the history of the Gentiles, beginning with the Jews' captivity and running on into the kingdom age. The period between the captivity and the second advent of Christ is named by him 'the times of the Gentiles.'"[100] Chafer continuously stresses that those prophets, like Daniel, who wrote of the Gentiles did not see the intercalation time of the Church or the present age. This age, according to Chafer, simply was not revealed to them.

The Jews are the third group that Chafer discusses. He traces their lineage to Abraham and stresses their distinct qualities. He claims that although they have been oppressed for many years without their own land, they will one day be a victorious people. "Their rightful king, the son of David, will occupy the Davidic throne forever (Ps. 89:34-37; Isa. 9:6-7; Jer. 33:16; Luke 1:31-33; Rev. 11:15)."[101]

He stresses that the Bible teaches during this present age there is no difference between the Jew and the Gentile spiritually; they are either with or without grace. "The present divine purpose is the outcalling from both Jews and Gentiles of that company who are the Bride of Christ, who are, therefore, every one to partake of His standing, being in Him, to be like Him, and to reign with Him on the earth (Rev. 20:4,6; 22:5)."[102]

At the completion of this present age, Israel must pass through the Great Tribulation, and Chafer draws this conclusion from such passages as Jeremiah 30:4-7; Daniel 12:1, and Matthew 24:21. This period will begin with the judgments of God in the earth. The millennium will ensue immediately after the tribulation and is described in Zechariah 14:1-21. He believes that Revelation 20:7-15 depicts the ending of the thousand-year period. Chafer gives more insight into his thinking concerning the Jewish nation:

As indicated before, Israel in all her generations — exclusive of those who have entered into the exalted privilege of the present age of grace — will come up for judgment, some to everlasting life and others to everlasting contempt (cf. Dan. 12:2; Ezek. 20:33-44; Matt. 24:37-25:30). The portion of this people who are destined to enter the kingdom become the "all Israel" who will be saved (cf. Isa. 63:1) when the Deliverer comes out of Zion according to God's unalterable covenant (Romans 11:26-27, 29). These, like all other creatures of God, are traced into the eternity to come; for the kingdom is "an everlasting dominion" (Dan. 7:13-14). Great grace from God will be upon those who enter the land (cf. Ezek. 20:44; Rom. 11:27).[103]

There will be Jews who are excluded from the land, according to Chafer. But he admits it is uncertain what their fate will be. "Whatever this estate thus described may be, it abides forever."[104] One outstanding quality Chafer possessed was his ever-present determination not to read into a text of Scripture his own particular views. He had his own personal biases and opinions, yet he remained remarkably objective.

The fourth group Chafer discusses is the Christians. He states:

> This company — composed of Jews and Gentiles who are saved and safe in Christ — is never divided in the divine purpose. They are one body.... All sectarian divisions of the church, ... are violence against this unity.... The entire notion that some believers are, through their supposed merit, better than other believers is an insult to that grace which perfectly saves.[105]

The purpose of God is presently centered in this group, and the Scriptures addressed to this company include the Gospel of John, the Acts, and the Epistles. The Synoptic Gospels, Chafer believes, present Christ as loyal to the Mosaic Law under which he lived. Jew and Gentile are one because spiritually there is no difference between them, since they are both in Christ.[106]

Thus, Chafer believes God distinguishes between groups in the dispensation of law and will again in the kingdom age. But during this age of grace, the Church is comprised of both Jew and Gentile.

The Covenants

Chafer strongly emphasizes in his dispensationalism four covenants: the covenant God made with Abraham, the covenant through Moses, the covenant made with David, and the New Covenant. Chafer explains the nature of the covenant:

> Whatever God declares He will do is always a binding covenant. If He in no way relates His proposed action to human responsibility, the covenant is properly termed *unconditional*. If He relates it to human responsibility or makes it to depend on cooperation on the part of any other being, the covenant is properly termed *conditional*.... A covenant which is unconditional cannot be conditional and a conditional covenant cannot be unconditional.[107]

Who is the recipient of God's covenants? Chafer believes the Israelite is an heir by virtue of his physical birth while the Christian is also an heir based solely on the grounds of a spiritual birth.[108]

The Abrahamic covenant is the first covenant Chafer considers. He draws the concept of this covenant from Genesis 12:1-3, 13:14-17, 15:4-21, 17:1-8 and 22:17-18. He claims it is also restated to Isaac and Jacob in Genesis 26:3-5 and Genesis 35:10-12. The covenant is unconditional and is everlasting in duration. The benefits of the covenant with respect to Abraham are as follows: (1) Abraham will be a great nation, fulfilled in his posterity, Ishmael and Isaac, and in their father's spiritual seed; (2) he will be blessed; (3) his name will be great; (4) he will be a blessing (Chafer saw this fulfilled not only in the Jewish race but also the Gentile); (5) he was promised land. Chafer claims the promise of land is amplified by the terms found in the Palestinian covenant, as contained in Deuteronomy 28:63-68; 30:1-10.[109] Chafer clarifies his thinking concerning the Abrahamic covenant:

Chafer's Dispensationalism

> This covenant reaches on through all time and into eternity and involves the blessedness of all the families of the earth. It is *unconditional* in the most absolute sense, being set forth in seven *I wills* of Jehovah.... The covenant anticipates the sovereign will of God in Abraham's personal blessing, in the everlasting mercy to Israel, and the coming of the Seed which is Christ....[110]

Chafer next discusses the Mosaic covenant. He believes this is the only conditional covenant, that is, that blessing from God is conditioned upon individual obedience.[111] Chafer claims the covenant is depicted in Exodus 20:1-31:18. This covenant was addressed to a people who had been in covenant relationship with God through a physical birth. Though this covenant had been broken, it will be superseded by a new covenant.

The unconditional Davidic covenant is contained in 2 Samuel 7:4-16. David has been promised a perpetual royal lineage, a throne, and a kingdom; all of these elements have been promised to be eternal. Chafer says:

> From the day that the covenant was made and confirmed by Jehovah's oath (Acts 2:30) to the birth of Christ, David did not lack for a son to sit on this throne (Jer. 33:21), and Christ the Eternal Son of God and Son of David, being the rightful heir to that throne and the One who will yet sit on that throne (Luke 1:31-33), completes the fulfillment of this promise to David that a son would sit on his throne forever.[112]

Chafer believes the covenant concerns an actual earthly throne and is related to a people whose expectation is earthly. He does not see this as a heavenly throne nor that the earthly reign will merge into a spiritual one. He states it will be established on the earth when the Lord returns, according to Matthew 25:31-32 and Luke 1:31-33.

The last covenant Chafer considers is the New Covenant, and this too is unconditional. Chafer draws this covenant from Jeremiah 31:31-33; Hebrews 8:6, 10-13; 10:16-17. It will not supersede the Abrahamic or

Davidic covenants, which will continue forever, but is placed over against the Mosaic covenant, which Israel could not keep. According to Chafer this covenant will be enacted between Israel and God upon entering the land.

The Controversy Concerning Dispensationalism

Without doubt, because of Chafer's dispensational teachings, he experienced great misunderstanding, denunciation, and even wrath. What was this issue, who was involved, and why was the misunderstanding so bitter?

Chafer battles with the anti-dispensationalists, who were of the adamant Reformed camp. James Bear makes this comment concerning Chafer's dispensationalism:

> It is the unanimous opinion of your Committee that Dispensationalism ... is out of accord with the system of doctrine set forth in the Confession of Faith, not primarily or simply in the field of eschatology, but because it attacks the very heart of the theology of our Church, which is unquestionably a Theology of one Covenant of Grace. As Dr. Chafer clearly recognizes, there are two schools of interpretation represented here which he rightly designates as "Covenantism" as over against "Dispensationalism."[113]

One cannot accuse Chafer of passivity in his comments concerning covenant theology:

> The theological terms, *Covenant of Works* and *Covenant of Grace*, do not occur in the Sacred Text. If they are to be sustained it must be wholly apart from Biblical authority. What is known as Covenant Theology builds its structure on these two covenants and is, at least a recognition — though inadequate — of the truth that the creature has a responsibility toward his creator. A theology which penetrates no further into

Scripture than to discover that in all ages God is immutable in His grace toward penitent sinners, and constructs the idea of a universal church, continuing through the ages, on the one truth of immutable grace, is not only disregarding vast spheres of revelation but is reaping the unavoidable confusion and misdirection which part-truth engenders.[114]

Covenant theologians derive the concept of the covenant from the belief that it is inherent in the Scriptures. *The Westminster Confession of Faith* cites two covenants, that of works and grace. According to this document, there is a need for a covenant relationship between God and humankind. Reformed theology, then, is based upon a two covenantal scheme, works and grace. Ryrie claims some Reformed theologians add a third covenant, the covenant of redemption. Berkhof is one theologian who speaks of a third covenant.[115]

Ryrie explains the use of this third covenant:

> Some Reformed theologians have introduced a third covenant, the covenant of redemption. It was made in eternity past and became the basis for the covenant of grace ... between God and the elect....
>
> These two or three covenants become the core and basis of operation for covenant theology in its interpretation of the Scriptures. Thus the theological system which makes these so-called theological covenants its base is covenant theology.[116]

The covenant of works is typically understood to have been instituted with Adam; because of Adam's failure, a new covenant had to be established, and this is the covenant of grace. The covenant of grace, then, spans both the Old and New Testaments. But Chafer offers this forthright indictment against a covenantal scheme:

> Since the days of Johannes Coccejus (1603 - 1669) who, more than any other, introduced a one-covenant-of-grace idea, many theologians have promoted the notion that God is undertaking but one objective throughout human history. Scripture

must be ignored or greatly misinterpreted to the end that such idealism may be advanced....[117]

The kernel of the issue between Chafer and his Reformed brethren is that Chafer was absolutely convinced that the Scriptures did not teach a two-covenantal scheme. Of course, he believes in covenants; he holds to at least four covenants, three of which are unconditional and must be fulfilled. But concerning a means of dividing and understanding the Scriptures, Chafer is convinced only a dispensational scheme is faithful to an honest comprehension of the Bible. Concerning the conflict between a dispensational and nondispensational interpretation of the Scriptures, he says:

> It has been claimed that Dispensationalism is in some respects "illogical" and leads to "disastrous consequences." No argument against this claim need be advanced here other than to point out that Dispensationalism has now become one of the most firmly established features of Christian education and is the acknowledged source of untold blessings as well as the inspiration to sacrificial service to uncounted multitudes who testify that the Bible became a new and transforming message to them when dispensational distinctions were observed.[118]

It took honesty and a forthright attitude on Chafer's part to admit his views concerning dispensationalism, since the denomination in which he held ordination is opposed to dispensationalism and in no uncertain terms believes it to be heresy. But to Chafer's credit, he does not hold to dispensationalism out of spite or rebellion; he is convinced *The Westminster Confession of Faith* is not as clear as Scripture concerning dispensationalism! He sums up his thought concerning the disputation between dispensationalism and covenant theology by stating:

> Because past, present and future ages (cf. Eph. 1:10; 3:1-6) are so clearly defined in the Scriptures, covenant theologians acknowledge different ages or time-periods, but then they treat

them as merely different ways of administering one and the same divine purpose. Regardless of every feature known to earlier ages, it will be seen that the Word of God builds all its doctrinal structure on an age past, a present age, and a future age. To deny these varied divisions, however, gathered as they are about the different revealed purposes of God, is to cease to be influenced duly by the precise Scripture which God has spoken.[119]

James E. Bear, former Professor of Literature and Interpretation of the New Testament at Union Theological Seminary in Richmond, Virginia, aims many remarks at Chafer's dispensationalism. He first of all sees dispensationalism as a recent occurrence, having come to America in the 1850s. He correctly states that the premillennial view dates to the early church and that this view is not dispensational premillennialism. Bear mentions the works of Feinberg, Scofield and Chafer and categorizes the three as holding similar dispensational views.[120] He especially places Scofield and Chafer in the same mold. In a footnote Bear reminds the reader that ordained ministers in the Presbyterian Church, U. S. must adopt and subscribe to *The Westminster Confession of Faith* as well as the *Catechisms*. There is no record that Chafer was ever questioned on an official basis concerning his dispensationalism.[121]

The misunderstanding between the Presbyterian Church, U. S., and those such as Chafer who held to dispensationalism continued to foment. Chafer gives insight into the heated debate:

> Of more moment than its own import would indicate is the action of the Presbyterian Church, U. S. at its recent General Assembly by which action an investigation of so-called *dispensationalism* is being conducted. The inquiry, according to the wording of the overture which promoted the investigation, is "as to whether the type of Bible interpretation known as *Dispensationalism* is in harmony with the Confession of Faith" (Minutes, 1941, p. 60). This move on the part of the Presbyterian Church, U. S. will doubtless be observed by other denominations. Since dispensational distinctions form an integral

The Promise of Dawn

feature of the premillennial interpretation of the Scriptures, all premillennialists are challenged by this investigation.[122]

Perhaps for the first time in the dispensational controversy we see Chafer digging in and defending himself:

> Since there is so much in the Confession of Faith which is in no way related to this discussion and which is the common belief of all, the issue should yet be narrowed to the difference which obtains between *Dispensationalism* and *Covenantism*. The latter is that form of theological speculation which attempts to unify God's entire program from Genesis to Revelation under one supposed Covenant of Grace. That no such covenant is either named or exhibited in the Bible and that the covenants which are set forth in the Bible are so varied and diverse that they preclude a one-covenant idea, evidently does not deter many sincere men from adherence to the one-covenant theory....[123]

Finally, he claims: "It is time for any theological Rip Van Winkle to awaken to the recognition of that which has developed doctrinally since a company of good men drew up the Confession of Faith."[124]

A lifetime of study convinced Chafer that the dispensational, premillennial approach was the correct means of biblical interpretation. But he at times exhibited a slightly defensive attitude toward those who were not in agreement with his dispensationalism. Admittedly, it took great courage on his part to state his views, yet Chafer never lost his courage.

A primary complaint which Bear raises is that Scofield and Chafer teach two means of salvation; obedience to the law as one means and salvation by grace through faith as the other. Bear declares: "We are led to the conclusion, then, that the Dispensational teaching about 'dispensations' gives two methods of salvation, works and grace."[125] Further, Bear states: "Again, let us say, under this heading we are simply emphasizing the fact that the Dispensationalists do not teach one plan of salvation, and here they seem to diverge radically from the teaching of our Church and from that of the church throughout the ages."[126] With tongue in cheek, Bear concludes his opinion of Chafer's dispensationalism: "But we must note further that Dr. Chafer himself feels that it [covenant teaching] is widely divergent from the belief held by those who are not of his group. We agree with him that his view is widely divergent from the view held by the Church through the ages."[127]

But Chafer claims repeatedly: "...There is, therefore, but one way to be saved and that is by the power of God made possible through the sacrifice of Christ."[128] How was salvation obtained before the time of Christ? Chafer says:

> That God has assigned different human requirements in various ages as the terms upon which He Himself saves on the ground of the death of Christ, is a truth of Scripture revelation and is recognized as true by those who receive their doctrine from the Sacred Text rather than from manmade creeds. Nevertheless, when the various human requirements of the different ages are investigated it is found that they come alike in the end to the basic reality that faith is exercised in *God*. And that one basic element of trust in God doubtless answers that which in every case God must require.[129]

However, Chafer in this issue did not get to the heart of the matter of salvation before the time of Christ. He is somewhat unclear. For instance, he does not state what the essential element of saving faith is in dispensations previous to that of the period of grace.

Chafer makes a statement which resulted in much controversy. He states concerning the subject of salvation:

> Whatever may have been the divine method of dealing with individuals before the call of Abraham and the giving of the Law by Moses, it is evident that, with the call of Abraham and the giving of the Law and all that followed, there are two widely different, standardized, divine provisions, whereby man, who is utterly fallen, might come into the favor of God.[130]

Chafer claims this statement led to much "misunderstanding and unjust criticism."[131] He explains that the word "salvation" is not used in the statement he made. He claims he is simply stating the truth that some have come into a right relationship with God, as is the case of Israel and Judaism, by a physical birth and others, as is the situation with Christians in Christianity, by a spiritual birth. Chafer says concerning the subject of salvation:

> But the determination persists that those who hold dispensational distinctions teach there are two ways to be saved. What they really teach, if at all, is that Judaism had its requirements summed up in works of the Law of Moses, which system, or religion, is not now in effect, and that Christianity has its requirements summarized in faith and is now the one and only basis of acceptance with God.[132]

However, again, it is stated Chafer did not always make clear the content of that pre-Christ faith and the grounds of salvation.

Conclusion

Chafer's entire *Systematic Theology* contains a dispensational perspective. He sees the English word "dispensation" as derived from the Latin *dispensatio*, and understands its meaning as "economic management," or "superintendence." The Greek equivalent is *oikonomia* and is translated "stewardship" or "economy." There are seven dispensations in Chafer's scheme, but he emphasizes only those of law, grace, and kingdom. He believes in God's arrangement there are four essential groups: angels, Gentiles, Jews, and Christians. Each is distinct and retains its separate identity. He concentrates upon four covenants, which God initiated, and these are the Abrahamic, Mosaic, Davidic, and New covenants. Chafer has been greatly misunderstood, misquoted, and in a sense ostracized because of his dispensational views. However, he had the courage to state his beliefs even though it would have been easier for him not to have done so.

Notes: Chapter 3

1. Lewis Sperry Chafer, *Systematic Theology*, vol. 1: *Prolegomena-Bibliology-Theology Proper* (Dallas: Dallas Seminary Press, 1947), p. v.

2. Ibid., p. 36.

3. Ibid., p. 11.

4. Ibid., p. 38.

5. Ibid., pp. 36-37.

6. Lewis Sperry Chafer, *Systematic Theology*, vol. 2: *Angelology-Anthropology-Hamartiology* (Dallas: Dallas Seminary Press, 1948), p. 55.

7. Ibid., p. 155.

8. Ibid., p. 217.

9. Ibid., p. 224.

10. Ibid., p. 365.

11. Lewis Sperry Chafer, *Systematic Theology*, vol. 3: *Soteriology* (Dallas: Dallas Seminary Press, 1948), pp. 188-89.

12. Lewis Sperry Chafer, *Major Bible Themes* (Dallas: Dallas Theological Seminary, 1926; rev. ed., Grand Rapids: Dunham Publications, 1963), p. 149.

13. Lewis Sperry Chafer, *Systematic Theology*, vol. 4: *Ecclesiology-Eschatology* (Dallas: Dallas Seminary Press, 1948), p. 47.

14. Ibid., p. 49.

15. Ibid., pp. 122-23.

16. Ibid., p. 124.

17. Ibid., p. 208.

18. Ibid., p. 224.

19. Ibid., pp. 243-44.

20. Ibid., p. 255.

21. C. I. Scofield, Introduction to *The Kingdom in History and Prophecy*, by Lewis Sperry Chafer (New York: Fleming H. Revell Co., 1915; reprint ed., Philadelphia: *The Sunday School Times*, 1926), p. 6.

22. Ibid., p. 9.

23. Ibid.

24. Lewis Sperry Chafer, *Systematic Theology*, vol. 6: *Pneumatology* (Dallas: Dallas Seminary Press, 1948), p. 65.

25. Chafer, *Prolegomena-Bibliology-Theology Proper*, pp. 11-12.

26. Lewis Sperry Chafer, *Dispensationalism* (Dallas; Dallas Theological Seminary, 1936; rev. ed., Dallas: Dallas Seminary Press, 1951) p. 8.

27. Lewis Sperry Chafer, *Systematic Theology*, vol. 7: *Doctrinal Summarization* (Dallas: Dallas Seminary Press, 1948), p. 122.

28. C. I. Scofield, ed., *Scofield Reference Bible* (New York: Oxford University Press, 1909), p. 5, quoted in Chafer, *Dispensationalism*, p. 9.

29. Chafer, *Prolegomena-Bibliology-Theology Proper*, p. 41.

30. Ibid.

Chafer's Dispensationalism

31. Chafer, *Dispensationalism*, p. 45.

32. Ibid., p. 47.

33. Ibid., p. 48.

34. Ibid., pp. 48-49.

35. Chafer, *Ecclesiology-Eschatology*, p. 164.

36. Lewis Sperry Chafer, *Grace* (n.p., 1922; rev. ed., Grand Rapids: Zondervan Publishing House, 1950), p. 147.

37, Chafer, *Ecclesiology-Eschatology*, p. 183.

38. Chafer, *Prologomena-Bibliology-Theology Proper*, p. 41.

39. Chafer, *Doctrinal Summarization*, p. 240.

40. Chafer, *Ecclesiology-Eschatology*, p. 186.

41. Ibid., p. 188.

42. Ibid., p. 190-91.

43. Chafer, *Dispensationalism*, p. 50.

44. Chafer, *Ecclesiology-Eschatology*, p. 168.

45. Ibid., p. 171-72.

46. Ibid., p. 173.

47. Ibid., p. 178.

48. Chafer, *Dispensationalism*, p. 9.

49. C. H. Mackintosh, *The Mackintosh Treasury* (Neptune, New Jersey: Loizeaux Bros., 1898; 1st ed. in one vol., 1976), p. 871.

50. Ibid., p. 874.

51. Ibid., p. 876.

52. Ibid., p. 886.

53. Ibid., pp. 886-87.

54. William L. Pettingill, *Simple Studies in Matthew* (Harrisburg: Fred Kelker, 1910), p. 32.

55. Ibid., p. 269.

56. Ibid., pp. 287-88.

57. Ibid., pp. 291-98.

58. William Kelly, *An Exposition of the Book of Isaiah* 4th ed. (St. Albans: Mayflower Press, n.d.; rev. ed., London: C. A. Hammond, 1947), pp. 274-75.

59. Ibid., p. 39.

60. Ibid., pp. 234-35.

61. William Kelly, *Lectures on the Gospel of Matthew*, with a foreward by Guernsey (London: n.p., 1868; new ed. rev., London. Pickering & Inglis, (n.d.), p. 440.

62. Ibid., p. 482.

63. Erich Sauer, *From Eternity to Eternity*, trans. G. H. Lang (Grand Rapids: William B. Eerdmans Publishing Co., 1954), pp. 78-80.

64. Ibid., p. 90.

65. Ibid., p. 93.

66. Ibid., p. 95.

67. E. Schuyler English, *Re-Thinking the Rapture* (Travelers Rest, South Carolina; Southern Bible Book House, 1954; rev. ed., Neptune, New Jersey: Loizeaux Bors., 1970). p. 122.

68. H. A. Ironside, *Isaiah,* with a foreward by Ann Hightower Ironside (Neptune, New Jersey: Loizeauz Bros., 1952). pp. 217-18.

69. Chafer, *Christology,* p. 130.

70. H. A. Ironside, *Matthew* (Neptune, New Jersey: Loizeaux Bros., 1948), p. 325.

71. A. C. Gaebelein, *The Conflict of the Ages* (n.p.: Arno C. Gaebelein, 1933; reprint ed., Neptune, New Jersey: Loizeaux Bros., 1983), pp. 155-56.

72. J. Barton Payne, *The Imminent Appearing of Christ* (Grand Rapids: Wm. B. Eerdmans Publishing Co., 1962), pp. 82-83.

73. George E. Ladd, *The Blessed Hope* (Grand Rapids: Wm. B. Eerdmans Publishing Co., 1956), pp. 11-12.

74. John F. Walvoord, *The Millennial Kingdom* (n.p.: Dunham Publishing Co., 1959; reprint ed., Grand Rapids: Zondervan Publishing House, 1976), pp. 248-49.

75. Albertus Pieters, *The Seed of Abraham* (Grand Rapids: Wm. B. Eerdmans Publishing Co., 1950), pp. 64-65.

76. Ibid., p. 67.

77. Ibid., p. 93.

78. Anthony A. Hoekema, "Amillennialism," in *The Meaning of the Millennium,* ed. Robert G. Clouse (Downers Grove, Illinois: Intervarsity Press, 1977), p. 162.

79. Ibid., p. 169-70.

80. Ibid., p. 178.

81. Ibid., p. 181.

82. Ibid.

83. Ibid., p. 183.

84. Ibid.

85. Charles Hodge, *Systematic Theology*, vol. 3: *Soteriology* (New York: Charles Scribner & Co., 1972; reprint ed., Grand Rapids: Wm. B. Eerdmans Publishing Co., 1940), p. 801.

86. Ibid., p. 838.

87. Ibid., p. 847.

88. Ibid., p. 857.

89. Ibid., p. 859.

90. Ibid., pp. 859-60.

91. Loraine Boettner, "Postmillennialism," in *The Meaning of the Millennium*, p. 117.

92. Ibid., pp. 117-18.

93. Ibid., p. 125.

94. Ibid., p. 137.

95. Walvoord, *The Millennial Kingdom*, p. 33.

96. Ibid., p. 59.

97. Chafer, *Dispensationalism*, pp. 19-20.

98. Chafer, *Angelology-Anthropology-Hanmartiology*, p. 4.

99. Chafer, *Dispensationalism*, pp. 22-23.

100. Chafer, *Ecclesiology-Eschatology*, p. 330.

101. Chafer, *Dispensationalism*, p. 22-23.

102. Ibid., p. 30.

103. Chafer, *Ecclesiology-Eschatology*, pp. 416-17.

104. Ibid., p. 417.

105. Ibid., p. 418.

106. Ibid., p. 12.

107. Chafer, *Dispensationalism*, p. 73.

108. Ibid., p. 76.

109. Ibid., p. 77

110. Chafer, *Major Bible Themes*, p. 106.

111. Chafer, *Dispensationalism*, pp. 89-90.

112. Chafer, *Major Bible Themes*, pp. 108-09,

113. Minutes of the Eighty-Fourth General Assembly of the Presbyterian Church in the United States, 25-30 May 1944 (Historical Foundation of the Presbyterian & Reformed Churches, Montreat, North Carolina), p. 126.

114. Chafer, *Ecclesiology-Eschatology*, p. 156.

115. Louis Berkhof, *Systematic Theology* (Grand Rapids: Eerdmans Publishing Co., 1974), pp. 265-71.

116. Charles C. Ryrie, *Dispensationalism Today* (Chicago; Moody Press, 1965), p. 178.

117. Chafer, *Doctrinal Summarization*, pp. 96-97.

118. Chafer, *Dispensationalism*, p. 12.

119. Chafer, *Doctrinal Summarization*, p. 123.

120. James E. Bear, "Dispensationalism and the Covenant of Grace," *Union Seminary Review* 49 (July 1939):285-307. Cf. Oswald T. Allis, "Modern Dispensationalism and the Doctrine of the Unity of the Scriptures," *The Evangelical Quarterly* 8 (January 1936):22-35; "Modern Dispensationalism and the Law of God," *Evangelical Quarterly* 8 (July 1936): 272-89; and John Wick Bowman, "Dispensationalism," *Interpretation* 10 (April 1956):170-86.

121. Joel L. Alvis, Jr., Local Church History Coordinator, Presbyterian Church, U.S., Montreat, North Carolina, personal letter, 24 January 1985. Mr. Alvis writes: "I have checked the General Assembly Minutes concerning Lewis Sperry Chafer and any charges of heresy. The General Assembly never charged Chafer with heresy per se.... Chafer requested that the 1945 General Assembly withdraw publication and circulation of that 1944 statement on the grounds that it misrepresented him. The Committee on Bills and Overtures reported in reply to the request that it was 'unable to see that Dr. Chafer's teaching had been misrepresented. It therefore is unable to rescind the statement or suppress the literature containing the same.'"

122. Lewis Sperry Chafer, "Dispensational Distinctions Challenged," *Bibliotheca Sacra* 100 (July 1943):337.

123. Ibid., p. 338.

124. Ibid., p. 341.

125. Bear, "Dispensationalism and the Covenant," p. 297.

126. Ibid., pp. 297-98.

127. Ibid., pp. 304-05.

128. Lewis Sperry Chafer, "Inventing Heretics Through Misunderstanding," *Bibliotheca Sacra* 102 (January 1945):1.

129. Ibid., p. 2.

130. Lewis Sperry Chafer, "Dispensationalism," *Bibliotheca Sacra* 93 (October 1936):410.

131. Lewis Sperry Chafer, "Are There Two Ways to Be Saved?" *Bibliotheca Sacra* 105 (January 1948):1.

132. Ibid.

Chapter IV
Chafer's Millennialism

Dispensational premillennialism is the crowning conclusion of Chafer's eschatology. He is convinced if one studies the Scriptures in a literal fashion distinct time periods, or dispensations, are obviously seen. But the central event is the establishing of Christ's kingdom which will occur only after the second coming. One's view of eschatology is not simply of secondary importance to Chafer; rather, in his thinking, eschatology is a central issue. He believes an understanding of the end times influences one's conclusions concerning prophecy, the resurrection, the judgment, the second advent, and the millennium itself.

In his work, *The Kingdom in History and Prophecy*, published in 1915, Chafer forcefully enunciates his convictions concerning the necessity of a premillennial interpretation:

> Accepted inferences of so-called Postmillennialism and Premillennialism as possible co-existing systems of interpretation constitute a serious challenge against the dignity and purpose of the Bible itself. Either the divine revelation follows a definite order in the development of the kingdom in the earth, or it does not. If it does, there could hardly be two distinct programs co-existing in the mind and purpose of God.[1]

Additional understanding into his thinking is offered:

> It is a thousand years which is said to intervene between the first and second of humanity's resurrections (Rev. 20:4-6); which resurrections are named in 1 Corinthians 15:23-26 as "they that are Christ's at His coming," and "the end" (resurrection). In the Corinthian passage, as in Revelation 20:4-6, these resurrec-

tions are separated by a kingdom reign when Christ, according to the Corinthian passage, before delivering this kingdom to the Father, shall have put down all rule, and authority and power, and shall have put all enemies under his feet.... In this thousand years ... every earthly covenant with Israel will be fulfilled — all, indeed, that belong to the Messianic kingdom.[2]

Chafer defends premillennialism by citing other scholars who held to this position, and he refers to Bengel, Olshousen, Gill, Stier, Alford, Lange, Lillie, Meyer, Kurtz, Stark, Fausset, Jones, Nast, Delitzsch, Bonar, Ryle, Seiss, and Cunningham.[3]

Perhaps Chafer should have been careful to explain that dispensational premillennialsim was not the view of the early Church. Even though he does not explicitly state that it was, he seems to give this impression. He says:

> Some modern writers seem to realize but little that chiliasm or premillennialism was the all-but-universal belief of the early church, or the extent of that conviction in all centuries when any truth has been received at all. It is hardly worthy of any scholar to assert this is a modern departure, or, if held in the early centuries, was looked upon as heresy.[4]

It is not the purpose of the present argument to examine the early church's concept of the millennium. It can be said that the early church was premillennial, but that belief is not identical to Chafer's premillennial system. Chafer cites other premillennialists, not to give credence to his own position, but because he himself was personally convinced and willing to promote premillennialism.

Though Chafer holds to a historical-grammatical, hermeneutical method and claims that Scripture must be interpreted in accordance with its plain meaning, he also believes Scripture contains figurative language. Regarding Reformed eschatology, Chafer does not speak against the fact of symbolism in Scriptures, but rather against the method of interpretation:

While some prophecy is couched in symbolic language, those portions which trace the forward movements of the kingdom in the earth are largely free from problems presented by such symbolism, and that body of truth appears in language and terms the meaning of which cannot reasonably be questioned.... A mixture of teachings concerning Israel, as a nation, with the revelations concerning the Church, the body of Christ, is groundless in Scripture. It is hopelessly confusing and grotesque, for under this plan only Israel's blessings are borrowed; her curses and penalties are, naturally, not wanted. No progress can be made in kingdom studies unless plain words are taken in their obviously plain meaning.[5]

Historical Context

In order to more fully understand the divergent views in eschatology, it is necessary to briefly cover eschatology's historical development. Ladd, a premillennialist though not a dispensationalist, offers a helpful summary of the Church Fathers' concept of the kingdom:

> In the early church two interpretations of the kingdom are to be found: an eschatological interpretation and a non-eschatological interpretation. During the first two centuries the kingdom of God in the Church Fathers was exclusively eschatological ... and with one exception there is no Church Father before Origin who opposed the millenarian interpretation, and there is no one before Augustine whose extant writings offer a different interpretation of Revelation 20 than that of a future earthly kingdom consonant with the natural interpretation of the language.[6]

Chafer is absolutely convinced that the Reformed eschatological position is not true to the Scriptures. The primary issue which divides dispensational premillennialism and Reformed eschatology is the view of

Israel and the Church. The promises of Israel of a literal, earthly kingdom were fulfilled by the Church, according to the Reformed position. Chafer, of course, believes God is pursuing a specific course for Israel and a unique course for the Church; therefore, Israel and the Church are kept separate in his scheme. Chafer is familiar with the eschatological position of the Hodges and Warfield. Chafer was also an ordained minister with the denomination which considered these postmillennial theologians to be of supreme value in the understanding of the Reformed eschatological position. It must be recalled that Chafer retained many beliefs which were peculiar to his denomination. Some of these have to do with infant baptism, the total depravity of the individual, election, irresistible grace, the perseverance of the saints, and the sovereignty of God. Chafer in his *Systematic Theology* does not cite amillennial theologians. He is familiar with the postmillennial theologians; therefore, it is more pertinent to discuss this view.

Charles Hodge

In the latter nineteenth and early twentieth centuries there were three theologians associated with Princeton who exerted a powerful influence upon postmillennial thought. These are: Charles Hodge, Archibald A. Hodge, and Benjamin B. Warfield.

Charles Hodge (1797 - 1878) graduated from Princeton in 1815 and from the seminary in 1819. He became an instructor at Princeton in 1820 and remained there his entire life. He was a professor of Biblical Literature during 1822 - 1840 and professor of theology the remaining years. His writings carry his influence beyond the three thousand students he taught. His most influential work is his *Systematic Theology* (1872 - 1873), which is still in print and is considered a classic in Reformed theology.

He begins his division on the second coming of Christ with a general outline of his eschatology:

> The common church doctrine is, first, that there is to be a second personal, visible, and glorious advent of the Son of God. Secondly, that the events which are to precede that advent are:

1. The universal diffusion of the Gospel; or, as our Lord expressed it, the ingathering of the elect; this is the vocation of the Christian Church.
2. The conversion of the Jews, which is to be national. As their casting away was national, although a remnant was saved, so their conversion may be national, although some may remain obdurate.
3. The coming of Antichrist.

Thirdly, that the events which are to attend the second advent are:
1. The resurrection of the dead, or the just and of the unjust.
2. The general judgment.
3. The end of the world. And
4. The consummation of Christ's kingdom.[7]

Hodge does not mention the binding of Satan (Revelation 20:1-3). The closest he comes to mentioning God's opposition is the coming of the Antichrist. He believes there are different uses of the word "Antichrist," but in the book of Revelation, he understands it as alluding to the ecclesiastical power of the papacy.

Hodge claims the Bible speaks of only one general resurrection. He cites three categories of passages as proof: (1) passages where the righteous and wicked are raised together (John 5:28-29; Matthew 25:31-32; Revelation 20:12-13; and 2 Thessalonians 1:7-10); (2) passages which teach that the resurrection of the righteous will take place at "the last day" when Christ shall appear in glory; therefore, there is not a thousand years before that event (John 11:24; 6:39-40, 44, 54; and 12:48); and (3) passages which teach that the resurrection of the saints will take place at the day of judgment or the final judgment (Matthew 24:30-31; 25:31-46; and 2 Timothy 1:7-10).[8] Hodge believes Christ will come the second time, the dead in Christ will rise, all nations will be judged, and the present order of things will cease.[9]

Hodge claims the possible exception to only one general resurrection is Revelation 20:4-6. He also admits that the passage taken by itself teaches two resurrections.[10]

Hodge believes that the Kingdom is to be brought in gradually. He writes:

> It is not only asserted that the kingdom of Christ is to attain this universal extension by slow degrees, but its gradual progress is illustrated in various ways. Our Lord compares his kingdom to a grain of mustard seed, which is indeed the least of all seeds, but when it is grown it is the greatest among herbs; and to leaven, which a woman took, and hid in three measures of meal, till the whole was leavened.[11]

God has always had a kingdom upon this earth, according to Hodge, and the Messianic form began when God's Son became flesh. Hodge also believes that "nothing, therefore, can be more opposed to the plain teaching of the New Testament, than that the kingdom of Christ is yet future and is not to be inaugurated until his second coming. This is to confound its consummation with its commencement."[12] He states the millennium does not need to be a thousand years. Hodge says, "Others, assuming that in the prophetic language a day stands for a year, assume that the so-called millennium is to last three hundred and sixty-five thousand years."[13]

Hodge describes the condition prior to the second coming:

> As therefore the Scriptures teach that the kingdom of Christ is to extend over all the earth; that all nations are to serve Him; and that all people shall call Him blessed; it is to be inferred that these predictions refer to the state of things which is to exist before the second coming of Christ. This state is described as one of spiritual prosperity; God will pour out his Spirit upon all flesh; knowledge will everywhere abound; wars shall cease to the ends of the earth, and there shall be nothing to hurt or destroy in my holy mountain, saith the Lord.[14]

Chafer respected Charles Hodge and quotes extensively the latter's works, though not his eschatology.

Archibald Hodge

Archibald Hodge, son of Charles Hodge, graduated from Princeton in 1846, and, after a brief period as a missionary in India, returned to America and became a pastor. He was professor of systematic theology at Western Theological Seminary, Allegheny, Pennsylvania, and served there until 1877. From 1878 until his death in 1886, he was professor of theology at Princeton.

A. A. Hodge's eschatology is identical to his father's. He claims the following events must occur before the second advent: Antichrist apostasy, the preaching of the gospel to every nation, the fullness of the Gentiles, the conversion of the Jews, the millennial prosperity of the Church, and the final defection.[15] He believes the millennium will be a thousand years when the gospel has influence over the entire earth. But this influence is to be done gradually through the spiritual presence of Christ.[16] Hodge believes all the dead, good and bad, are to rise and be judged at the second advent.[17] He writes concerning the kingdom:

> As to the fact that the Kingdom of Christ has already come. He has sat upon the throne of his Father David ever since his ascension.... The Old Testament prophecies, therefore, which predict this kingdom, must refer to the present dispensation of grace, and not to a future reign of Christ on earth in person among men in the flesh.[18]

Chafer also read and quoted extensively from A. A. Hodge, especially his Outlines of Theology. But as stated previously, Chafer apparently was not convinced by their eschatological conclusions, though he was aware of them.

Benjamin B. Warfield

Benjamin B. Warfield (1851 - 1921) graduated from Princeton Seminary in 1878 and was appointed professor of New Testament Literature and Exegesis at Western Theological Seminary, Allegheny, Pennsylvania. In 1887, he became a professor of theology at Princeton Theological Seminary, where he succeeded A. A. Hodge. He served in this capacity for thirty-three years.

Warfield expounds principles which he believes are important for understanding the book of Revelation and prophecy in general: (1) recapitulation and successive visions — Warfield believes it is exegetically questionable to view the Apocalypse as one continuously progressive vision. He sees it as a series of seven, each reaching to the end, not in repetition of one another, but unfolding in ever increasing development; (2) symbolism—he claims that the language of the Apocalypse has its own laws of interpretation; (3) ethical purpose — it is the spiritual and ethical impression that rules the presentation and not a chronological intent; (4) fulfillment of prophecy — the fulfillment of prophecy is to be interpreted separately. It is only when one understands the book fully can the question of prophetic fulfillment be comprehended.[19]

Warfield claims the nineteenth and twentieth chapters of Revelation must be pictured as a unit. He states:

> The picture of this conquering church is given us in the nineteenth chapter. But there is also the church waiting there above, but not waiting merely, but living and reigning with Christ, free from all strife and safe from all assaults of the evil one. This is depicted for us in the opening verses of the twentieth chapter. Not the one only, but both together — the church militant and the church expectant — constitute the church of Christ; and not the one alone but both together pass unscathed through the great trial (latter part of ch. xx) to inherit the new heavens and new earth (ch. xxi).[20]

Warfield pictures chapter nineteen as the Church engaging in war and gaining victory by means of preaching of the gospel.[21] It is evident that Warfield believes in a "golden age" for the Church. In one of his articles, he mentions the divergent views of premillennialism and postmillennialism. In this article, Warfield strongly intimates that he is a postmillennialist.[22]

Warfield's understanding of the "binding of Satan" is as follows:

> It is a description of the form of a narrative: the element of time

and chronological succession belongs to the symbol, and not the thing symbolized. The "binding of Satan" is therefore, in reality, not for a season, but with reference to a sphere; and his "loosing" again is not after a period but in another sphere; it is not subsequence but exteriority that is suggested. There is, indeed, no literal "binding of Satan" to be thought of at all: what happens, happens not to Satan but to the saints, and is only represented as happening to Satan for the purposes of symbolical picture. What actually happens is that the saints described are removed from the sphere of Satan's assaults.[23]

He also sees the first resurrection as spiritual. The martyrs of Revelation 20:4 are symbols for all of Christ's saints in the world. It is those saints who have died and now are in paradise with the Lord which Warfield calls the first resurrection.[24] The second resurrection Warfield sees as literal. He writes: "The 'first resurrection' is here, therefore the symbolic description of what has befallen those who while dead yet live in the Lord; and it is set in contrast with the 'second resurrection,' which must mean the restoration of the bodily life."[25]

Warfield admits the difficulty with his interpretation of Revelation 20:1-10 lies with the word "nation." The word normally represents the anti-Christians in the book of Revelation. But Warfield thinks the word "nation" may have a double sense like the word "world." Therefore, he understands "the 'nations' here, not of the anti-Christian world in contrast to the Christian, but of the world on earth in contrast with the saints gathered in paradise."[26]

In a sense it is difficult to place Warfield in the postmillennial camp, as he seemingly has traits of amillennial thought. He claims "The millennium of the Apocalypse is the blessedness of the saints who have gone away from the body to be at home with the Lord."[27] But conversely, it is difficult to place him in the amillennial camp since, after he denies the earthly millennium, he claims that his view of the millennium does not deny a "golden age" in a spiritual sense for the church in the future. The vision in the latter half of chapter nineteen of the book of Revelation emphasizes that the gospel is to completely conquer the world. The gospel must be preached to the whole world before the second advent, but the winning of the world will most likely not eliminate all evil.[28] He summarized this point:

> There is a "golden age" before the Church — at least an age relatively golden, gradually ripening to higher and higher glories as the Church more and more fully conquers the world and all the evil of the world; and ultimately an age absolutely golden when the perfected Church is filled with the glory of the Lord in the new earth and under the new heavens.[29]

Though he apparently has elements of both amillennialism and postmillennialism, his eschatology is characterized by the latter.

Charles A. Hodge, Archibald A. Hodge, and Benjamin B. Warfield exercised a great influence upon Reformed theology during the latter decades of the nineteenth century and well into the twentieth century. Chafer knew their writings and respected them with one qualification — he was convinced their eschatology was both unbiblical and out of touch with the times. It took great courage on the part of Chafer to claim in no uncertain terms that these respected theological giants of his own denomination were in error. When pressed and forced to do such, he denounced postmillennialism and amillennialism. Chafer challenged the citadel of Reformed thought concerning eschatology; this challenge remained lifelong for him.

The Role of Prophecy

According to Chafer, the Old Testament prophets spoke of a future time of blessing for the Israelite nation. What does Chafer believe prophecy to be?

> The comparative importance of predictive prophecy as related to other aspects of Bible truth is indicated by the fact that at least one-fifth of the Bible was, at the time it was written, an anticipation of the future. Of this extended material much

Chafer's Millennialism

has now been fulfilled, and much remains to be fulfilled. In each step of human progress it has pleased God to declare beforehand precisely what He was about to do....[30]

Why is prophecy so important to Chafer? First, he believes at least one-fifth of the Bible at the time written was predictive. Second, prophecy attests to the divine authority of the Scripture; prophecy verifies the Bible as the Word of God in distinction to mere human opinion. Third, prophetic themes enable the believer to more fully interpret the Scripture. Fourth, prophecy gives to the individual a "blessed hope" concerning the future.

We see further insight into Chafer's view of prophecy: "In all ages it has pleased God to pre-announce certain things He proposed to do. These announcements are termed prophecies. All prophecy is history pre-written and it is as credible as any word God hath spoken."[31]

The prophets, Chafer writes, spoke primarily during one period; it was during a dismal time of Israel's history as she was about to be dispersed. But it was during this period that the prophets spoke of Israel's coming glory. He says, "It was in the darkest hour of their history that these seers, as by contrast, set forth the unprecedented light of the nation's coming glory."[32] What is the predominant theme of which these prophets spoke?

> While they spoke with individual purpose and style, they were united as one voice on certain great themes. They condemned the nation's sin and predicted the coming chastisement. They saw the judgments about to fall upon the surrounding nations.... Above all they saw their own future blessings, the form and manner of which are too accurately described by them to be misunderstood. Their prophecies expanded into magnificent detail the covenanted reign of David's Son over the House of Jacob forever.[33]

Chafer claims that "The Bible lends itself to one program of events and to this program all Scripture is in perfect accord."[34] He believes the kingdom will be theocratic, centered in Jerusalem and established by the power of the returning King. According to Chafer, Jeremiah 23:5 speaks of the reign of the king during a time when justice will be upon the earth. He also cites Ezekiel 37:24 and Hosea 3:4,5 to give credence that the kingdom will be a theocratic reign. The prophets forecasted that this reign will be centered in Jerusalem where Israel has been regathered and converted (Jeremiah 33:7-9; Ezekiel 36:16-38, 37:21-25). He believes the prophets Zechariah and Malachi spoke of the kingdom's establishment through the power of the returning king (Zechariah 2:10-12; Malachi 3:1-4). The kingdom is also spiritual in the sense that the will of God will be effective in all matters of conduct and government.[35] It is clearly seen, then, that Chafer holds that prophecy is of great importance concerning the subject of the kingdom. He believes that "the prophet was God's representative to man as the priest was man's representative to God."[36] God gave to the prophet a message which he in turn gave to the nation. One subject of which the prophet spoke was that of the kingdom.

Chafer does acknowledge that much prophecy has been fulfilled. He offers this summary of prophetic events which have been fulfilled and those which are still future:

> A brief survey of the many features of unfulfilled prophecy is here given: the last days for the Church, the first resurrection, the rapture, the Church in heaven, her rewards, the marriage of the Lamb, the great tribulation on earth, the man of sin, Israel's last sufferings, the beginning of the Day of the Lord, the second coming of Christ, the battle of Armageddon, the destruction of ecclesiastical Babylon, the destruction of political Babylon, the binding of Satan, the regathering and judgment of sorrowing Israel, the judgment of the nations, the seating of Christ upon His throne, the resurrection of the "tribulational saints," the millennial kingdom, the loosing of Satan and the last revolt, the doom of Satan, the great white throne, the destiny of the wicked, the destiny of the saved, the new heaven and new earth.[37]

The Second Advent

In dispensational, premillennial thought, the second coming of Christ is the event which signifies the imminent commencement of the millennium, the thousand-year reign of Christ. Why is a correct understanding of the second advent important to Chafer? One reason is he believes a correct interpretation will produce the conclusion of a premillennial advent. But another important reason is the vibrant hope it gives to individuals, since Chafer believes the rapture of the Church will occur before the time of tribulation upon the earth. The second advent, then, indeed signifies hope in Chafer's eschatological scheme.

At the first advent, the kingdom was not established. Jesus preached the gospel of the kingdom as well as did the disciples, but always with the same result — rejection of the message by the Jews. However, at the second advent, the kingdom will be established, and the King will commence His reign.

In order to better understand Chafer's views, one must realize he believes the prophets did not fully understand these predictions.

> From 1 Peter 1:10, 11 it is clear that the prophets of the Old Testament were unable to distinguish two advents of the Messiah. So perfectly was the present age a secret in the counsels of God that, to the prophets, these events which were fulfilled at His first coming and those which are yet to be fulfilled at His second coming were in no way separated as to the time of their fulfillment.[38]

The first advent, of course, has been fulfilled, but the second waits consummation, according to Chafer. The second advent is central to the kingdom since he believes the millennial period cannot be initiated until this event occurs. Chafer claims there are seven achievements which will be consummated in the second coming of Christ:

> (a) Christ Himself returns as He went, in the clouds of heaven and with power and great glory.

(b) Christ takes the throne of His father David, which is the throne of glory, and reigns forever.
(c) Christ comes, not to a converted world, but to the earth in rebellion against Jehovah and against His Messiah, and conquers it by the might of His own infinite power.
(d) At Christ's coming, judgment will fall upon Israel, upon the nations, upon Satan, and upon the man of sin.
(e) Christ's coming is accompanied by the convulsion of nature and accomplishes her release from the curse.
(f) Christ's coming provokes Israel's long-predicted repentance and brings her salvation.
(g) At His coming Christ establishes His kingdom of righteousness and peace, with converted Israel regathered to their own land, united and blessed under "their King," and Gentiles as a subordinate people, sharing in that kingdom.[39]

The second coming, then, will be a type of catalyst setting into action many events. However, there are specific events even prior to the second coming which must be fulfilled, and Chafer believes there is a definite pattern and chronological order, which he bases upon the Scriptures.

The Church at this present time finds herself in the dispensation of grace, or that period which extends from the death of Christ until the translation of the saints. The taking out of the saints is a possibility at any time and Chafer calls this the "rapture of the living saints":

> The Apostle goes on to declare a mystery, or a sacred secret hitherto unrevealed (1 Cor. 15:51-57), namely, that "we shall not all sleep," but with essential changes which are wrought in a moment, the child of God goes on in this body to meet the Lord in the air (cf. John 14:1-3; 1 Cor. 15:51-52; 1 Thess. 4:13-18; 2 Thess. 2:1; Heb. 9:28).[40]

Immediately following the rapture, the tribulation period of seven years will commence. Chafer states the Church will not be involved with this period, but it will be specifically for Israel since she has remained spiritually aloof. In Chafer's eschatological perspective, Israel is unique.

Chafer's Millennialism

"The election of Israel is continually emphasized throughout the Scriptures."[41] Chafer writes:

> Israel has never been the Church, is not the Church now, nor will she ever be the Church. A form of covenant theology which would thread all of Jehovah's purposes and undertakings upon His one attribute of grace could hardly avoid confusion of mind in matters related to His varied objectives.... The Church is thought to be a spiritual remnant within Israel to whom all Old Testament blessings are granted and the nation as such is allowed to inherit the cursings.[42]

He states concerning Israel that "the Jewish nation is the center of all things related to the earth. The Church is foreign to the earth and related to it only as a witnessing people."[43]

Chafer claims that Israel's national entity will never be lost even through centuries of dispersion. But a future of tribulation lies ahead for Israel. The tribulation period will be a time of refinement and rejuvenation spiritually for Israel. Chafer says:

> At the end of this age, Israel must pass through the great tribulation, which is specifically characterized as "the time of Jacob's trouble" (Jer. 30:4-7; Dan. 12:1; Matt. 24:21); and, before entering her kingdom, she must come before her King in judgment.... The Day of Jehovah, which extended period occupies so large a part of the Old Testament prophecy....[44]

Chafer, then, sees this seven-year period not for the Church since she will be taken out before this time; this view is called the pretribulational position. However, Chafer at times is not specific or clear how the seven-year period will be consummated. He at times does not clearly distinguish the translation of the saints with the second coming of Christ. Chafer apparently uses the term "second coming" to encompass both the translation of the Church before the tribulation period and the return of the Church before the establishment of the millennium.[45] The former occurs before the seven-year period while the latter occurs at the conclusion of the seven years. An example of an unclear statement by Chafer concerning the translation is: "Whether it be that coming of Christ to the earth in glory when Israel is to be delivered or that coming into the air to receive His Bride, the coming is imminent.... In both instances the return of Christ is unannounced and therefore impending."[46]

Chafer often spoke of imminency, but at times does not distinguish between the rapture and the second coming; thus, this lack of distinction causes confusion. A clearer presentation of the two events is the following:

> A clear distinction should be observed between the Scriptures which announce the coming of Christ into the air to receive His Bride, the Church, ... and those Scriptures which announce the coming of Christ to the earth in power and great glory, ... in the first event the movement is upward from earth to heaven, as in 1 Thessalonians 4:16-17 ... in the second advent the movement is downward from heaven to earth, as in Revelation 19:11-16. These events, though not always clearly distinguished in every Scripture, are naturally classified by the character of conditions and incidents accompanying them.[47]

The Resurrections

Chafer does not believe in a general resurrection at the end of the age, but he believes a correct interpretation of the Scriptures teaches three resurrections. In Chafer's thought, the various resurrections actually show a unity. God's resurrection program for the Church is specifically identified, as is a resurrection for Israel and a final resurrection for the Gentiles, or those outside of the faith. At the time of the translation of the Church, the Church age saints will be resurrected. Chafer sees the Old Testament passage of Daniel 12:1-3 as promising a resurrection for Israel at the completion of the seven-year period; some will be raised to life while others to everlasting comtempt.[48] However, the doctrine of the resurrection of the Christian is contained in two parts. First, he has already been raised spiritually and seated with Christ, according to Ephesians 2:6.

Second, if the believer dies and does not experience the rapture, his body is yet to be raised.[49] Chafer believes the Christian "may go the way of death and resurrection, or he may go by translation; yet a standardized reality awaits him. He will have a body like unto Christ's glorious body (Phil. 3:20-21)."[50] Chafer expresses his thinking concerning this subject:

> As to be expected, there is a central and exhaustive portion of Scripture bearing on so great a theme as the resurrection of the believer's body; and that Scripture is 1 Corinthians 15:20-23; 35-37. In the first section — 15:20-23 — the resurrection of the believer's body is seen in its order as preceded by the resurrection of Christ, with the present period between the first and second advents intervening, and followed by the resurrection of all humanity — which resurrection is termed "the end" resurrection, or the last in the order of resurrections (cf. Rev. 20:12-15) — and separated from the believer's resurrection by Christ's reign and authority which must continue until all enemies are under His feet.[51]

There is a logical order, then, according to Chafer. Christ's own resurrection is the prototype for all future resurrections. At the same moment of the translation of the saints, those who have died in the Lord since the beginning of the Church age will be resurrected into the presence of the Lord. At the end of the tribulation period, the resurrection of the tribulation saints as well as the Old Testament saints will occur. The unsaved dead will be resurrected at the close of the millennial reign of Christ.[52] This company of people will be judged according to their works and not by grace because of their lack of standing in Christ. Their judgment will follow immediately after their resurrection.[53] Chafer explains the two classes of humanity:

> From this Scripture [John 5:25, 28, 29] it is clear that all — both good and evil — are to be raised from the dead at the command of the Son of God, and while, at the present time, there is some difference to be observed between the saved and

the lost, it is not until the resurrection that men find themselves separated into an unalterable two-fold classification with eternal destinies assigned which are removed from each other as Heaven is removed from hell.[54]

The key passage, of course, for Chafer is Revelation 20:4,5. The first resurrection alludes to those who will perish during the tribulation period while the "rest of the dead" refers to that vast company of unredeemed who have died out of grace.

How does Chafer understand the nature of the resurrected body of the redeemed?

> An exception to his clear teaching on the universality of the resurrection of bodies of Christians is the abrupt statement that "we shall not all sleep" (1 Cor. 15:51), that is, not all Christians are to experience death. By these arresting words a hitherto unrevealed purpose of God, here termed a *mystery*, is disclosed. As elsewhere declared, some will be alive and remain unto the coming of the Lord (1 Thess. 4:15-17); but these do not enter heaven in the present body of limitation. For these, this body will be changed, and that "in a moment, in the twinkling of an eye" (vss. 51-52). The change here indicated is not with respect to residence, though such a change is determined (1 Thess. 4:17), but rather the change is one of the nature of the body itself....[55]

The Tribulation Period

Chafer understands the seven-year period of tribulation to be a future event. The Church will be taken out before this occurrence. He recognizes the tribulation as one of the major highways of prophecy which can be traced through the Scriptures, and he supports his beliefs from the following passages: Daniel 12:1; Matthew 24:9-26; 2 Thessalonians 2:1-12; Revelation 3:10; 6:1 - 19:6.[56] He explains the tribulational period:

The great tribulation is the period known as Daniel's seventieth week (Daniel 9:24-27), the order of events being the same in Daniel as in Matthew 24 and 2 Thessalonians 2. The final week or heptad is seven years in duration, which is proved by the fact that it was exactly 69 x 7 years between the order to rebuild Jerusalem and the cutting off of Messiah. The remaining seventieth "week" of years belongs to Israel's age and will be characterized by the same general conditions as obtained in the past Jewish age. The time is shortened a little (Matt. 24:22). It is known as "the time of Jacob's trouble" (Jer. 30:4-7) out of which Israel will be saved. The great tribulation is the time of God's unavoidable judgments on a Christ-rejecting world (Ps. 2:5). It is characterized by:
1. The removal of the Holy Spirit together with the Church from the earth (2 Thess. 2:7)
2. The casting of Satan into, thus restricting him to, the earth (Rev. 9-12).
3. The development of sin which was hitherto restrained (2 Thess. 2:11).
4. The rule of the man of sin (John 5:43).
5. Termination by the second coming of Christ, the battle of Armageddon, and the smiting stone of Daniel 2.[57]

The tribulation period is a time in which Israel will be chastised; she is brought to her knees because of perpetual rejection of God as revealed in Christ. It will be a period of purging in order that she may enter the millennial kingdom. Chafer believes that "at the end of this age, Israel must pass through the great tribulation, which is specifically characterized as 'the time of Jacob's trouble' (Jer. 30:4-7; Dan. 12:1; Matt. 24:21); and, before entering her kingdom, she must come before her King in judgment."[58] According to Chafer, the times of the Gentiles will be completed with the end of the seven-year period. Chafer says:

> Whatever belongs to the Gentile times began with the Babylonian captivity and aside from the intercalary age of the Church is revived and consummated in the yet 7 future years....

Again, the purpose of the great tribulation is wholly extraneous to the Church. That period is declared to be for the final judgments of God upon a God-and-Christ-rejecting world. It is the ending of the *cosmos* system. Over against this, the Church is neither a part of the *cosmos* ... nor is she ever to be brought into condemning judgment (John 5:24; Rom. 8:1).[59]

The Judgments

Chafer is convinced the Scriptures do not each one general judgment; he holds to eight judgments:

Again, many theologians have erred greatly in contending there is one general judgment and in seeking to merge several other judgments into this particular one. For instance they are convinced that the judgment of the nations (Matt. 25:31-46) is the same as the judgment of the great white throne (Rev. 11:15).[60]

He enumerates the judgments as the judgment of the cross, self, believers, the believers' works, Israel, the nations, angels, and unbelievers at the Great White Throne.[61] However, he devotes most of his thought to only three: the judgment of the works of the believer, the judgment of the nations, and the Great White Throne judgment. Chafer sees three essential judgments as they portray the distinction between the sheep and the goats, or those who are redeemed and those who are lost.

Why is a correct understanding of the judgments important to Chafer? The Judgment Seat of Christ gives incentive to believers. At this judgment, the believer will not be judged according to his sins, but only according to the merits he has performed for the Lord during his journey upon earth. A correct understanding of this judgment on the part of the believer acts as an incentive for one to give of his best to the Master daily. The Great White Throne judgment gives confidence to the child of God that he will not stand before God to have his works reviewed in a negative manner, and this last judgment is specifically for those outside of God's grace. The judgment of the nations is in a sense at the heart of his premillennialism, as it will determine who will enter the kingdom.

> In the context of Matthew, chapters 24 and 25, and continuing to 25:31, Christ is seen executing judgment over regathered Israel. Beginning with 25:31, He is seen judging the nations, which judgment is to determine who among the nations shall enter the kingdom prepared for them from the foundation of the world (Matt. 25:34).... The test in this judgment will be the treatment the nations will have accorded to Israel, who are here called by the Lord "my brethren." This is not a reference to the Church; that company will have been with the Lord in heaven and will have returned with Him to reign (Rev. 19:7-14) before He sits upon the throne of His glory. The "brethren" are Israel — His brethren according to the flesh.[62]

There are reasons why the judgment of the nations has not been fully understood or even recognized. First, there is a failure to recognize Israel and her relationship to other nations. Second, there has been a general failure to comprehend the importance of Israel as the chosen people of God. "They are dear to Him as the apple of His eye, and are graven on His hand (Isa. 49:16)."[63] Chafer believes that "the kingdom belongs to Israel, and only the nations who have proven themselves kindly disposed to that people are to be permitted to share their earthly glory."[64] Furthermore, Chafer says:

> The judgment of the nations, which prepares for the kingdom, is too often confused with the final Great White Throne judgment with which the kingdom ends. The judgment of the nations is distinctly said to be at the Second Coming of Christ. There is no resurrection, the throne of judgment is on earth ... and no books are opened. All of this is in contrast to those conditions which are predicted for the judgment of the Great White Throne (Rev. 20:11-15).[65]

The believer's judgment will differ from the Great White Throne judgment. At the accounting of the Great White Throne, God will judge the unbeliever according to his works because all who are present at this judgment do not have saving faith. The result of this judgment is eternal separation from God. At the judgment of believers, each one stands before Christ, justified by faith. But what a radical difference! He will never be separated from God's presence because of personal saving faith in Christ. His works will be judged, but this judgment will not determine each person's eternal destiny but only his rewards or loss of rewards. Chafer calls this judgment of believers, the "Judgment Seat of Christ." He writes:

> The saved, when standing before the judgment seat of Christ at His coming, are judged according to their works, and this judgment does not determine whether they are saved or lost; it rather determines the reward or loss of reward for service which will be due each individual believer.[66]

Passages which pertain to this judgment include 1 Corinthians 3:9-15 and 1 Corinthians 9:16-27. This judgment occurs in heaven sometime after the translation of the saints.[67] Chafer says:

> All the saved must come before the ... judgment seat of Christ. This experience occurs in spite of the assurance given by John 5:24 that the child of God shall not come into judgment. Although his sins have been judged at the cross and will not be brought up again, at the judgment seat of Christ his works or service must be judged.[68]

This judgment Chafer sees in a very positive light; fear is kept at a minimum and the motivation is for the Christian to live life to the fullest. "The doctrine of rewards is the necessary counterpart of the doctrine of salvation by grace."[69] Chafer claims this judgment "is more for the bestowing of rewards than for the rejection of failure; and it is clearly asserted in 1 Corinthians 4:5 that, in spite of every failure, every (Christian) ... shall have praise of God."[70]

Chafer sees the Bible teaching that the Christian life is compared to a race, and it is only through much effort on the individual's part that he can in the end, when his works are judged, expect to obtain a reward from his Lord. This anticipation calls for obedience and a daily reliance upon the grace of God.

The Great White Throne judgment is the third judgment to which Chafer devotes considerable thought. Though Chafer's life and thought are characterized by grace and the love of God, he believes that the Scriptures teach that God, even though He has infinite love for the sinner, will commit the unrepentant sinner to eternal retribution. His years as an evangelist had instilled in his thinking both the love and the justice of God. Chafer believes:

> That all unsaved humanity must be raised to judgment is taught by Christ in John 5:28-29. Nobody has any authority to modify the terrible revelation that God has made in connection with the final reckoning. The Word of God must stand as it is.[71]

Chafer, then, understands Revelation 20:11-15 as the major passage which illustrates the Great White Throne judgment. He understands this judgment as the greatest numerically since the unregenerate from all periods of time will stand before God, who will judge them according to their works. Their fate will be final — eternal separation from God, but there will be the need for determining the extent of punishment in accordance with the measure of sin. What is the nature of this judgment?

> This, the final judgment which consummates the judgment of the cross and the judgment of all people who are unredeemed, occurs at the close of the millennium. These people will be raised for that judgment and will be judged according to their works.... The doom that awaits them is terrible beyond comprehension; for it is the last word of a holy God respecting sin and all unrighteousness.[72]

Chafer states that the tendency is to confuse the Great White Throne judgment with the judgment of nations. At the former, there will only be the unregenerate while at the latter there will be sheep and goats, that is, saved and unsaved. The judgment of nations will occur on earth while the Great White Throne will take place in space. At the judgment of the nations, the issue will be the treatment of the Jew while at the Great White Throne, it will be evil works which are judged. At the judgment of nations, some enter the kingdom while others enter the lake of fire, and all those judged at the Great White Throne will enter the lake of fire.

Chafer believes in the reality of a future judgment. His dispensationalism and premillennialism led him to the conclusion that there are eight judgments, though he primarily emphasizes only three, those of the judgment of the believer's works, the judgment of nations and the judgment of the unregenerate.

The Millennium

Chafer believes that only with the personal coming of Christ will the millennium be established. Though he holds the preaching of the gospel in high esteem, even this medium will not initiate the thousand-year reign of Christ. The millennium will be a foretaste of the eternal estate itself. The world will be restored. The judgment of the nations will assure that only those who are the Lord's sheep will be allowed to enter.

One must keep in mind the essential premise upon which Chafer has built his doctrine of the kingdom:

> One of the greatest errors of theologians is an attempt as essayed now, to build a kingdom on the first advent of Christ as its basis, whereas according to the Scriptures it will be realized only in connection with the second advent. All Scriptures conform to this arrangement, strange though it may look.[73]

The first advent resulted in the death and resurrection of Christ. Though He won victory over darkness, sin, Chafer believes, still reigns and will continue until the second advent itself.

The Covenants and Their Relationship to the Millennium

The promise that the kingdom will occur is grounded in the Abrahamic and Davidic covenants. The covenants act as a thread of unity throughout the dispensations. These two are unconditional; thus, their fulfillment is assured. With the Abrahamic covenant, Abraham's seed was promised to become an everlasting nation. This is an unconditional covenant, Chafer believes, and even though Israel spurned the offer given to them by God, the promise given to Abraham will still be fulfilled. The covenant was made in Genesis 12, and Chafer sees it continuing to the end of the New Testament. The Palestinian covenant, which Chafer views as an outgrowth of the Abrahamic, was first announced to Abraham and then reiterated to Isaac and Jacob. It is seen more fully in Deuteronomy 30:3-8. The Palestinian covenant extends the land to Abraham and his physical seed, and it is an everlasting covenant.

The Davidic covenant and its promises are contained in 2 Samuel 7:16. Chafer writes:

> Since the coming theocratic kingdom is the divine objective with respect to the earth and since it forms the national hope of Israel, the covenant with David which introduces the revelation of the kingdom declares the precise nature of all this.... This earthly kingdom, the throne, and the King are among the dominant themes of the Old Testament. The revelation respecting these great features in the Davidic covenant is both explicit and extended. Difficulty arises only for those who are determined to metamorphose a literal, earthly throne and kingdom into some vague and wholly imaginary spiritual idealism.[74]

Chafer believes there is only one reservation in the covenant — that those succeeding David would be chastised — and this event is seen in the Babylonian captivity. Nevertheless, the terms of the covenant will not be destroyed.[75] Chafer traces Scripture to portray the promises of this fact in both the Old and New Testaments. He draws from Isaiah 9:6-7, Hosea 3:4-5, Luke 1:31-32, Acts 2:25-31, and Revelation 22:16.[76] All of these passages show the reigning King will be of the line of David. Chafer, then, interprets literally these passages and sees Christ as fulfilling the requirements of the King who will reign.

The Teachings of Christ Concerning the Millennium

There are two major teachings of Christ concerning times future to Him, and these are the Olivet Discourse and the Sermon on the Mount. Chafer sees the former pertaining to the time of tribulation upon the earth. However, both are addressed to Israel. The Olivet Discourse is contained in Matthew 24 and 25. According to Chafer, the discourse begins with a description of the tribulation period and concludes with the judgments which will fall upon Israel and then the nations. The Church is not present in the Gospel of Matthew, thus, the address is given only to Israel. Chafer says:

> The disciples knew nothing of the present Church age (cf. Acts 1:6-7) and therefore could have known nothing of its end. They were living in the Mosaic age, the latter part of which Daniel had predicted would continue for 490 years. He predicted also that the last seven years of that period — Daniel's seventieth week — would be the time of the greatest human upheaval, including the great tribulation, and the presence of the man of sin.... In other words, the great tribulation and the man of sin belong to the Mosaic age that is past and are wholly unrelated to the present age of the Church.[77]

According to Chafer, the gospel of the kingdom will also be preached during the time of tribulation. The Olivet discourse speaks of judgment upon Israel and the Lord's coming in glory with the heavenly hosts. His coming marks the end of the time of tribulation. The next event to occur on the prophetic calendar is the thousand-year reign.

The Sermon on the Mount is the second important eschatological message which Christ spoke. This message is found in Matthew 5, 6, 7, and Chafer believes its primary application is not to the present age of grace but to the kingdom period.[78]

Chafer remarks that the sermon itself commences with the proclamation of blessedness to those whose quality of spiritual life meets specific requirements. During the kingdom reign, a paradox will exist — the humble in spirit will reign. Chafer explains the requirements:

> If the warnings respecting hell fire do not fit into the grace system — and they do not — it is because the entire kingdom program of relationship and conduct is far removed from that which belongs to grace. The kingdom rule of life is an extension of the Mosaic system in the direction of a more drastic law; it is not the modification of law in the direction of grace. To say as some have done that they accept the Sermon on the Mount as the rule of their lives, but omit those portions which threaten hell fire, is to disregard the revealed truth respecting the law, namely, that someone who assumes the least portion of it is a debtor to do the whole law (cf. Gal. 5:3; James 2:10).[79]

The Announcement of the Kingdom

John the Baptist announced with great vigor the coming of the kingdom. Chafer understands that John the Baptist fulfilled the prophetic words of Isaiah 40:3, which states: "A voice of one calling in the desert prepare the way for the Lord; make straight in the wilderness a highway for our God." Chafer points out that those who are opposed to premillennialism have a problem with John the Baptist. Those who advocate a spiritual kingdom or no kingdom must minimize John's message, or even say that he was mistaken. Chafer believes that John came preaching a literal, earthly kingdom to be established by the Messiah.[80] Chafer recognizes that John's message was not one of salvation by faith in Christ, "But rather to a correction of daily life on the part of those who should be thus prepared for their King."[81] The kingdom message, then, had been offered by Christ and Israel rejected this offer. The message will again be offered to the same people, and if accepted, they will be allowed to enter the kingdom itself.

The Conditions of the Kingdom

Only those who have passed through the tribulation period and have been judged as sheep will be allowed to enter the kingdom. Chafer explains:

> Some will have nourished Israel and some will have afflicted them.... Some inherit their share — according to much prophecy — in Israel's kingdom and as designed by the Father from the foundation of the world; those that have afflicted Israel are dismissed into the lake of fire prepared for the devil and his angels. They go to the lake of fire on the ground of their lost estate and as those who are not prepared to enter the kingdom.[82]

Chafer recognizes the Scriptures teach that there are three classes of nations at the judgment of the nations. The designation, "my brethren," alludes to Israel herself while the "sheep" refers to those who spiritually belong to God. The designation "goats," speaks to those who have rejected God. Does the judgment of the nations concern literal nations or individuals? Chafer explains:

> The question inevitably intrudes as to whether this judgment is of nations as entities, or of the individual people who comprise the nations. There are arguments advanced in support of each contention. It is likely that to some extent both claims are true.... It should not be overlooked that even now, as never before, the nations are taking sides for or against the Jew. Among those favorable there are individuals who are anti-semitic, and among those unfavorable there are those who are semitic in their sympathies. The King alone can and will render the right judgment.[83]

Gentiles will enter the kingdom too, but only those who have been gracious to Israel, and these individuals will be subservient to Israel.[84]

The means by which one is in a covenanted relationship with God during the millennial age is not conditioned upon grace, as in the present age. Chafer sees the beatitudes as a kingdom message:

> The intense emphasis on the covenant of meritorious works

is obvious in this message; but John did not preach Moses and the prophets. The law and the prophets were *until* John. It is to be concluded that the preaching of John the Baptist was wholly new, and was according to his mission as herald of the King; but that message is legalistic and not gracious. It is a covenant of works and not a covenant of faith.[85]

Chafer, then, recognizes that the emphasis during the kingdom will be on conduct and righteousness. He claims that "kingdom teaching extends into finer detail the law of Moses and never ceases to be the very opposite of the principle of grace."[86] Chafer enumerates three characteristics of the kingdom message: (1) the message is that of the kingdom of heaven, or the earthly reign of Christ; (2) two key words in the kingdom are those of "righteousness" and " peace"; (3) the kingdom teachings are based upon a covenant of works.[87] Chafer believes the kingdom teachings have never been applied to any individual:

> The teachings of the kingdom have not been applied to men in all ages; nay, more they have not yet been applied to any man. Since they anticipate the binding of Satan, a purified earth, and restoration of Israel, and the personal reign of the King, they cannot be applied until God's appointed time when these accompanying conditions on the earth have been brought to pass.[88]

The King will reign with an iron hand; iniquity will be punished immediately and all forms of sin will be judged in perfect righteousness. There are at least five characteristics of the kingdom: (1) the kingdom will be theocratic; (2) the kingdom will be heavenly in character; (3) it will be over regathered and converted Israel; (4) the kingdom will be established by the returning King; (5) the reign will be spiritual.[89] In summary, the King will reign over His people, and His authority will be unquestioned.

Satan, Chafer believes, will be bound at the beginning of the millennial reign; therefore, he cannot entice the saints. Chafer comments:

> The Scriptures abundantly testify that, while there will be far

less occasion to sin, for the sufficient reason that Satan is then bound and in a pit and the glorious King is on His throne, there will be need of immediate execution of judgment and justice in the earth, and even the King shall rule, of necessity, with a "rod of iron."[90]

There will be a limited amount of evil manifested in the millennium because it will be judged quickly. Chafer refers to three sources of sin: Satan, the world system or *cosmos*, and the flesh. the latter is the only one of the three which will be present during the millennial period. The reality of the lust of the flesh is ever-pervasive; therefore, the Lord must rule with an iron hand.

Chafer does not go into great detail concerning what the condition of the environment will be during the millennial reign of Christ. He does, however, quote Isaiah 11:6-9, which refers to the subduing of the animal kingdom. If interpreted literally, Isaiah 55:12-13 speaks of the absence of thorns and briars. Micah 4:3 anticipates a time when the nations will know no more war. The promise of God's total forgiveness of the sins of Israel is promised in Jeremiah 31:33-34. The millennium is a time of peace.

The Close of the Millennial Period

The thousand-year reign of Christ will close with specific and cataclysmic events just as the age of law had closed with the death of Christ and the age of grace will close with the translation of the saints. Chafer argues there are seven events which mark the transition from the kingdom age to eternity:

> There are seven stupendous events which mark the transition to be wrought between the kingdom age and eternity to come: (1) the release of Satan from the abyss, (2) the revolt on earth with judgments upon Satan and his armies, (3) the passing of the old heaven and the old earth, (4) the great white throne judgment, (5) creation of a new heaven and a new earth, (6) the descent of the bridal city from God out of heaven, and (7) the surrender of the mediatorial aspect of Christ's reign; and adjustment to the eternal state following immediately.[91]

Chafer's Millennialism

The release of Satan occurs at the end of the kingdom age; he bases his interpretation for this event upon Revelation 19:7-8. Satan, then, is the catalyst behind a final battle on earth, which Chafer terms Gog and Magog. Chafer vividly writes concerning the conduct of this fallen angel:

> Thus it is intimated that Satan is ever deceiving the nations, excepting for the period of his biding and until his final dismissal to the lake of fire. Much like the unceasing pressure of the sin nature on the individual's life is the influence of Satan upon the mass of humanity, inciting to war, greed, self manifestations, and impious conduct. What even a day's release of the individual from the pressure of the sin nature would mean in actual experience or a day's release for humanity from the deceptions of Satan cannot be imagined.... It will be noted that the last army to be assembled will be drawn from the four quarters of the earth and "Gog and Magog;" which designation is perhaps more a reference to the event in question than to any locality or specific peoples.[92]

Chafer looks to Revelation 20 to substantiate that the present order of the earth and heavens will pass away. The final resurrection and the Great White Throne judgment are events which are concerned with the same class of people, those who are unregenerate. According to Revelation 21:1, a new heaven and earth will be created. Chafer believes:

> It may yet be observed that, in this picture of the new earth, the all-important feature is that "the tabernacle of God" will be with men. Such a situation has not obtained before. Earth has been the sphere of sin and corruption unsuited to the presence of God; but it will then be as holy as heaven, and in the new earth He will delight to dwell among men and to be their God.[93]

Chafer claims the heavenly city will come into view for those who are upon the earth. Chafer finds his biblical support for the city from Revelation 21.

Chafer calls attention to the debate concerning the mediatorial role of Christ in the future. Some Bible scholars think Christ will withdraw as King at the end of the thousand-year reign, according to 1 Corinthians 15:24-28. However, Chafer believes there are literally scores of passages which state the opposite; Christ will reign forever on the throne of David. Such passages include 2 Samuel 7:16; Psalm 89:3-4, 34-37; Hebrews 1:8; Jeremiah 33:14-17, 20-21; and Ezekiel 37:24-28. Chafer answers the problem by stating that Christ will still reign as He always has, under the rule and authority of the Father. The authority for Christ's kingship is an outgrowth of His deity. "He will, as so fully assured elsewhere, reign on the throne of David forever."[94]

Dispensational Premillennialism as Central to Chafer's Thought

Dispensational premillennialism is of primary importance in Chafer's understanding and interpretation of the Scripture. In every volume of Chafer's *Systematic Theology* a dispensational, premillennial interpretation is woven into each doctrine. The question arises as to why it is important for Chafer to interpret with such a method. Concerning the millennium itself, why is it essential for Chafer to understand the millennium as literal? If the millennium is fulfilled in the Church or in heaven by the saints, then the prophecies which promise a literal kingdom are not to be understood literally but are spiritualized away. The covenants, such as the Davidic covenant, are not seen to be literally fulfilled in the future by Christ, but are again somehow fulfilled by the reigning Church during the present period, according to the Reformed position.

Premillennialism, according to Chafer, claims the Church cannot be found in the Old Testament; the Church did not begin until Pentecost. However, the Reformed understanding is that the Church can be found in the Old Testament. This view says that there is not a separate future program for the Church; she will not be raptured and taken out in order that the tribulation, God's special program for Israel, may occur. In amillennial eschatology, there is no other age after the present; hence, there is not a future for Israel. The Church today is Israel and inherits all the promises given to her. What a vast difference, then, exists between dispensational premillennialism and the amillennial understanding of the nature of the Church. The promise to Israel of a literal kingdom is a theme throughout the Scriptures, and this theme gives a unity to Chafer's dispensational, premillennial thought.

There is also a difference in the area of the Holy Spirit. Chafer, along with a majority of dispensational premillennialists, stresses the peculiar work of the Holy Spirit during this present age. Since the time of the recording of the work of the Spirit in the book of Acts, the Spirit has been with the Church. Chafer emphasizes that there is a distinct ministry of the Holy Spirit during the age of grace; however, the amillennial position tends to treat the work of the Holy Spirit as the same in all ages. The dispensationalist claims the Spirit came upon an individual temporarily in the Old Testament, whereas in the present era, the indwelling is of a permanent nature.

This is why Chafer gave so much attention to the work of the Holy Spirit in his book, *He that is Spiritual*. During this present age the spiritual life is enhanced by allowing the Spirit of God to control the individual's walk with God. Reformed theology tends to say that the Spirit regenerated individuals in the Old Testament while the dispensationalist does not.

Dispensational premillennialism, as articulated by Chafer, stresses a difference in angelology in comparison to an amillennial view. The latter perspective minimizes angels, ignores them, or even denies their existence. Concerning Satan, Chafer is emphatic. Those who hold to the amillennial view believe a binding of Satan has occurred, and that to a degree, his power has been curtailed. Chafer stresses that the Scriptures refer to him as the "god of this world" who is raging in demonic activity even against the Church. Chafer believes that the binding of Satan is yet future, and it will occur at the beginning of the millennium. At the end of the thousand-year reign, he will again be loosed for a short period, after which he will be eternally damned. Chafer, then, has a greatly contrasting view of the power of Satan and his present role in the world and his relationship to the Church.

Concerning eschatology itself, as has already been displayed, there is a great divergence between the Reformed and dispensational, premillennial methods. Both positions hold to the essential doctrines of the second coming of Christ, the resurrection of the dead, the final judgment, and the eternal estate. But with the amillennial position, these events all occur in quick succession and are intimately associated with the second coming itself. Concerning a period of tribulation, the amillennial position typically understands this period sometime before the second advent of Christ. There is then, no literal calculating of the seventieth week of Daniel 9 and interpreting this last week as the tribulation itself. Dispensational premillennialism, as seen in Chafer's writings, interprets in a literal fashion this last prophetic week and claims it pertains to a period after the Church is raptured. An example is the judgment found in Matthew 25:31-46. The dispensational premillennialist claims this judgment pertains to a judgment of the nations to decide who will enter the millennium. This view is held since nothing is said in the passage about resurrected individuals appearing before God, neither is anything mentioned about the Church. The dispensationalist claims only the nations, or the Gentiles, are mentioned. Amillennial theology, however, traditionally has interpreted this passage as the last judgment itself; it is the final separation of those who will either be in the presence of God or eternally separated from Him. Here again, the vast difference in interpretation between dispensational premillennialism and Reformed theology is evident.

Conclusion

Dispensational premillennialism is the crowning conclusion of Lewis Sperry Chafer's eschatology. He was apparently convinced that a postmillennial or an amillennial approach is not intellectually and experientially defensible. Chafer was aware of the standard interpretations of eschatology since he had read works by Hodge and Warfield. But he was convinced they were especially amiss in their interpretation of Revelation 20 and their interpretation of the first and second resurrections contained in verses five and six of that chapter. Chafer argues that there is prophecy concerning the kingdom age, and that prophecy and its fulfillment are as certain as the fulfillment and record of historical sections of the Scriptures. The golden age is yet future, but it is assured. There are specific

Chafer's Millennialism

events which must take place relative to the kingdom. The present age of grace will continue until the translation of the saints occurs, at which time the seventieth week of Daniel will commence. This period is terminated by the Battle of Armageddon. Chafer as well as other dispensationalists believe that Armageddon will begin near the Hill of Megiddo on an extended plain in Northern Palestine. However, it is believed that all of Palestine will be engulfed in warfare by several Middle East countries. Chafer believes that Revelation 19:17-21 teaches Christ will defeat this Middle East coalition at the time of the Second Coming. The saints will have already experienced their judgment at the Judgment Seat of Christ. The judgment of the nations will determine who will enter the millennial kingdom over which the Lord Himself will rule. The millennium will be terminated by a battle, Gog and Magog, and the outcome is that all evil principalities will be defeated. The heavens and the earth will be recreated and the eternal state will commence.

Notes: Chapter 4

1. Lewis Sperry Chafer, *The Kingdom in History and Prophecy* (New York: Fleming H. Revell Co., 1915; reprint ed., Philadelphia: *The Sunday School Times*, 1926), p. 17.

2. Lewis Sperry Chafer, "An Introduction to the Study of Prophecy," *Bibliotheca Sacra* 100 (January 1943):108-09.

3. Ibid.

4. Lewis Sperry Chafer, *Systematic Theology*, vol. 4: *Ecclesiology-Eschatology* (Dallas: Dallas Seminary Press, 1948), p. 271.

5. Chafer, *The Kingdom in History and Prophecy*, p. 15.

6. George Elden Ladd, *Crucial Questions about the Kingdom of God* (Grand Rapids: Wm. B. Eerdmans Publishing o., 1952), pp. 22-23.

7. Charles Hodge, *Systematic Theology*, vol. 3: *Soteriology* (New York: Charles Scribner & Co., 1872; reprint ed., Wm. B. Eerdmans Publishing Co., 1940), p. 792.

8. Ibid., pp. 840-41.

9. Ibid., p. 840.

10. Ibid., p. 841.

11. Ibid., p. 856.

12. Ibid., p. 857.

13. Ibid., pp. 858-59.

14. Ibid., p. 859.

15. Archibald A. Hodge, *Outlines of Theology* (n.p.:Robert Carter & Bros., 1878; rewritten & enl., New York: A. C. Armstrong & Son, 1895), p. 568.

16. Ibid.

17. Ibid., p. 571.

18. Ibid., p. 570.

19. Benjamim B. Warfield, "The Millennium and the Apocalypse," *Princeton Theological Review* 2 (October 1904):601; Cf. Benjamin B. Warfield "The Book of Revelation," in *Selected Shorter Writings of Benjamin B. Warfield*, ed. John E. Meeter (Nutley, New Jersey: Presbyterian & Reformed Publishing co., 1973), pp. 87-89.

20. Benjamin B. Warfield, "The Gospel and the Second Coming," in *Selected Shorter Writings of Benjamin B. Warfield*, p. 349.

21. Warfield, "The Millennium and the Apocalypse," p. 602.

22. Warfield, "The Gospel and the Second Coming," pp. 349-51.

23. Warfield, "The Millennium and The Apocalypse," pp. 605-06.

24. Ibid., p. 607.

25. Ibid.

26. Ibid., p. 611.

27. Ibid., p. 615.

28. Ibid., p. 616.

29. Ibid.

30. Lewis Sperry Chafer, *Systematic Theology*, vol. 1:*Prolegomena-Bibliology-Theology Proper* (Dallas: Dallas Seminary Press, 1947), pp. xxxii-xxxiii.

31. Lewis Sperry Chafer, *Major Bible Themes* (Dallas: Dallas Theological Seminary, 1926; rev. ed., Grand Rapids: Dunham Publications, 1964), p. 265.

32. Chafer, *The Kingdom in History and Prophecy*, p. 26.

33. Ibid., pp. 26-27.

34. Chafer, *Major Bible Themes*, p. 266.

35. Chafer, *The Kingdom in History and Prophecy*, pp. 27-38.

36. Chafer, *Major Bible Themes*, p. 266.

37. Chafer, *Prolegomena-Bibliology-Theology Proper*, pp. xxxiv-xxxv.

38. Chafer, *Major Bible Themes*, p. 270.

39. Chafer, *Ecclesiology-Eschatology*, pp. 306-07.

40. Ibid., p. 395.

41. Ibid., p. 310.

42. Ibid., p; 311.

43. Ibid., p. 313.

44. Ibid., pp. 10-11.

45. Lewis Sperry Chafer, *Systematic Theology*, vol. 5: *Christology* (Dallas: Dallas Seminary Press, 1948), pp. 128-40.

46. Chafer, *Ecclesiology-Eschatology*, p. 367.

47. Chafer, *Christology*, p. 288.

48. Chafer, *Ecclesiology-Eschatology*, p. 23.

49. Ibid., pp. 32-34.

50. Ibid., p. 124.

51. Ibid.

52. Lewis Sperry Chafer, *Systematic Theology*, vol. 2: *Angelology-Anthropology-Hamartiology* (Dallas: Dallas Seminary Press, 1948) p. 154, and also in Lewis Sperry Chafer, *Must We Dismiss the Millennim?* (Crescent City, Florida: Biblical Testimony League, 1921), p. 12.

53. Chafer, *Major Bible Themes*, pp. 294-95.

54. Ibid., p. 294.

55. Chafer, *Angelology-Anthropology-Harmartiology*, pp. 152-53.

56. Lewis Sperry Chafer, *Systematic Theology*, vol. 7: *Doctrinal Summarization* (Dallas: Dallas Seminary Press, 1948), p. 306.

57. Ibid., p. 307.

58. Chafer, *Ecclesiology-Eschatology*, pp. 10-11.

59. Ibid., pp. 364-65.

60. Chafer, *Doctrinal Summarization*, pp. 213-214.

61. Ibid., pp. 213-16.

62. Chafer, *Major Bible Themes*, p. 290.

63. Ibid., p. 291.

64. Ibid.

65. Ibid., p. 292.

66. Ibid., p. 283-84.

67. Chafer, *Ecclesiology-Eschatology*, p. 406.

68. Chafer, *Doctrinal Summarization,* p. 215.

69. Chafer, *Major Bible Themes*, p. 286.

70. Chafer, *Ecclesiology-Eschatology*, p. 406.

71. Chafer, *Doctrinal Summarization*, p. 217.

72. Chafer, *Ecclesiology-Eschatology*, p. 411-12.

73. Chafer, *Doctrinal Summarization*, p. 224.

74. Chafer, *Christology*, p. 321.

75. Ibid.

76. Ibid., pp. 323-29.

77. Ibid., pp. 119-20.

78. Ibid., p. 97.

79. Ibid., p. 108.

80. Chafer, *Ecclesiology-Eschatology*, p. 293.

81. Ibid., p. 294.

82. Lewis Sperry Chafer, "What Will God Do with the Cosmos?" in *Light for the World's Darkness,* ed. John W. Bradbury (New York: Loizeaux Bros., 1944), p. 110.

83. Lewis Sperry Chafer, "The Future of the Gentiles." *Moody Monthly* 4 (November 1940):155.

84. Ibid., p. 156.

85. Chafer, *Ecclesiology-Eschatology*, pp. 214-15.

86. Chafer, *Christology*, p. 344.

87. Chafer, *Ecclesiology-Eschatology*, pp. 215-16.

88. Ibid., p. 207.

89. Chafer, *Christology*, pp. 334-40.

90. Ibid., p. 346.

91. Ibid., pp. 359-60.

92. Ibid., p. 361.

93. Ibid., p. 366.

94. Ibid., p. 374.

Conclusion

Lewis Sperry Chafer's life and theological contribution are of great significance. Specifically, this work about Chafer displays his contribution to biblical eschatology. Chafer has been somewhat overlooked, misunderstood, and even misrepresented. When one objectively views what he accomplished during his life and posthumously, the vastness of the import of his life is realized. He was the first to bring together in a unified, cohesive, and scholarly manner dispensational, premillennial eschatology by writing a systematic theology based upon such an eschatological stance.

He had a thorough understanding of evangelical eschatological thought since throughout his life he was associated with such endeavors as the Bible conference movement. He associated with the leading conservative theologians of his day. But Chafer attracts attention in that he promotes a balanced view of fundamentalism, and his life and writings are exemplary because they suggest theological differences must not divide the true Church. He is important in his influence and his role in establishing a seminary and becoming its first professor of systematic theology and president. He, with the assistance of W. H. Griffith Thomas, constructed the curriculum and doctrinal statement of Dallas Theological Seminary, today the largest nondenominational seminary in the world. His life, writings, and influence have exerted a tremendous impact upon the Church.

The biographical data explains the formative influences upon his mature eschatological thought. One sees a journey in awareness on his own part of the development and maturation of his great gifts. Even in the early years of his ministry, he questioned and searched for accuracy and precision, as was the situation with his argument against the traditional evangelistic methods of his time and his resulting work, *True Evangelism*. One does not find in Chafer a rebel or iconoclast; he was simply enamored with the belief that God's full revelation is contained in the Scriptures and that through an inductive study one can understand, though to a limited degree, the mind of God concerning the end time.

He developed traits at an early age which characterized his entire life: hard driving, responsible, able to give and receive love, but also a longing for insight into the eternal. Perhaps the loss of his father, who was a minister, at an early age, instilled these traits and desires in Chafer. His conversion experience and his lifelong remembrance that this event was by the grace of God became inbred in the warp and woof of his theological and specifically, his eschatological position.

Though it was not until Chafer was well into his middle years that he achieved recognition, his earlier life laid the foundation for the heavy responsibilities and resultant achievements. His work as an evangelistic singer, evangelist, teacher at Northfield's Mount Hermon School for Boys, pastor, and Bible teacher provided the foundation for an amazing career as professor, seminary president, and author. It is not possible to state which of these three was the most influential upon his eschatology. Each one played a vital role in the dissemination of his dispensational premillennialism. As a professor, he had intimate contact with literally thousands of students who studied his view of the end. As president of Dallas Theological Seminary, he charted the course of the seminary's doctrinal position, and as author it is not possible to judge how extensively his writings have impacted eschatological thought not only in the United States, but internationally. Many of his current disciples on a popular and academic level are better known than Chafer himself, but the fact is, his life and influence helped them.

There are three sources of Chafer's eschatological conclusions: the Northfield conferences, C. I. Scofield, and Chafer's personal study. At Northfield, he was actively involved with many who held to dispensational premillennialism. This eschatological position was a very prevalent one, and the idea must not be entertained that only an isolated individual here and there held to it. Chafer heard Moody, Webb-Peploe, A. T. Pierson, G. Campbell Morgan, George F. Pentecost, and many others. Through such individuals, Chafer was heavily exposed to dispensational premillennialism. The collective impact of the speakers at

Conclusion

Northfield influenced Chafer.

The man who exerted the greatest impact on Lewis Sperry Chafer's eschatology was C. I. Scofield. In a sense, Chafer found in Scofield the father he had never really known. It was Scofield who altered his life and aspirations. From Scofield, he learned firsthand the importance of a dispensational, premillennial interpretation.

However, Chafer was personally convinced by arduous study that the Scriptures themselves teach dispensational premillennialism. This personal study entailed above all an inductive method of studying the Bible, and the result was a belief in the premillennial return of the Lord. Also, his personal study included the reading of many theologians' works, and in particular George N. H. Peters. Peters' *The Theocratic Kingdom* articulates a dispensational, premillennial interpretation of eschatology, and Chafer, who was most impressed with the work, quotes extensively from it.

Though he believes there are seven dispensations, he understands only three to be of primary importance, and these are the dispensations of law, grace, and kingdom. It was because of Chafer's dispensationalism that he incurred the wrath of his Reformed brethren who held to a covenantal scheme of interpretation and considered dispensationalism as somewhat heretical. Chafer's entire *Systematic Theology* is written from a dispensational, premillennial perspective, and such writers as George E. Ladd and Daniel Fuller acknowledge it as the first such work.

Dispensational premillennialism is the crowning conclusion of his millennial thought. His scheme is not as simplistic as a postmillennial or amillennial structure. There are various events which Chafer believes must occur, and specific time sequences to be fulfilled. The millennium is essentially Jewish, although other nations will be allowed to enter. The Jewish people will turn to the One whom they rejected, and this revival will take place during the time of tribulation. There is specific prophecy predicting the millennial reign of Christ and the fact that He indeed will reign with an iron hand. Chafer rejects the millennialism of the Princeton theologians, as he is convinced they have erred in not understanding the millennial reign to be earthly and a fulfillment of specific Old Testament covenants. As there was a transition from the dispensation of law and the age of grace, so too, there will be distinct events which will mark the transition from the kingdom age to the eternal estate itself. The promise of dawn, the second coming of Christ, ultimately ushers in the eternal state of light and glory.

Lewis Sperry Chafer left this earth in 1952, but the influence of his eschatology continues.

Selected Bibliography

Primary Sources

Books by Lewis Sperry Chafer

Analytical Questionnaire: First, Second, and Third Books. Dallas: Evangelical Theological College, n.d.

Dispensationalism. Dallas: Dallas Theological Seminary, 1936; rev. ed., Dallas: Dallas Seminary Press, 1951.

The Ephesian Letter. New York: Loizeaux Bros., 1935.

Grace. N.p., 1922; rev. ed., Grand Rapids: Zondervan Publishing House, 1950.

He That Is Spiritual. Foreword by John F. Walvoord. N.P., 1918; rev. ed., Grand Rapids: Zondervan Publishing House, 1967.

The Kingdom in History and Prophecy. Introduction by C. I. Scofield. New York: Fleming H. Revell Co., 1915; reprint ed., Philadelphia: The Sunday School Times, 1926.

Major Bible Themes. Dallas: Dallas Theological Seminary, 1926; rev. ed., Grand Rapids: Dunham Publications, 1964.

Must We Dismiss The Millennium? Crescent City, Florida: Biblical Testimony League, 1921.

Salvation. Introduction by W. H. Griffith Thomas. N.p., 1917; rev. ed., Grand Rapids: Zondervan Publishing House, 1955.

Satan. Foreword by C. I. Scofield. N.p., 1919; rev. ed., Grand Rapids: Zondervan Publishing House, 1964.

Selected Hymns. New York: Biglow & Main Co., n.d.

Systematic Theology. Vol. 1: *Prolegomena-Bibliology-Theology Proper*; vol. 2: *Angelology-Anthropology-Hamartiology*; vol. 3: *Soteriology*; vol. 4: *Ecclesiology-Eschatology*; vol. 5: *Christology*; vol. 6: *Pneumatology*; vol. 7: *Doctrinal Summarization*; vol. 8: *Biographical Sketch and Indexes.* Biographical Sketch of the Author by C. F. Lincoln. Dallas: Dallas Seminary Press, 1947-48.

True Evangelism. N.p., 1919; rev. ed., Grand Rapids: Zondervan Publishing House, 1967.

Articles in Periodicals and Books by Lewis Sperry Chafer

"Abiding." *Bibliotheca Sacra* 107 (January 1950):1-5.

"Adam." *Bibliotheca Sacra* 107 (April 1950):129-32.

"Adoption." *Bibliotheca Sacra* 107 (October 1950):385-86.

"After This War What?" *Bibliotheca Sacra* 101 (April 1944):129.

"All Truth." *Bibliotheca Sacra* 99 (April 1942):129-31.

"Angelology." *Bibliotheca Sacra* 98 (October 1941):389-420; 99 (January 1942):6-25; 99 (April 1942):135-36; 99 (July 1942):262-96; 99 (October 1942):391-417; 99 (1942):135-56.

"Anniversary Past," *Bibliotheca Sacra* 101 (January 1944):1.

"Annual Report of the Seminary." *Bulletin of Dallas Theological Seminary* 26 (September-October 1950).

"Anthropology." *Bibliotheca Sacra* 100 (April 1943):220-43; 100 (July 1943):354-73; 100 (October 1943):479-96; 101 (January 1944):8-29; 101 (April 1944):132-48; 101 (July 1944):264-82;

Selected Bibliography

101 (October 1944):391-402.

"Are There Two Ways To Be Saved?" *Bibliotheca Sacra* 105 (January 1948):1-2.

"Astonishing Book Sales." *Bibliotheca Sacra* 106 (January 1949):2-3.

"An Attack Upon a Book." *Bibliotheca Sacra* 104 (April 1947):130-34.

"Authors." *Bibliotheca Sacra* 100 (January 1943):3-4.

"The Baptism of the Holy Spirit." *Bibliotheca Sacra* 109 (July 1952):199-216.

"The Bible's Place in the Theological Seminary." *Bulletin of Dallas Theological Seminary* 16 (July-September 1940).

"Biblical Evangelism." *Bulletin of Dallas Theological Seminary* 20 (October-December 1944).

"Biblical Theism." *Bibliotheca Sacra* 95 (October 1938):390-416; 95 (January 1939):5-37; 96 (April 1939):138-63; 96 (July 1939):264-84; 95 (October 1939):390-404.

"Bibliology." *Bibliotheca Sacra* 94 (October 1937):389-409; 95 (January 1938):7-21; 105 (April 1938):137-56.

"The Black Story of Judas, Then and Now." *The Sunday School Times* 59 (19 May 1917):283-84.

"Breaking Bands and Casting Cords." *Bibliotheca Sacra* 96 (July 1941):257-58.

"Bullingerism." *Bibliotheca Sacra* 104 (1947):257-58.

"The Calvinistic Doctrine of Security." *Bibliotheca Sacra* 107 (1950):9-41.

"Canonicity and Authority." *Bibliotheca Sacra* 95 (1938):137-56.

"Careless Misstatements of Vital Truth." *Our Hope* 30 (March 1924):540-41.

"Dr. Rollin Thomas Chafer." *Bibliotheca Sacra* 97 (April 1940):129.

"Christian Love and Faith." *Bibliotheca Sacra* 106 (July 1949):257-58.

"Christian Problems." *Bibliotheca Sacra* 106 (January 1949):1.

"The Cognomen." *Bibliotheca Sacra* 97 uly 1940):260-61.

"The Coming Destruction of Ecclesiastical and Political Babylon." In *Light for the World's Darkness*, pp. 52-62. Edited by John W. Bradbury. New York: Loizeaux Bros., 1944.

"Congress on Propohecy." *Bibliotheca Sacra* 101 (January 1944):1-3.

"The Consummating Scripture on Security." *Bibliotheca Sacra* 107 (April 1950):136-53.

"The Cosmos, Its Beginning and Its End." *Moody Monthly* 40 (January 1940):250-51, 279.

"Daily Scripture Calendar." Our Hope 24 (June 1918):763-68; 25 (July 1918):60-64; 25 (August 1918):124-28, 25 (September 1918):188-92; 25 (October 1918):251-56; 25 (November 1918):315-20; 25 (December 1918); 378-84; 25 (January 1919):443-48; 25 (February 1919);507-12; 25 (March 1919):570-76; 25 (April 1919):636-40; 25 (May 1919):698-704; 26 (December 1919):349-59.

"Description of Courses." *Evangelical Theological College Bulletin* 3 (June 1927):14-21; *Bulletin of Dallas Theological Seminary* 28 (September-October 1952).

"Dispensational Distinctions Challenged." *Bibliotheca Sacra* 100 (July 1943):337-45.

"Dispensationalism." *Bibliotheca Sacra* 93 (October 1936):390-449;

Selected Bibliography

106 (January 1949):2.

"The Doctrine of Sin" *Bibliotheca Sacra* 91 (October 1934):390-408; 92 (January 1934):7-25; 92 (April 1934):134-53; 92 (October 1935):394-411; 93 (January 1936):5-25; 93 (April 1936):133-61; 93 (July 1936):263-88.

"Does Your Congregation Sing Well?" *The Sunday School Times* 60 (28 September 1918):528.

"Effective Ministerial Training." *Evangelical Theological College Bulletin* 1 (May 1925):7-11.

"The Ephesian Letter." *Revelation Magazine* 2 (July 1932):288, 310-13; 2 (August 1932):328, 350-52; 2 (September 1932):370, 390-92; 2 (October 1932):410, 432-34; 2 (November 1932):452, 471-72; 2 (December 1932):490, 515-16; 3 (January 1933):8, 30-32; 3 (April 1933):211, 236-37; 3 (July 1933):250, 274-75; 3 (August 1933):287, 313-14.

"The Essentials in Christian Education." *Evangelical Theological College Bulletin* 4 (November 1927):11-13.

"The Eternal Retribution of the Lost." *Our Hope* 47 (July 1940):28-34.

"Eternal Security of the Believer." *Bibliotheca Sacra* 106 (July 1949):260-90; 106 (October 1949):392-420.

"The Evangelical Theological College." *The Sunday School Times* 80 (June 1931):322.

"Evils Resulting from an Abridged Systematic Theology." *Bibliotheca Sacra* 91 (April-July 1934):134-54, 261-85.

"Expository Preaching." *Bibliotheca Sacra* 104 (October 1947):385-88.

"Faith and Finances." *Bulletin of Dallas Theological Seminary* 19 (October-December 1943).

"Fellowship with God." *Bibliotheca Sacra* 106 (April 1949):129.

"The First Sin on Earth and Its Effect.' *Bibliotheca Sacra* 97 (1935):7-25.

"Following Beaten Paths." *Bibliotheca Sacra* 98 (October 1941):385.

"For the Glory of God." *Evangelical Theological College Bulletin* 7 (Nobember 1930):4-6.

"For Whom Did Christ Die?" *Bibliotheca Sacra* 105 (January 1948):134-35, 155-57.

"Dr. A. C. Gaebelein." *Bibliotheca Sacra* 102 (January 1946):1.

"God in Financial Depressions." *Evangelical Theological College Bulletin* 9 (November 1932).

"God Is Propitious." *Bibliotheca Sacra* 102 (October 1945):385-86.

"God and Morals." *Bibliotheca Sacra* 98 (July 1941):258-59.

"Gospel Preaching." *Bibliotheca Sacra* 95 (July 1938):343-64.

"The Highest Standard." *Bulletin of Dallas Theological Seminary* 19 (April-June 1943).

"Historical Sketch." *Bibliotheca Sacra* 97 (April 1940):129-32.

"I Believe God." *Bibliotheca Sacra* 102 (October 1946):387.

"The Imminent Coming of Christ." *Bulletin of Dallas Theological Seminary* 17 (October-December 1941).

"In Memoriam — Dr. A. B. Winchester." *Bibliotheca Sacra* 100 (October 1943):465-68.

"The Incarnation of Christ." *Bibliotheca Sacra* 94 (January 1937):8-14.

"Infinite Grace." *Bibliotheca Sacra* 98 (April 1941):131-32.

Selected Bibliography

"The Iniquity of the Amorites." *Bibliotheca Sacra* 98 (April 1941):129-30.

"Inspiration." *Bibliotheca Sacra* 94 (1937):389-409; 95 (1938):7-21.

"Introduction to Bibliology." *Bibliotheca Sacra* 94 (April 1937):137-52.

"An Introduction to Eschatology." In *Christ and Glory*, pp. 158-173. Edited by Arno C. Gaebelein. New York: Publication Office "Our Hope," n.d.

"An Introduction to the Study of Prophecy." *Bibliotheca Sacra* 100 (January 1943):98-133.

"Inventing Heretics through Misunderstanding." *Bibliotheca Sacra* 102 (April 1948):129-30.

"Is Philosophy A Substitute for Systematic Theology?" *Bibliotheca Sacra* 105 (April 1948):129-30.

"Is This the End?" *Bibliotheca Sacra* 97 (October 1940):388-89.

"Is This the Era of the Teacher?" *The Sunday School Times* 61 (26 April 1919):228.

"Is War Murder?" *Bibliotheca Sacra* 98 (January 1941):1-3.

"Is The World Getting Better? *Bibliotheca Sacra* 97 (July 1940):257-58.

"The Jew a World Issue." *Bibliotheca Sacra* 102 (April 1945):129-30.

"Judaism." *Bibliotheca Sacra* 104 (April 1947):129-30; 106 (October 1949):385-86.

"Justification." *Bibliotheca Sacra* 103 (October 1946):129-34.

"Knowing Christ." *Bulletin of Dallas Theological Seminary* 18 (October-December 1942).

"Look We for a Revival?" *Bibliotheca Sacra* 104 (January 1947):1.

"A Love Story Infinitely True." *Bibliotheca Sacra* 105 (April 1948):134-44.

"Man's Present State as a Sinner." *Bibliotheca Sacra* 92 (1935): 134-53.

"Ministerial Education." *Bibliotheca Sacra* 107 (July 1950):257-59.

"Modern Evangelism." *Bibliotheca Sacra* 103 (October 1946):385-86.

"A Moving Population." *Bibliotheca Sacra* 107 (APril 1950):132-33.

My Lord Delayeth His Coming." *Bibliotheca Sacra* 108 (April 1951):129-31.

"The Names of Diety." *Bibliotheca Sacra* 96 (1939):390-404.

"National Prayer." *Bibliotheca Sacra* 97 (July 1940):258-60.

"A New Departure in Theological Training." *Our Hope* 24 (January 1928):432-35.

"A Notable Increase." *Bibliotheca Sacra* 103 (October 1946):387 88.

"Notes on Open Letters." *The Sunday School Times* 83 (25 October 1941):854.

"The Olivet Discourse." *Bibliotheca Sacra* 109 (1952):4-36.

"One Hundred Years of Testimony." *Bibliotheca Sacra* 99 (April 1942):129.

"One Man's Power." *Bibliotheca Sacra* 99 (January 1942):1-2.

"Our Assurance of Infant Salvation." *The Sunday School Times* 70 (10 November 1928):653-54.

"The Pastor's Objective." *Bibliotheca Sacra* 99 (July 1942):257-59.

Selected Bibliography

"Plain Teaching about the Spirit." *The King's Business* 13 (December 1922):1248-49.

"Pleeroma." *Bibliotheca Sacra* 99 (July 1942):257.

"Populating the Third Heaven." *Bibliotheca Sacra* 108 (April 1951):138-52; (July 1951):263-69.

"Preaching and Teaching A Supernatural Work." *Moody Monthly* 24 (September 1923):8-10.

"Preaching in These Times." *Bibliotheca Sacra* 98 (July 1941):374-75.

"Prophecy Concerning Evil and Its End." In *The Sure Word of Prophecy*, pp. 209-13. Edited by John W. Bradbury. New York: Fleming H. Revell Co., 1943.

"Prophecy in This Lesson." *The Sunday School Times* 65 (22 September 1923):551; 65 (29 September 1923):565; 65 (6 October 1923):584; 65 (13 October 1923):599; 65 (20 October 1923):625; 65 (27 October 1923):641; 65 (3 November 1923):144; 65 (10 November 1923); 677; 65 (17 November 1923):700; 65 (24 November 1923):717; 65 (1 December 1923):743; 65 (8 December 1923):760; 65 (15 December 1923):783; 66 (5 January 1924):10; 66 (12 January 1924):26; 66 (19 January 1924):40; 66 (26 January 1924):53; 66 (2 February 1924):74-75; 66 (9 February 1924): 89; 66 (16 February 1924):107-08; 66 (23 February 1924):127; 66 (1 March 1924):148; 66 (8 March 1924):163; 66 (15 March 1924):177; 66 (22 March 1924):196; 66 (29 March 1924):211; 66 (5 April 1924): 225; 66 (12 April 1924):243; 66 (19 April 1924):255; 66 (26 April 1924):271; 66 (3 May 1924):285; 66 (10 May 1924):301; 66 (17 May 1924):317; 66 (24 May 1924): 332; 66 (7 June 1924):357; 66 (14 June 1924):376; 66 (21 June 1924):387; 66 (28 June 1924):399; 66 (5 July 1924):414; 66 (12 July 1924):428; 66 (19 July 1924): 439; 66 (26 July 1924):452; 66 (2 August 1924):466; 66 (9 August 1924):483; 66 (16 August 1924):496; 66 (23 August 1924):507; 66 (30

August 1924):519; 66 (6 September 1924):533; 66 (13 September 1924):547; 66 (20 September 1924):559; 66 (27 September 1924):574; 66 (4 October 1924):591; 66 (11 October 1924):604; 66 (18 October 1924):627; 66 (25 October 1924):642; 66 (1 November 1924):661; 66 (8 November 1924); 677; 66 (15 Novwember 1924):700; 66 (22 November 1924):716-17; 66 (29 November 1924):740; 66 (6 December 1924):757; 66 (13 December 1924):778-79.

"Public Evangelism." *Bibliotheca Sacra* 105 (October 1948):385-86.

"Purpose." *Bibliotheca Sacra* 100 (January 1943):2-3.

"Recognition of the Centennial Issues." *Bibliotheca Sacra* 100 (April 1943):209.

"The Recognition of God's Program Essential to a Right Interpretation (1) & (2)." In *Winona Echoes*, pp. 39-45. Grand Rapids: Zondervan Publishing House, 1944.

"A Recognized Need Fulfilled." *Evangelical Theological College Bulletin* 9 (November 1932).

"Repentance." *Bibliotheca Sacra* 108 (April 1951):131-32.

"Responsibility for the Training of Preachers and Missionaries." *Evangelical Theological College Bulletin* 7 (March 1931):9-11.

"Responsibility of a Union Church." *Bibliotheca Sacra* 108 (April 1951):132-33.

"The Resurrection of Christ." *Revelation Magazine* 1 (April 1931):115-16, 140-41.

"Revelation." *Bibliotheca Sacra* 94 (July 1937):264-80.

"Salient Facts Regarding Evangelism." *Bibliotheca Sacra* 101 (October 1944):385-88.

Selected Bibliography

"Satan and the Jew." *Bibliotheca Sacra* 98 (July 1941):259-60.

"The Saving Work of the Triune God." *Bibliotheca Sacra* 105 (July 1948):261-85; 105 (October 1948):387-403; 106 (January 1949):5-26; 106 (April 1949):133-48; 107 (July 1950):263-80; 107 (October 1950):389-419.

"Scholarship." *Bibliotheca Sacra* 105 (October 1948):385.

"Dr. C. I. Scofield." *Bibliotheca Sacra* 100 (January 1943):4-7.

"Cyrus Ingerson Scofield, D.D." In *And in Samaria*, pp. 1-4. by Mildred W. Spain, Dallas: Central American Mission, 1940.

"The Scofield Bible." *Bibliotheca Sacra* 109 (April 1952):97-99.

"Scourging." *Bibliotheca Sacra* 107 (January 1950):5.

"Should Premillennialism Be Blamed?" *The Sunday School Times* 83 (18 January 1941):45-46.

"Sin in the Believer."*The King's Business* 13 (November 1922): 1109-11.

"The Sins of Christians." *Bibliotheca Sacra* 109 (January 1952):2-7.

"Soteriology." *Bibliotheca Sacra* 102 (January 1945):8-26; 102 (April 1945):135-52; 102 (July 1945):263-79; 102 (October 1945):390-404; 103 (January 1946):4-15; 103 (April 1946):140-60; 103 (July 1946):261-82; 103 (October 1946):391-410; 104 (January 1947):3-24; 104 (April 1947):135-53; 104 (July 1947):263-81; 104 (October 1947):393-414.

"Sovereignty." *Bibliotheca Sacra* 107 (January 1950):5-6.

"Specialists." *Bibliotheca Sacra* 105 (October 1948):385.

"The Specific Character of the Christian's Sin." *Bibliotheca Sacra* 92

(1935):394-411.

"Study." *Bibliotheca Sacra* 98 (January 1941):3-5.

"Summer Bible Conferences: Their Meaning." *The Sunday School Times* 62 (24 April 1920):235.

"The Teachings of Christ Incarnate." *Bibliotheca Sacra* 108 (October 1951):389-414; 109 (January 1952):4-36; 109 (April 1952):103-36.

"Theism." *Bibliotheca Sacra* 95 (1938):260-90.

"Theology." *Bibliotheca Sacra* 104 (January 1947):2.

"Henry C. Thiessen." *Bibliotheca Sacra* 104 (July 1947):257.

"Things New and Old." *Bibliotheca Sacra* 97 (October 1940):386-88.

"Time for a Theological Education." *Bibliotheca Sacra* 109 (January 1952):1-2.

"A Timely Report." *Bibliotheca Sacra* 97 (April 1940):132-36.

"A Timely World of Instruction." *Bibliotheca Sacra* 103 (October 1946): 386-87.

"A Tribute, A Record, and a Memory." *The Sunday School Times* 86 (17 June 1944):437.

"Trinitarianism." *Bibliotheca Sacra* 97 (January 1940):5-26; 97 (April 1940):137-65; 97 (July 1940): 262-88; 97 (October 1940):385-89; 98 (January 1941):728; 98 (April 1941):133-54; 98 (July 1941):264-84.

"Twenty Years of Experience." *Bulletin of Dallas Theological Seminary* 19 (July-September 1943):3.

Selected Bibliography

"Unabridged Systematic Theology." *Bibliotheca Sacra* 91 (January 1934):3-23.

"United Action of Evangelicals." *Bibliotheca Sacra* 99 (October 1942):385-86.

"The Upper Room Discourse." *Bibliotheca Sacra* 109 (1952):103-35.

"Was Paul Mistaken in Going to Jerusalem?" *The Sunday School Times* 63 (October 1921):579.

"What does Being Lost Mean?" *The Sunday School Times* 82 (27 January 1940):69-70.

"What and If a Christian Would Sin?" *Bibliotheca Sacra* 108 (January 1951):1-3.

"What Is Revival" *Bibliotheca Sacra* 108 (April 1951):132.

"What Really Is The Gospel?" *The Sunday School Times* 59 (22 December 1917):743-44.

"What Will God Do with the Cosmos?" In *The Sure Work of Prophecy*, pp. 67-71. Edited by John W. Bradbury. New York: Fleming H. Revell Co., 1943.

"What Will Jehovah Do?" *Bibliotheca Sacra* 98 (April 1941):130-31.

"When I Learned from Dr. Scofield." *The Sunday School Times* 64 (4 March 1922):120.

"Why a Denominationally Unrelated Theological College?" *Evangelical Theological College Bulletin* 2 (February 1926):3-7.

"Why Music Reaches Souls." *The Sunday School Times* 60 (23 February 1918):108-09.

"Why Substitutes?" *Bibliotheca Sacra* 97 (October 1940):385-86.

"Why Was It Necessary for Christ to Die?" *The Sunday School Times* 60 (27 April 1918):241.

"Yes a Phenomenon." *Bibliotheca Sacra* 109 (July 1052):193-94.

Tapes and Letters by Lewis Sperry Chafer

"The Believer and the Holy Spirit." Dallas Theological Seminary.

Lewis Sperry Chafer to Scofield Memorial Church. 11 April 1923.

"The Christian's Sin." Dallas Theological Seminary.

"Doctrine of Grace." Dallas Theological Seminary.

"Forgiveness." Dallas Theological Seminary.

"The Founding of Dallas Theological Seminary." Dallas Theological Seminary.

"The History of the Scofield Bible." Dallas Theological Seminary.

"The Love of God." Dallas Theological Seminary.

"The Olivet Discourse." Dallas Theological Seminary.

"Propitiation." Dallas Theological Seminary.

"Three Riches of Grace." Dallas Theological Seminary.

Secondary Sources
Books

Ahlstrom, Sydney E. *A Religious History of the American People.* 2 vols. Garden City, New York: Doubleday & Co., Image Books, 1975.

Selected Bibliography

_____. *Theology in America: The Major Protestant Voices from Puritanism to Neo-Orthodoxy.* Indianapolis: Bobbs-Merrill Co., 1967.

Allis, Oswald T. *Prophecy and the Church.* Philadelphia: Presbyterian & Reformed Publishing Co., 1945.

Anderson, Sir Robert. *The Coming Prince.* London: Pickering & Ingles, n.d.

Armerding, Carl E. and W. Ward Gasque. *A Guide to Biblical Prophecy.* Peabody, Massachusetts: Hendrickson Publishers, 1989.

Bacchiocchi, Samuel. *The Advent Hope for Human Hopelessness.* Berrien Springs Michigan: Biblical Perspectives, 1986.

Bass, Clarence, *Backgrounds to Dispensationalism: Its Historical Genesis and Ecclesiastical Implications.* Grand Rapids: Wm. B. Eerdmans Publishing Co., 1965.

Berkhof, Louis, *The Second Coming of Christ.* Grand Rapids: Wm. B. Eerdmans Co., 1953.

_____. *Systematic Theology.* Grand Rapids: Wm. B. Eerdmans Co., 1974.

Bernard, John. *From Evangelicalism to Progressivism at Oberlin College, 1866-1917.* Columbus: Ohio State University Press, 1969.

Bible Studies at Northfield. Terre Haute, Indiana: Ambassadors for Christ, n.d.

Blackstone, William E. *Jesus is Coming.* 3rd ed. rev. New York: Fleming H Revell Co., 1917.

Boardman, George N. *A History of New England Theology.* Chicago:1899

Boettner, Loraine. *The Millennium.* Philadelphia: Presbyterian & Reformed Publishing Co., 1957.

_____. "Postmillenniasm." In *The Meaning of the Millennium,* pp. 117-41. Edited by Robert G. Clouse, Downers Grove, Illinois: Intervarsity Press, 1977.

Brauer, Jerald C. *Protestantism in America: A Narrataive History.* Philadelphia: Westminster Press, 1965.

Brooks, James H. *"I am Coming" : A Setting Forth of the Second Coming of Our Lord Jesus Christ as Personal-Private Premillennial.* Edinburg: Pickering & Ingles, n.d.

_____. *Maranatha: Or the Lord Cometh.* New York: Fleming H. Revell Co., 1889.

Brunner, Heinrich E. *Eternal Hope.* Trans. Harold Knight. Philadelphia: Westminster Press, 1954.

Burr, Nelson R. *A Critical Bibliography of Religion in America.* 2 vols. Princeton, New Jersey: Princeton University Press, 1961.

Carnell, Edward J. *The Case for Orthodox Theology.* Philadelphia: Westminster Press, 1959.

Cauthen, Kenneth. *The Impact of American Religious Liberalism.* New York: Harper & Row, 1962.

Cherry, Conrad. *The Theology of Jonathan Edwards.* Garden City, New York: Doubleday & Co., 1966.

Clouse, Robert G., ed. *The Meaning of the Millennium.* Downers Grove, Illinois: Intervarsity Press, 1977.

Cole, Stewart G. *The History of Fundamentalism.* New York: Richard R. Smith, 1931.

Cox, William E. *An Examination of Dispensationalism.* Philadelphia:

Selected Bibliography

Presbyterian & Reformed Publishing Co., 1963.

Cross, Whitney R. *The Burned-Over District: The Social and Intellectual History of Enthusiastic Religion in Western New York, 1800-1850.* Ithaca: Cornell University Press, 1950.

Darby, John N. *Lectures on the Second Coming.* London: W. Broom, 1868.

_____. *Letters.* 3 vols. Kingston-on-Thames Bible & Tract Depot, n.d.

Davidson, A. B. *Old Testament Prophecy.* Edited by J. A. Paterson. Edinburgh: T & T Clark, 1904.

Ellingsen, Mark. *The Evangelical Movement: Growth, Impact, Controversy, Dialog.* Minneapolis: Augsburg Publishing House, 1988.

English, E. Schuyler. *Rethinking the Rapture.* Travelers Rest, South Carolina:Southeren Bible Book House, 1954; rev. ed., Neptune, New Jersey: Loizeaux Bros., 1970.

Erickson, Millard J. *Christian Theology.* Grand Repids: Baker Book House, 1986.

Fairbairn, Patrick. *The Interpretation of Prophecy.* London: Banner of Truth, 1856.

Feinberg, Charles L. *Millennialism: The Two Major Views.* Foreward to the First Edition by Lewis Sperry Chafer. Chicago: Moody Bible Institute, 1936; 3rd ed. rev. & enl., Chicago: Moody Press, 1982.

Findlay, James F. Jr. *Dwight L. Moody: American Evangelist, 1837-1899.* Chicago: University of Chicago Press, 1969.

Forrest, William M. *Do Fundamentalists Play Fair?* New York: Macmillan Co., 1925.

Foster, Frank H. *The Modern Movement in American Theology.* New York: Fleming H. Revell Co., 1939.

Froom, Leroy Edwin. *The Prophetic Faith of our Fathers.* 4 vols, Washington, D.C.: Review & Herald, 1946.

The Fundamentals. 12 vols. Chicago: Testimony Publishing Co., 1910-12.

Furniss, Norman. *The Fundamentalist Controversy, 1918-1931.* New Haven: Yale University Press, 1954.

Gaebelein, Arno C. *Christianity and Religion: A Study of the Origin and Growth of Religion and the Supernatural of Christianity.* New York: Publication Office "Our Hope," 1927.

_____. *The Conflict of the Ages.* New York: Arno C. Gaebelein, 1933; reprint ed., Neptune, New Jersey: Loizeaux Bros., 1983.

_____. *The Gospel of Matthew.* 2 vols. New York: Publication Office "Our Hope," 1910.

_____. *Half a Century.* New York: Publication Office "Our Hope," 1930.

_____. *The Harmony of the Prophetic Word: A Key to the Old Testament Prophecy Concerning Things to Come.* New York: Publication Office "Our Hope," n.d.

_____. *The Prophet Daniel.* New York: Publication Office "Our Hope," 1911; reprint ed., Grand Rapids: Kregel Publications, 1955.

_____. *The Revelation.* New York: Our Hope Press, n.d.; reprint ed., Neptune, New Jersey: Loizeaux Bros., 1961.

_____. *World Prospects: How Is It All Going To End.* New York: Arno C. Gaebelein, 1934.

Selected Bibliography

Gasper, Louis. *The Fundamentalist Movement*. Haguel Mouton & Co., 1963.

Hamilton, Floyd. *Basis of the Millennial Faith*. Grand Rapids: Wm. B. Eerdmans Publishing Co., 1932.

Henry, Carl F. H. *Evangelical Responsibility in Contemporary Theology*. Grand Rapids: Wm. B. Eerdmans Publishing Co., 1957.

_____. *The Uneasy Conscience of Modern Fundamentals*. Grand Rapids: Wm. B. Eerdmans Publishing Co., 1947.

Hodge, Archibald A. *Outlines of Theology*. N.p.: Robert Carter & Bros., 1878; rewritten & enl., New York: A. C. Armstrong & Son, 1895.

Hodge, Charles. *Systematic Theology*. Vol. 3: *Soteriology*. New York: Charles Scribner & Co., 1872; reprint ed., Wm. B. Eerdmans Publishing Co., 1940.

Hoekema, Anthony A. "Amillennialism." In *The Meaning of the Millennium*, pp. 155-187. Edited by Robert G. Clouse. Downers Grove, Illinois: Intervarsity Press, 1977.

Hoyt, Herman A. *The End Times*. Chicago: Moody Press, 1969.

Ironside, H. A. *Expository Notes on the Gospel of Matthew*. London: Pickering & Ingles, 1959.

_____. *Isaiah*. Foreward by Ann Hightower Ironside. New York: Loizeaux Bros., 1952.

_____. *The Lamp of Prophecy: Or Signs of the Times*. Grand Rapids: Zondervan Publishing House, 1940.

_____. *Lectures on Daniel*. New York: Loizeaux Bros., 1920.

_____. *Lectures on Revelation.* Neptune, New Jersey: Loizeaux Bros., 1944.

_____. *Matthew.* New York: Loizeaux Brox., 1948.

_____. *Not Wrath but Rapture.* New York: Loizeaux Bros., n.d.

_____. *Wrongly Dividing the Word of Truth.* Neptune, New Jersey: Loizeauzx Bros., n.d.

Johnson, Elliott E. *Expository Hermeneutics: An Introduction.* Grand Rapids: Zondervan Publishing House, 1990.

Kelly, William. *An Exposition of the Book of Isaiah.* 4th ed. St. Albans: Mayflower Press, n.d.; rev. ed., London: C. A. Hammond, 1947.

_____. *Lectures on the Gospel of Matthew.* Foreward by Guernsey. London: n.p., 1868; new ed. rev., Glasgow: Pickering & Inglis, n.d.

Kerr, Hugh T., ed. *Calvin's Institutes: A New Compend.* Louisville, Ky: Westminster/John Knox Press, 1989.

Konig, Adrio, *The Eclipse of Christ in Eschatology.* Grand Rapids: Wm. B. Eerdmans Publishing Co., 1989.

Kraus, C. Norman. *Dispensationalism in America: Its Rise and Development.* Richmond: John Knox Press, 1958.

Kromminga, D. H. *The Millennium in the Church: Studies in the History of Christian Chiliasm.* Grand Rapids: Wm. B. Eerdmand Publishing Co., 1954.

_____. *The Millennium: Its Nature, Function and Relation to the Consummation of the World.* Grand Rapids: Wm. B. Eerdmans Publishing Co., 1948.

Selected Bibliography

Ladd, George E. *The Blessed Hope*. Grand Rapids: Wm. B. Eerdmans Publishing Co., 1956.

_____. *Crucial Questions about the Kingdom of God*. Grand Rapids: Wm. B. Eerdmans Publishing Co., 1952.

_____. *The Gospel of the Kingdom*. Grand Rapids: Wm. B. Eerdmans Pubishing Co., 1959.

Light on Prophecy: Proceedings and Addresses of the Philadelphia Prophetic Conference. New York: New York Chirstian Herald, 1918.

Lightner, Robert P. *Neo-Evangelicalism*. Des Plains, Illinois: Regular Baptist Press, 1965.

_____. *Evangelical Theology*. Grand Rapids: Baker Book House, 1987.

Mabie, Janet. *The Years Beyond, The Story of Northfield, Moody, and the Schools*. East Northfiled, Massachusetts: Northfield Bookstore, 1960.

Machen, J. Gresham. *Christianity and Liberalism*. Grand Rapids: Wm B.Eerdmans Publishing Co., 1946.

_____. *What Is Faith?* New York: Macmillan, 1925.

Mackintosh, C. H. *The Mackintosh Treasury*. Neptune, New Jersey: Loizeaux Bros., 1898; 1st ed. in one vol., 1976.

Marsden, George M. *Fundamentalism and American Culture*. New York: Oxford University Press, 1980.

Marty, Martin E. *Righteous Empire: The Protestant Experience in America*. New York: Dial Press, 1970.

McKelway, Alexander J. *The Systematic Theology of Paul Tillich*. Richmond: John Knox Press, 1964.

McLoughlin, William G., ed. *Religion in America*. Boston: Houghton Mifflin Co., 1968.

Moody, D. L. *Heaven*. N.p.; reprint ed., Springdale, Pennsylvania: Whitaker House, 1982.

Morgan , G. Campbell. *The Parables and Metaphors of Our Lord*. New York: Fleming H. Revell Co., 1943.

_____. *Sunrise, Behold He Cometh*. London: Hodder & Stoughton, 1912.

Nash, Ronald. *The New Evangelicalism*. Grand Rapids: Zondervan Publishing House, 1963.

Noel, Napolean. *The History of the Plymouth Brethren*. 2 vols. Denver: W. F. Knapp, 1936.

Payne, J. Barton. *The Imminent Appearing of Christ*. Grand Rapids: Wm. B. Eerdmans Publshing Co., 1962.

Pentecost, Dwight. *Things To Come*. Grand Rapids: Zondervan Publishing House, 1958.

Peters, George N. H. *The Theocratic Kingdom*. 3 vols. Preface by Wilbur M. Smith. New York: Funk & Wagnalls Co., reprint ed., Grand Rapids: Kregel Publications, 1957.

Pettingill, William L. *Simple Studies in Matthew*. Harrisburg: Fred Kelker, 1910.

Pierson, Delevan L., ed. *Northfield Echoes, Northfield Conference Addresses for 1902*. East Northfield, Massachusetts: Northfield Bookstore, 1902.

_____. *The Victorious Life, the Post Conference Addresses Delivered at East Northfield, Massachusetts, August 17-25, 1895*. New York: Baker & Taylor Co., 1896.

Selected Bibliography

Pieters, Albertus. *A Candid Examination of the Scofield Bible*. Swengel, Pennsylvania: Bible Truth Depot, 1938.

_____. *The Seed of Abraham*. Grand Rapids: Wm. B. Eerdmans Publishing Co., 1950.

Premillennial Essays: *Proceedings of The 1879 Prophetic Conference*. Chicago: Fleming H. Revell Co., 1886.

Rall, Harris. *Modern Premillennialism and the Christian Hope*. New York: Abingdon Press, 1920.

Rian, Edwin H. *The Presbytrian Conflict*. Grand Rapids: Wm. B. Eerdmans Publishing Co., 1940.

Riley, William B. *The Evolution of the Kingdom*. New York: Charles C. Cook, 1913.

_____. *The Menace of Modernism*. New York: Christian Alliance Publishing Co., 1917.

Robertson, O. Palmer. *The Christ of the Covenants*. Grand Rapids: Wm. B. Eerdmans Publishing Co., 1980.

Robinson, Haddon W. *Biblical Preaching*. Grand Rapids: Baker Book House, 1985.

Ryrie, Charles C. *The Basis of the Premillennial Faith*. Neptune, New Jersey: Loizeaux Bros., 1953.

_____. *Dispensationalism Today*. Chicago: Moody Press, 1965.

Sandeen, Ernest. *The Roots of Fundamentalism*. Grand Rapids: Baker Book House, 1978.

Sauer, Erich. *From Eternity to Eternity*. Translated by G. H. Lang. Grand Rapids: Wm. B. Eerdmans Publishing Co., 1954.

Schaff, Philip, et al., gen. eds. *The American Church History Series.* 13 vols. New York: Christian Literature Co., 1893-97.

Scofield, C. I. *Addresses on Prophecy.* New York: A. C. Gaebelein, 1919.

_____. *Rightly Dividing the Word of Truth.* Neptune, New Jersey: Loizeaux Bros., [1896].

_____, ed. *The Scofield Reference Bible.* New York: Oxford University Press 1909.

_____. *What Do The Prophets Say?* Philadelphia: The Sunday School Times, 1918.

Shelly, Bruce L. *The Gospel and The American Dream.* Portland, Or: Multnomah Press, 1989.

Smith, Timothy L. *Revivalism and Social Reform in Mid-Nineteenth Century America.* Nashville, Tennessee: Abingdon Press, 1957.

Snowden, James H. *The Coming of the Lord: Will It Be Premillennial?* New York: Macmillan Co., 1919.

Stonehouse, Ned B. *J. Gresham Machen: A Biographical Memoir.* Grand Rapids: Wm. B. Eerdmands Publishgin Co., 1955.

Sweet, William W. *Revivalism in America: Its Origin, Growth and Decline.* New York: Charles Scribner & Sons, 1944.

_____. *The Story of Religion in America.* New York: Harper & Bros., 1950.

Taylor, Mrs. Howard. *Empty Racks and How to Fill Them.* Dallas: Evangelical Theological College, n.d.

Thompson, Ernest T. *Presbyterianism in the South.* Richmond, Virginia: John Knox Press, 1963.

Selected Bibliography

Torrey, R. A. *The Fundamental Doctrine of the Christian Faith.* Doran, New York, 1918.

Trumbull, Charles. *The Life Story of C. I. Scofield.* New York: Oxford University Press, 1920.

Walvoord, John F. *Inspiration and Interpretation.* Grand Rapids: Wm. B. Eerdmans Pyublishing Co., 1957.

_____, ed. *Lewis Sperry Chafer's Systematic Theology Abridged Edition.* Wheaton, Illinois: Scripture Press, 1988.

_____. *The Millennial Kingdom.* Findlay, Ohio: Dunham Publishing Co., 1959; reprint ed., Grand Rapids: Zondervan Publishing House, 1976.

_____. *The Rapture Question.* Findlay, Ohio: Dunham Publishing Co., 1957.

_____. *The Return of the Lord.* Findlay, Ohio: Dunham Publishing Co., 1955.

Warfield, Benjamin B. *Selected Shorter Writings of Benjamin B. Warfield.* Edited by John E. Meeter. Nutley, New Jersey: Presbyterian & Reformed Publishing Co., 1973.

Weber, Timothy. *Living in the Shadow of the Second Coming.* New York: Oxford University Press 1979.

Wells, David F. *Reformed Theology in America: The Princeton Theology.* Grand Rapids: Baker Book House, 1990.

_____. *Reformed Theology in America: Dutch Reformed Theology.* Grand Rapids: Baker Book House, 1990.

_____. *Reformed Theology in America: Southern Reformed Theology.* Grand Rapids: Baker Book House, 1990.

Wood, Leon. *Is The Rapture Next?* Grand Rapids: Zondervan Publishing House, 1958.

Woodward, C. Vann. *The Burden of Southern History.* Baton Rouge: Louisiana State University Press, 1960.

Periodicals

Allis, Oswald T. "Modern Dispensatinalism and the Doctrine of the Unity of the Scriptures." *The Evangelical Quarterly* 8 (Januery 1936):22-35.

_____. "Modern Dispenationalism and the Law of God." *The Evangelical Quarterly* 8 (15 July 1936):285-307.

Bear, James E. "Dispensationalism and the Covenant of Grace." *Union Seminary Review* 49 (July 1938):285-307.

_____. "The People of God." *Union Seminary Review* 52 (October 1940):33-63.

Bennetch, John H. "The Biography of *Bibliotheca Sacra.*" *Bibliotheca Sacra* 100 (January 1943):8-30.

Bowman, John Wick. "Dispensationalism." *Interpretation* 10 (April 1956):170-86.

Briggs, Charles. "The Origin and History of Premillennialsim." *Lutheran Quarterly* 9 (1879):207-45.

Brookes, James H. "Brethren Fighting." *The Truth* 21 (July 1895):309-12.

_____. "Caught Up Together." *The Truth* 6 (February 1880):109-12.

_____. "How I Became A Premillennialist." *The Truth* 22 (June 19 1896):331-33.

Selected Bibliography

_____. "Four Prophetic Periods." *The Truth* 19 (April 1893):197-200.

_____. "Israel and the Church." *The Truth* 7 (February 1881):117-20.

_____. "Notes by the Way." *The Truth* 20 (April 1895):181-87.

_____. "Who Shall Be Caught Up?" *The Truth* 20 (April 1894):204-07.

Brown, J. A. "The Second Advent and the Creed of Christendom." *Bibliotheca Sacra* 24 (1867):629-51.

Case, Shirley Jackson. "The Premillennial Menace." *Biblical World* 52 (July 1918):16-23.

Dallas Morning News, 4 November 1909; 25 September 1924; 1 October 1924; 20 July 1928; 29 October 1933; 13 July 1948; 23 August 1952.

"Dispensationalism and the Scofield Reference Bible:Are They Heresies?" *The Sunday School Times* (20 February 1937), pp. 130, 132, 133.

Ehlert, Arnold. "A Bibliography of Dispensationalism." *Bibliotheca Sacra* 101 (Jaunary 1944):95-101; 101 (April 1944):199-209; 101 (July 1944):319-328; 101 (October 1944):447-60; 102 (January 1945):84-92; 102 (April 1945):207-334; 102 (October 1945):455-67; 103 (January 1946):57-67.

_____. "Genealogical History of *Bibliotheca Sacra*." *Bibliotheca Sacra* 100 (January 1943):31-52.

English, E. Schuyler. "E. Schuyler English Looks at Dispensationalism." *Christian Life* 18 (September 1956):25.

Findlay, James F., Jr. "Preparation for Flight: D. L. Moody in Illinois and the Midwest, 1865-1873." *Journal of Presbyterian History* 41 (June 1963):103-16.

Gaebelein, Arno C. "The Kingdom in the Old Testament." *Our Hope* 22 (Feberuary 1906):460.

_____. "The Story of the Scofield Reference Bible." *Moody Monthly* 43 ()ctober 1942):65-66, 97; 43 (November 1942):128-135; 43 (December 1942):202-233; 43 (January 1943):277-79; 43 (February 1943):343-45; 43 (March 1943):400-02.

Goen, C. C. "Jonathan Edwards, A Departure in Eschatology." *Church History* 28 (1959):25-40.

Houghton, George C. "Lewis Sperry Chafer, 1871-1952." *Bibliotheca Sacra* 128 (October 1971):291-99.

Hague, Dyson. "Dr. W. H. Griffith Thomas." *The Evangelical Christian* 20 (July 1924):276-77.

Howard, Wally. "Accident Man." *Sunday School Promoter* 6 (June 1944):15-20, 54-56.

Kellogg, Samuel H. "Premillennialism: Its Relation to Doctrine and Practice." *Bibliotheca Sacra* 45 (April 1888):234-74.

Kelly, Robert L. "Tendencies in Theological Education in America." *Journal of Religion* 4 (January 1924):16-31.

Lincoln, C. F. "Lewis Sperry Chafer." *Bibliotheca Sacra* 109 (October 1952):332-37.

Macartney, Clarence. "The Crux of the Present Protestant Controversy." *The Sunday School Times* 65 (April 1923):247-48.

Mason, Clarence. "A Readable and Thrilling Theology." *Our Hope* 55 (March 1949):535-43.

Selected Bibliography

Moody, Dale. "Present Theological Trends." *Review and Expositor* 47 (1950):9-11.

Nichols, Robert Hastings. "Fundamentalism in the Presbyterian Church." *Journal of Religion* 5 (January 1925):14-36.

Our Hope (New York). Edited by Arno C. Gaebelein until death in 1945. 64 vols. 1894-1957.

Pace, E. H. "One of God's Noblemen, Dr. Griffith Thomas." *The Sunday School Times* 66 (July 1924):450.

Parker, T. Valentine. "Premillennialsim: An Interpretation and An Evaluation." *Biblical World* 53 (1919):37-40.

Rall, Harris Franklin. "Premillennialism." *Biblical World* 53 (1919):339-47, 459-69, 617-27.

Rand, James F. "Problems in Literal Interpretation of the Sermon on the Mount." *Bibliotheca Sacra* 112 (January 1955):28-29.

Scroggie, W. Graham. "Dr. GriffithThomas — Scholar, Teacher, Friend." *The Sunday School Times* 66 (21 June 1924):383.

Smith, Wilbur M. "Some Much Needed Books." *Bibliotheca Sacra* 91 (April 1934):193.

Snowden, James H. "Summary of Objections to Premillennialism." *Biblical World* 53 (1919):165-73.

"The Stewarts as Christian Stewards: The Story of Milton and Lyman Stewart." *Missionary Review of the World* 47 (1924):595-602.

Thomas, W. H. Griffith. "Great Facts about Our Lord's Coming." *The Sunday School Times* 65 (December 1923):792-93.

"A True Theological Seminary." *The Sunday School Times* 66 (6 September 1924):525-26.

Walvoord, John F. "The Abrahamic Covenant and Premillennialism." *Bibliotheca Sacra* 108 (October 1951):414-22.

_____. "Amillennialism as a Method of Interpretation." *Bibliotheca Sacra* 107 (January 1950):42-50.

_____. "Lewis Sperry Chafer." *The Sunday School Times* 94 (11 October 1952):855, 868-70.

_____. "The Kingdom Promises to David." *Bibliotheca Sacra* 110 (January 1953):97-110.

_____. "The Millennial Issue in Modern Theology." *Bibliotheca Sacra* 106 (January 1949):34-47.

_____. "The New Covenant with Israel." *Bibliotheca Sacra* 110 (April 1953):193-205.

_____. "Premillennialism and the Church." *Bibliotheca Sacra* 110 (October 1953):289-98.

_____. "A Review of Lewis Sperry Chafer's Systematic Theology." *Bibliotheca Sacra* 105 (January 1948):115-27.

Warfield, Benjamin B. "Book Review of *He That Is Spiritual*." *Princeton Theological Journal* 17 (April 1919):322-27.

_____. "The Millennium and the Apocalypse." *Princeton Theological Journal* 2 (October 1904):599-617.

_____. "The Present Problem of Inspiration." *Homiletic Review* 21 (1891):410-16.

Watchword and Truth (Boston). Edited by Robert Cameron. 23 vols. 1898-1921.

Witmer, John A. "What Hath God Wrought — Fifty Years of Dallas Theological Seminary." *Bibliotheca Sacra* 130 (October 1973):291-304.

Selected Bibliography

Woelfkine, Cornelius. "The Religious Appeal of Premillennialism." *Journal of Review* 1 (1921):255-63.

Dissertations

Boles, Joseph. "The Theology of Lewis Sperry Chafer in the Light of His Theological Method." Th.D. dissertation, Southwestern Baptist Theological Seminary, 1963.

Campbell, Donald Keith. "Interpretation and Exposition of the Sermon on the Mount." Th.D. dissertation, Dallas Theological Seminary, 1953.

Cobb, John William. "The Origin, Development and Meaning of Dispensational Premillennialism." Th.D. dissertation, Southwestern Baptist Theological Seminary, 1945.

Fuller, Daniel P. "Hermeneutics of Dispensationalism." Th.D. dissertation, Northern Baptist Seminary, 1957.

Grant, Reg. "Lewis Sperry Chafer: Provisions." Project presented to the Faculty of Pastoral Ministries Department, Dallas Theological Seminary, 1981.

Hannah, John D. "The Social and Intellectual History of The Evangelical Theological College." Ph.D. dissertation, University of Texas at Dallas, 1988.

Harrington, Caroll E. "The Fundamentalist Movement in America, 1870-1920." Ph.D. dissertation, University of California, Berkely, 1959.

McBirnie, Robert S. "Basic Issues in the Fundamentalism of William Bell Riley." Ph.D. dissertation, State University of Iowa, 1952.

Nelson, John O. "The Rise of Princeton Theology." Ph.D. dissertation, Yale University, 1935.

Perry, Everett L. "The Role of Socioeconomic Factors in the Rise and Development of American Fundamentalism." Ph.D. dissertation, University of Chicago, 1959.

Renfer, Rudolph A. "A History of Dallas Theological Seminary." Ph.D. dissertation, University of Texas, 1959.

Wilson, Talmage. "A History of Dispensationalism in the United States of America." Th.M. Thesis, Pittsburgh-Xenia Theological Seminary, 1956.

Pamphlets and Reports

Dallas Theological Seminary Catalogue with a Doctrinal Statement, 1949-50.

Minutes of the Eighty-Eighth Stated Meeting of the Presbytery of Dallas of the Presbyterian Church in the United States, Called Meeting of 4 July 1923. Historical Foundation of the Presbyterian and Reformed Churches, Montreat, North Carolina.

Minutes of the Eighty-Fourth General Assembly of the Presbyterian Church in the United States, 25-30 May 1944. Reports of the Interim Committees, pp. 123-27. Foundation of the Presbyterian and Reformed Churches, Montreat, North Carolina.

Scofield Memorial Church Manual, Dallas, Texas, 1924.

The Westminster Confession of Faith. Philadelphia: Committee on Christian Education, n.d.

Personal Letters

Aldrich, Willard M. President Emeritus, Multnomah School of the Bible, Portland, Oregon, 9 January 1984.

Alvis, Joel L., Jr. Local Church History Coordinator, The Historical

Selected Bibliography

Foundation of the Presbyterian and Reformed Churches, Montreat, North Carolina, 7 January 1985 and 24 January 1985.

Ashcraft, Neil. Senior Pastor, Scofield Memorial Church, Dallas, Texas, 6 January 1984.

Campbell, Donald K. President, Dallas Theological Seminary, Dallas, Texas, 28 December 1983.

Deibler, Edwin C. Emeritus Professor of Historical Theology, Dallas Theological Seminary, Dallas, Texas, 17 January 1984.

Howe, Frederick R. Emeritus Professor of Systematic Theology, Dallas Theological Seminary, Dallas, Texas, 26 December 1983.

Robinson, Haddon. President, Denver Conservative Baptist Seminary, Denver, Colorado, 20 December 1983.

Ryrie, Charles C. Emeritus Professor of Systematic Theology, Dallas Theological Seminary, Dallas, Texas, 5 January 1983.

Seume, Richard H. Former Chaplain, Dallas Theological Seminary, Dallas, Texas, 30 December 1983.

Stanley, Charles F. Senior Pastor, First Baptist Church, Atlanta, Georgia, 6 March 1990.

Walvoord, John F. Chancellor, Dallas Theological Seminary, Dallas, Texas, 22 December 1983.

Witmer, John A. Emeritus Professor of Systematic Theology, Dallas Theological Seminary, Dallas, Texas, 3 June 1983.

Indexes

Persons

Abraham, 3, 65, 113, 120, 142, 144, 151, 187
Adam, 141, 147
Ahlstrom, Sydney, 13, 224
Aldrich, Willard, 40, 242
Alexander, W. Lindsey, 92
Alford, 164
Allis, O. T., 225, 236
Alvis, Joel L., 242
Anderson, Sir Robert, 96, 225
Anderson, William M., 34, 35
Apostle Paul, 77, 93, 121, 176
Augustine, 165

Bear, James E., 146, 149, 150-51, 236
Bengel, 164
Berkhof, L., 147, 225
Boettner, Loraine, 3, 138-39, 226
Boles, Joseph, 56, 83, 241
Bonar, 164
Broadus, John A., 61
Brooks, James H., 56, 67, 226, 236
Bullinger, E. W., 93-94

Calvin, John, 41
Cameron, Robert, 95, 96, 133
Campbell, Donald K., viii, 41, 83, 241
Case, Ella Loraine, 15
Cauthen, Kenneth, 31, 236
Chadwick, Samuel, 57
Chafer, Loraine, 20, 41
Chafer, Maryette, 12, 13

Chafer, Rollin, 12, 35
Chafer, Thomas Franklin, 6, 12, 56
Chafer, William, 12
Chapman, J. Wilbur, 55
Christ, vii, viii, 3, 4, 15, 17, 18, 26, 28, 29, 39, 43, 56, 57, 59, 61, 62, 64, 65, 70, 73, 74, 75, 76, 77, 79, 81, 82, 88, 90, 93, 94, 95, 96, 110, 112, 113, 114, 115, 117, 118, 119, 120, 121, 122, 123, 124, 126, 127, 128, 129, 130, 133, 134, 135, 136, 137, 138, 139, 140, 142, 143, 145, 151, 152, 163, 167, 168, 169, 170, 171, 174, 175, 176, 177, 178, 179, 181, 182, 183, 184, 186, 188, 189, 192, 194, 197, 207, 208
Cole, Stewart G., 1, 226
Cunningham, 164

Daniel, 81, 92, 96, 117, 120, 131, 142, 181, 188, 197
Darby, John Nelson, 3, 56, 82, 83, 227
David, 3, 65, 79, 86, 91, 121, 126, 142, 144, 145, 169, 173, 176, 187, 194
Deibler, Edwin C., viii, 12, 13, 18, 40, 243
Delitzsch, 164
Drummond, Henry, 61
Duncan, A. H. D., 42

Edwards, John, 4
Edwards, Jonathan, 4
Eerdman, William B., 20, 24
Eerdman, W. J., 67, 68, 133

245

Ehlert, Arnold D., 3, 4, 237
English, E. Schuyler, 131-132, 227, 237
Evans, Anthony, 7

Fausset, 164
Feinberg, Charles, L., 84, 149, 227
Findlay, Jr., James F., 60, 227, 237
Finney, Charles G., 13
Fleming, Robert O., 41
Fuller, Daniel P., 7, 56, 207, 241

Gaebelein, A. C., 1, 35, 37, 66, 68, 94-95, 96, 132-33, 228, 238
Gerhard, E. V., 92
Gill, 164
Gordon, Charles, 57
Gouge, William, 4
Graham, James R., 133
Griffith Thomas, W. H., 1, 2, 6, 11, 20, 24, 33, 35, 45, 57, 205, 234
Gray, James M., 24, 68
Guille, George E., 20

Hannah, John A., viii, 241
Harper, W. R., 61
Harris, Elmore, 68
Hendricks, Howard, 7
Hodge, A. A., 3, 91, 166, 169, 172, 196, 229
Hodge, Charles A., 3, 91, 92, 137-38, 166-68, 169, 172, 196, 229
Hoekema, Anthony, 135-37, 229
Hooker, 90
Howard, Wally, 14, 17, 21, 55, 238

Ironside, H. A., 1, 20, 35, 66, 92, 93, 94, 96, 229
Isaac, 144, 187

Jacob, 144, 173, 177, 181, 187
Jeremiah, David, 7
Jesus, vii, viii, 17, 28, 61, 64, 73, 79, 88, 89, 91, 95, 115, 116, 118, 121, 129, 134, 175,
John the Baptist, 26, 189, 191
Jones, 164

Kelly, William, 129-30, 230
Kelman, John, 57
Kraus, Norman, 7, 230
Kurtz, 164
Kyle, Marvin Grove, 39

Ladd, George E., 134, 165, 207, 230
Landrum, Lynn, 53-54
Lange, 164
Lillie, 164
Lincoln, C. F., 5, 12, 20, 38, 56, 86, 119, 238
Lindsey, Hal, 7

Mabie, Janet, 61, 231
Macartney, Clarence, 31, 238
Mackintosh, C. H., 92, 127-28, 231
Marsden, George M., 1, 92, 231
Mason, Clarence, 42, 238
McGee, J. Vernon, 7
McPheeters, Thomas, 67
McPherson, Norman, 134
Messiah, 78, 79, 88, 116, 124, 125, 130, 132, 133, 175, 176, 181, 189
Meyer, 20, 66, 164
Miley, John, 92
Moody, D. L., 1, 2, 19, 20, 21, 57, 58, 60-61, 68, 206, 232
Moody, Dale, 238
Moody, Mrs. W. R., 21
Morehead, W. G., 68
Morgan, G. Campbell, 20, 25, 57, 62-64, 66, 206, 232
Müller, George, 62

Nast, 164

Olshousen, 164

Persons Index

Parsons, H. M., 67
Payne, J. Barton, 133, 232
Pentecost, George F., 64-65, 206
Perpetuo, A. H., 35
Peters, George N. H., 83, 89, 90-91, 97, 119, 207, 232
Pettingill, William, 24, 68, 128-29, 232
Pierson, A. T., 58, 61-62, 66, 68, 206
Pierson, Delevan L., 20, 24, 232
Pieters, Albertus, 134, 35, 232
Poiret, Pierre, 4

Reed, Arthur T., 15
Reese, Alexander, 134
Renfer, Rudolph, 34, 37, 242
Richards, Larry, 7
Richey, Russell E., viii
Riley, W. B., 1, 233
Robinson, Haddon, viii, 233, 243
Ryle, 164
Ryrie, Charles C., 7, 147, 233, 243

Sandeen, Ernest, 1, 19, 58, 62, 95, 96, 233
Sankey, Ira, 20, 21
Satan, 5, 25, 26, 69, 75, 79, 88, 95, 111, 114, 116, 121, 130, 135, 136, 167, 170, 171, 174, 181, 191, 192, 193, 195
Sauer, Erich, 130-31
Scofield, C. I., 1, 2, 4, 6, 18, 20, 22, 23, 24, 34, 35, 56, 57, 66-82, 83, 84, 85, 89, 93, 96, 97, 116-117, 120, 149, 206, 207, 234
Scott, Moses, 14
Seiss, 164
Shedd, W. G. T., 92
Smith, Oswald J., 133
Smith, Wilbur M., 38, 43, 90, 91, 239
Snowden, James H., 3, 234, 239
Speer, Robert E., 57
Sperry, Ann, 12
Sperry, Asa, 6, 12
Sperry, Lois Lomira, 12
Sprunt, James, 25
Stanley, Charles, 7, 243

Stark, 164
Stibbins, George, 20
Stier, 164
Strong, A. H., 92
Sutcliffe, B. B., 33, 35
Swindoll, Charles R., 7

Torrey, R. A., 1, 24, 234
Towner, D. B., 20
Truett, George, 70
Trumbull, C. G., 67, 235

Walvoord, John F., viii, 23, 41, 42, 44, 57, 83, 84, 134, 139, 140, 235, 239, 240, 243
Warfield, Benjamin B., 1, 3, 91, 137, 166, 169-72
Watson, Richard, 92
Webb-Peploe, H. W., 20, 58-60, 66, 206
Weber, Timothy P., 1, 235
West, Nathaniel, 67
Weston, Henry G., 57, 68
White, W. P., 33
Wilson, Robert Dick, 37
Wilson, Woodrow, 57
Winchester, A. B., 1, 6, 20, 25, 33, 35
Witmer, John A., viii, 14, 22, 82, 83, 243, 240

Zuck, Roy B., 44

Subject

A System of Biblical Theology, 92
abrahamic covenant, 111, 135, 144, 145-146, 187
adamic covenant, 111
Allegheny, Pennsylvania, 169
American religion, 11,31, 56
amillennial, 3, 84, 85, 134, 135, 136, 137, 139, 140, 166, 171, 172, 195, 196, 207
Analytical Questionnaire, 43
Andover Theological Seminary, 39
Antichrist, 78, 79, 88, 91, 167, 169
angelology, 2, 43, 44, 119, 195
angels, 26,110, 111, 121, 140, 141, 152, 182, 190, 195
Anglican, 2, 6, 11, 58
anthropology, 2, 43, 44, 119
apostle of grace, vii, viii, 14
Armageddon, viii, 91, 174, 197
Arminian, 1, 3, 13,
Ashtabula County, 12
Atlanta, Georgia, 33
Auburn Theological Seminary, 6, 11

Babylon, 62, 92, 174
baptism, 93, 166
Beatitudes, 190
Bible conferences, 2, 12, 20,21, 22, 24, 25, 30, 34, 40, 41, 43, 65, 67, 84, 95, 205
bibliology, 43, 44, 119
Bibliotheca Sacra, 5, 39, 41, 42, 44, 89
Buffalo, New York, 16

calvinism, 37, 83
Calvinist, 1, 3, 80
Catechisms, 149
chiliasm, 85, 116, 164
Christians, 5, 21, 28, 57, 59, 61, 63, 64, 80, 86, 93, 110, 121, 127, 140, 141, 143, 152
christology, 2, 44, 119
Church, 3, 4, 5, 18, 38, 43, 59, 60, 64, 73, 74, 76, 77, 78, 79, 80, 81, 85, 86, 88, 91, 93, 94, 95, 96, 109, 111, 113, 114, 116, 117, 119, 123, 128, 129, 131, 132, 133, 134, 135, 136, 137, 138, 139, 142, 143, 144, 146, 147, 149, 150-151, 164, 165, 166, 167, 169, 170, 171, 172, 174, 175, 176, 177, 178, 179, 180, 181, 182, 183, 188, 194, 195, 196, 205
Church Fathers, 4, 90, 134, 165
Church of God,73, 80, 128
Church of the Holy Trinity, New York, 19
Civil War, 67
Coming Prince,The, 96
Confederate Cross of Honor, 67
Conflict of the Ages, The, 96
Congregational Church, 6, 67, 69
conscience, 74, 115, 120
conversion, 13, 14, 15, 67, 136, 138, 167, 169, 206
cosmos, 27, 114, 182, 192
covenant, 79, 91, 111, 114, 115, 116, 143, 144, 145, 146, 147, 148, 150, 151, 164, 177, 187, 190-191
covenant of works, 115, 146, 147, 191

covenant of grace, 115, 146, 147, 150
covenant of redemption, 115, 147
Crozer Theological Seminary, 68
cult, 87

Dallas, Texas, 2, 67, 68, 69, 93
Dallas Theological Seminary, viii, 55, 83, 92, 205, 206
davidic covenant, 27, 111, 145, 146, 187, 194
Day of Jehovah, 177
Day of the Lord, 63, 64, 74, 174
deeper life, 57, 61, 65
Denver, Colorado, 33
Denver Conservative Baptist Theological Seminary, viii, 40
dispensationalism, 3, 4, 6, 7, 22, 27, 28, 60, 61, 65, 69, 71, 80, 83, 84, 88, 109, 120, 121, 126, 127, 140, 144, 146, 148, 149, 150, 152, 186
Dispensationalism, 41, 86, 120
dispensation, 3, 4, 7, 28, 29, 63, 72, 73, 74, 76, 79, 87, 89, 93, 94, 110, 111, 113, 114, 115, 119, 120, 121, 122, 123, 124, 125, 127, 128, 130, 131, 132, 133, 134, 135, 137, 139, 141, 143, 150, 151, 152, 163, 164, 165, 169, 175, 176, 187, 194, 195, 196, 207,
Doctrinal Summarization, 42
Dogmatic Theology, 92

East Northfield, Massachusetts, 20, 57, 68 71
East Orange, New Jersey, 15, 25, 71
ecclesiology, 2, 14, 16, 43, 44, 113, 119, 122
edenic covenant, 111
Egypt, 62
election, 3, 112, 166, 177
Ephesian Letter, 41
epistles, 95, 111, 143
eschatology, 2, 3, 4, 6, 7, 11, 28, 35, 43, 44, 56, 58, 59, 72, 76, 80, 82, 83, 88, 89, 91,

The Promise of Dawn

92, 93, 94, 96, 97, 116, 117, 118, 119, 122, 131, 132, 133, 136, 137, 146, 163, 164, 165, 166, 168, 172, 194, 195, 196 205, 206, 207, 208
eschaton, vii
eternal estate, 60, 75, 88, 116, 118, 137, 138, 186, 196, 208
eternal security, 112
eternity, 86, 113, 141, 143, 145, 147, 192
European Common Market, viii
Evangelical Theological College, 33, 35, 36, 39, 86, 92
evangelist, vii, 11, 13, 14, 15, 16, 17, 19, 23, 24, 32, 33, 41, 57, 58, 61, 70, 71, 185, 206

Fall, 111, 112, 120, 141
first advent, 39, 64, 110, 175, 186
First Baptist Church of Dallas, Texas, 23, 70
First Baptist Church of San Diego, 18
First Congregational Church, 16
First Presbyterian Church, Dallas, Texas, 34
Fuller Theological Seminary, 90
fundamentalism, 6, 31, 36, 37, 43, 56, 205
Fundamentals, 95
Fundamentals Association, 36
futurist, 59

Gentiles, 5, 73, 74, 80, 85, 86, 88, 91, 96, 110, 111, 114, 116, 117, 121, 125, 128, 140, 141, 142, 143, 152, 169, 176, 178, 190, 196
Gentiles, times of the, 91, 181
goats, 141, 182, 185, 190
Gog and Magog, 193, 197
gospel of the kingdom, 65, 126, 130, 175, 188
Gospels, 3, 28, 67, 70, 77, 80, 81, 88, 122, 126, 130, 136, 137, 139, 141, 143, 167, 169, 170, 171, 186
government, 63, 74, 79, 114, 115, 117,

Subject Index

120, 121, 174
grace, vii, 4, 14, 16, 17, 26, 27, 29, 30, 45, 58, 67, 73, 74, 76, 77, 78, 79, 81, 91, 94, 113, 114, 115, 116, 117, 120, 121, 122, 123, 124, 125, 126, 130, 141, 142, 143, 144, 146, 147, 150, 151, 152, 166, 169, 176, 177, 179, 180, 183, 184, 185, 188, 189, 190, 191, 192, 195, 197, 206, 207
Grace, 28, 29, 71, 122
Great White Throne Judgment, 60, 75, 76, 81, 95, 131, 182, 183, 184, 185, 186, 192, 193,

hamartiology, 44, 112, 119
Harrisburg Circuit of Bible Conferences, 41
He That Is Spiritual, 1, 28, 57, 69, 195
historical-grammatical interpretation, 83, 89, 164
historicist, 59
History of Fundamentalism, The, 1
History of the Work of Redemption, 4
Holy Spirit, 15, 17, 18, 28, 59, 77, 78, 87, 181, 195
humanity, 3, 16, 80, 111, 112, 133, 163, 179, 185, 193

infant baptism, 166
innocence, 74, 115, 120
inspiration of Scripture, 3
Institutes of the Christian Religion, 92
irresistable grace, 3, 166
Israel, vii, 73, 74, 77, 80, 86, 88, 96, 110, 111, 113, 114, 115, 116, 121, 122, 125, 126, 127, 130, 131, 133, 134, 135, 136, 141, 142, 143, 145, 146, 152, 164, 165, 166, 173, 174, 176, 177, 178, 181, 192, 183, 187, 188, 189, 190, 191, 192, 194, 195
Jacob's Trouble, 177, 181
Jews, 73, 110, 114, 117, 121, 123, 128, 130, 132, 133, 140, 141, 142, 143, 144, 152, 167, 169, 175, 186, 190

judgment of the nations, 76, 81, 128, 129, 130, 174, 182, 183, 185, 186, 190, 196, 197
Judgment Seat of Christ, 81, 94, 131, 137, 182, 184, 197
justice of God, 185

Kanas State Legislature, 67
Keswick Movement, 58
kingdom, 4, 26, 27, 29, 59, 65, 74, 77, 79, 80, 81, 86, 88, 89, 91, 92, 93, 111, 114, 115, 116, 117, 118, 121, 123, 124, 125, 126, 128, 129, 130, 131, 132, 135, 136, 138, 140, 141, 142, 143, 145, 152, 153, 163, 164, 165, 166, 167, 168, 169, 173, 174, 175, 176, 177, 181, 183, 186, 187, 188, 189, 190, 191, 192, 193, 194, 196, 197, 207, 208
Kingdom in History and Prophecy, The, 27, 85, 99, 116, 117, 119, 163
kingdom of God, 79, 80, 81, 126, 131, 136, 139, 140, 165
kingdom of heaven, 79, 80, 81, 126, 128, 191
King's Business, 41

lake of fire, 26, 186, 190, 193
law, 4, 17, 26, 29, 67, 74, 76, 81, 93, 113, 114, 115, 120, 121, 122, 123, 125, 126, 128, 143, 150, 152, 207
Lectures on Daniel, 92
Lectures on Revelation, 92, 94
League of evangelical students, 1
Lewistown, New York, 16
Lord's Supper, 93
love of God, 28, 185

Major Bible Themes, 41, 44
Medo-Persia, 92
midtribulationalism, 134
millenarian, 19, 64, 95
millennial, 79, 80, 81, 82, 85, 114, 135, 139, 142, 163, 169, 174, 175, 179, 181,

251

190, 191, 192, 197
millennium, 3, 7, 117, 128, 131, 132, 136, 137, 138, 142, 163, 164, 168, 169, 171, 175, 177, 185, 186-189, 192, 194, 195, 196, 197, 207
Millennialism: The Two Major Views, 84
modernism, 6, 31
Moody Bible Institute, 68, 73, 84, 87
Moody Monthly, 41
mosaic covenant, 111, 145, 146
mosaic law, 120, 121, 143
Mount Hermon, 21, 22, 24
Mount Hermon Schools, 30
Mount Hermon School for Boys, 21, 206
Multnomah School of the Bible, 40
mystery, 123, 128, 176, 180

New Covenant, 111, 130, 134, 135, 144, 145
new earth, 121, 138, 170, 172, 174, 192, 193
new heaven, 121, 138, 170, 172, 174, 192, 193
New Lyme Institute, 12
New Lyme, Ohio, 12
New Scofield Reference Bible, 72
New York City, 2, 24, 25
Niagara Bible Conference, 67
noahic covenant, 111
Northfield, 2, 19, 20, 21, 22, 23, 24, 30, 57, 58, 60, 61, 62, 63, 64, 65, 66, 68, 69, 89, 92, 97, 206, 207
Northfield Bible Training School, 66
Northfield Congregational Church, 20, 66
Northfield Schools, 2
Not Wrath but Rapture, 93

Oberlin College, 13, 15, 39
Oberlin College and Conservatory of Music, 13
Old Testament, vii, 4, 5, 26, 28, 111, 114, 117, 118, 119, 123, 124, 125, 127, 128, 140, 169, 172, 175, 177, 178, 179, 187, 194, 195, 207
Olivet Discourse, 117, 188
Our Hope, 5, 41, 94, 95
Outline of Theology, 91
Oxford University Press, 72

palestinian covenant, 111, 144, 187
parable, 59, 80
partial-rapture, 134
pastor, 11, 13, 20, 23, 34, 35, 37, 117, 169, 206
Pentecost, 114, 135, 194
perseverence,
perseverence of the saints, 3, 166
Philadelphia, 33, 40
Philadelphia College of the Bible, 2, 25
Piedmont Hotel, 33
Pietism, 83
Pittsburgh, 33
Pittsburgh-Xenia Theological Seminary, 39
pneumatology, 2, 44, 119
postmillennial, 3, 84, 85, 137, 138, 139, 140, 163, 166, 170, 171, 172, 196, 207
posttribulational, 95, 133, 134
premillennial, 2, 3, 6, 11, 18, 19, 20, 23, 31, 39, 42, 43, 44, 45, 58, 60, 61, 62, 64, 65, 71, 72, 83, 84, 86, 89, 90, 95, 96, 97, 109, 114, 119, 127, 128, 131, 132, 133, 134, 135, 137, 139, 140, 149, 150, 163, 164, 165, 170, 175, 183, 186, 189, 194, 195, 196, 205, 207
Presbyterian Church, 6, 11, 67, 149
pretorist, 59
pretribulational, 81, 95, 96, 120, 133, 177
Princeton Theological Seminary, 37, 169
professor of Systematic Theology, 169, 205
promise, vii, 3, 57, 59, 74, 112, 114, 115, 120, 135, 144, 145, 187, 192, 194, 208
prophecy, viii, 27, 43, 56, 59, 61, 62, 65, 77, 78, 79, 81, 84, 88, 89, 90, 96, 116, 117, 118, 119, 129, 134, 140, 141, 163,

Subject Index

165, 170, 172, 173, 174, 177, 180, 190, 196, 207
Prophet Daniel, The, 96
prophets, 26, 63, 64, 77, 78, 79, 95, 172, 173, 174, 175, 191

rapture, 59, 60, 64, 74, 81, 85, 93, 95, 127, 128, 131, 132, 133, 134, 174, 175, 176, 178, 179, 194, 196
Reformed theology, 3, 42, 43, 77, 81, 91, 115, 146, 147, 148, 195, 196
resurrection, 56, 60, 75, 88, 111, 114, 127, 133, 135, 136-137, 138, 163, 164, 167, 171, 174, 178, 179, 180, 183, 186, 193, 196
Revelation Magazine, 5
Richmond, Virginia, 25
righteousness, 26, 29, 79, 112, 125, 128, 129, 138, 139, 176, 191
Rightly Dividing the Word of Truth, 73
Rock Creek, Ohio, 12
Roman Empire, 92

salvation, 14, 16, 17, 27, 29, 39, 58, 83, 113, 122, 123, 150, 151, 152, 176, 184, 189
Salvation, 27, 28
Satan, 22, 25
Scofield Memorial Church, 35, 39
Scofield Reference Bible, 23, 43, 72, 95, 128
scripture, 5, 62, 66, 71, 72, 73, 74, 75, 76, 77, 81, 82, 83, 85, 86, 87, 89, 90, 91, 97, 113, 117, 119, 124, 125, 129, 142, 143, 146-147, 147-148, 149, 151, 163, 164, 165, 168, 173, 176, 178, 179, 180, 182, 185, 186, 187, 190, 191, 194, 195, 196, 206, 207
Seattle, Washington, 33, 41
second advent, 56, 64, 117, 142, 163, 167, 169, 171, 175, 178, 186, 196,
second coming, 39, 74, 75, 81, 88, 93, 95, 163, 166, 168, 174, 175, 176, 177, 178, 181, 183, 208
seed of Abraham, 65, 11, 187
Selected Hymns, 13
Sermon on the Mount, 80, 188, 189
seventieth week, 4, 78, 81, 120, 131, 181, 188, 196, 197
sheep, 141, 182, 185, 190
sin, 26, 28, 74, 76, , 112, 114, 124, 132, 133, 136, 139, 173, 174, 176, 181, 185, 186, 188, 191, 192
sixty-nine weeks, 4, 78
soteriology, 2, 43, 44, 119
Southland Bible Conference, 2
sovereignty of God, 3, 166
stewardship, 120, 152
Studies in Theology, 91
St. Louis, Missouri, 34, 67
Sunday School Times, The, 5, 24, 39, 41, 43
Synopsis of the Books of the Bible, 82
synoptic gospels, 124, 143
Systematic Theology, 2, 5, 6, 7, 14, 41, 42, 43, 44, 45, 56, 62, 64, 82, 84, 85, 89, 91, 92, 109, 112, 116, 117, 119, 120, 122, 128, 140, 152, 166, 194, 207

Theocratic Kingdom, The, 89, 90, 91, 207
Theological Institutes, 92
theology proper, 43, 44, 119
third heaven, 15
total depravity, 3, 166
translation, 60, 81, 88, 114, 123, 127, 129, 131, 133, 134, 176, 177, 178, 179, 184, 192, 197
tribulation, 4, 59, 60, 74, 76, 78, 79, 81, 88, 93, 94, 95, , 116, 128, 129, 130, 131, 132, 133, 134, 136, 141, 142, 174, 175, 176, 177, 179, 180, 181, 182, 188, 189, 194, 207
Trinitarian Congregational Church, 68
Troy, New York, 20
True Evangelism, 11, 17, 18, 19, 22, 27, 205

tuberculosis, 16

Union Theological Seminary, 25, 62
University of Virginia, 67
ultra-dispensationalism, 93, 94

virgin birth, 3

Western Theological Seminary, 169
Westminster Confession of Faith, The, 147, 148, 149
Wheaton, Illinois, 33, 34
Wittenberg College, 90
Word of God, 16, 23, 43, 87, 96, 111, 125, 149, 173, 185
Wrongly Dividing the Word of Truth, 93

York, England, 12

Scripture
Old Testament

GENESIS
12	189
12:1-3	144
13:14-17	144
15:4-21	144
17:1-8	144
22:17-18	144
26:3-5	144
35:10-12	144

EXODUS
19	101
20:1-17	121
20:1-31:18	145
21:1-24:11	121
24:12-31:18	121-22

DEUTERONOMY
28:63-68	144
30:1-10	144
30:3-8	187

II SAMUEL
7:4-16	145
7:16	187, 194

NEHEMIAH
2	78

PSALMS
2:5	181
10:16	77
80:17-19	133
89:3-4	194
89:34-37	194

ISAIAH
2:1-2	125
9:6-7	142, 189
11:1-5	125
11:6-9	192
40:3	189
49:16	183
55:12-13	192
63:1	143
63:15-64:1-8	131

JEREMIAH
23:3-8	125
23:5	174
30:4-7	142, 177, 181
31:31-33	145
31:33-34	192
33:7-9	174
33:16	142
33:14-17	194
33:20-21	194
33:21	145

EZEKIEL
20:33-34	143
20:44	143
36:16-38	174

37:21-25	174	HOSEA	
37:24	174	3:4-5	125, 187, 194
37:24-28	194		
		MICAH	
DANIEL		4:3	192
2	181		
2:35	131	ZECHARIAH	
2:44	131	2:10-12	174
7	78, 92	14:1-21	142
7:13-14	143		
7:17	92	MALACHI	
9	4, 78, 196	3:1-4	174
9:24-27	180		
9:26	78		
12:1	142, 177, 180, 181		
12:1-3	178		
12:2	143		
12:11	79		

New Testament

		25:31-32	145, 167
MATTHEW		25:31-46	81, 167, 182, 196
5, 6, 7	188	25:34	182
11	80	25:41	140
13	128	35:31 46	141
16:18	76		
18:3	138		
24	129, 181, 183, 188	LUKE	
24:9-26	180	1:31-32	187
24:15	79	1:31-33	142, 145
24:21	142, 177, 181	12:39-40	64
24:22	181		
24:30-31	167	JOHN	
24:31	134	3:3	73
24:36-41	132	3:5	138
24:37-25:30	143	3:16	73
24:43	64	6:39-40	167
25	183, 188	6:44, 54	167
25:1-13	59	11:24	167
25:31	182	12:48	167

Scripture Index

14:1-3	127, 176	**EPHESIANS**		
14:3	127	1:10	148	
5:24	182, 184	1:22-23	73	
5:25, 28, 29	179	2:6	178	
5:28-29	167, 185	2:7	14, 74	
5:43	181	2:11	74	
		2:14	73	
ACTS		3:1-6	148	
1:6-7	188	3:1-10	77	
2	73, 77	3:2	74	
2:25-31	187	3:9-10	77	
2:30	145			
10, 11, 13	141	**PHILIPPIANS**		
		1:23	15	
ROMANS		3:20-21	114, 179	
8:1	182			
11:26-27, 29	143	**I THESSALONIANS**		
11:27	143	4	73, 77	
14:17	138	4:13-16	75	
		4:13-18	176	
I CORINTHIANS		4:15-17	180	
3:9-15	184	4:16-17	4, 127, 178	
4:5	184	4:17	180	
6:2-3	131	4:51-52	180	
9:16-27	184	5:1-2	64	
12:2	74	5:2	64	
12:12-13	73			
12:13	73	**II THESSALONIANS**		
15:20-23	179	1:7-10	167	
15:23-26	163	2	181	
15:35-37	179	2:1	176	
15:24-28	194	2:1-12	180	
15:51	180	2:3-4	79	
15:51-52	127, 176	2:7	181	
15:51-57	176	2:11	181	
II CORINTHIANS		**I TIMOTHY**		
5:8	15	1:17	77	
GALATIANS		**II TIMOTHY**		
3	121	1:7-10	167	
3:11	122			
3:28	74	**HEBREWS**		
5:3	189	1:8	194	

8:6	145	17:12	viii
8:10-13; 16-17	145	19	134, 170
9:28	176	19:7-8	193
		19:7-14	183
JAMES		19:11-16	178
2:10	189	19:11-21	131
		20	135, 136, 165, 170, 193, 196
I PETER			
1:10-11	175	20:1-3	167
		20:1-10	171
II PETER		20:4	142, 171
1:21	78	20:4, 5	180
3:8-12	64	20:4-6	75, 163, 167
3:10	64	20:5-6	127
		20:6	142
REVELATION		20:7-10	111
1-3	60, 94	20:7-15	142
3:10	182	20:11-15	81, 183, 185
4	94	20:12-13	169
4-22	59, 60, 94, 95	20:12-15	179
6:1-19:6	180	21	135, 170, 193
9-12	181	21:1	74, 193
11:15	131, 142, 182	22:5	142
13	92	22:16	187
16:15	64		

www.ingramcontent.com/pod-product-compliance
Lightning Source LLC
Chambersburg PA
CBHW062006220426
43662CB00010B/1246